# Rashomon Effects

Akira Kurosawa is widely known as the director who opened up Japanese film to Western audiences, and following his death in 1998, a process of reflection has begun about his life's work as a whole and its legacy to cinema. Kurosawa's 1950 film *Rashomon* has become one of the best-known Japanese films ever made, and continues to be discussed and imitated more than sixty years after its first screening.

This book examines the cultural and aesthetic impacts of Akira Kurosawa's *Rashomon*, as well as the director's larger legacies to cinema, its global audiences and beyond. It demonstrates that these legacies are manifold: not only cinematic and artistic, but also cultural and cognitive. The book moves from an examination of one filmmaker and his immediate social context in Japan, and goes on to explore how an artist's ideas might transcend their cultural origins to ultimately provide global influences. Discussing how *Rashomon*'s effects began to multiply with the film being reimagined and repurposed in numerous media forms in the decades that followed its initial release, the book also shows that the film and its ideas have been applied to a wider range of social and cultural phenomena in a variety of institutional contexts. It addresses issues beyond the realm of *Rashomon* within film studies, and extends to the Rashomon effect, which itself has become a widely recognized English term referring to the significantly different interpretations of different eyewitnesses to the same dramatic event.

As the first book on *Rashomon* since Donald Richie's 1987 anthology, it will be invaluable to students and scholars of film studies, film history, Japanese cinema and communication studies. It will also resonate more broadly with those interested in Japanese culture and society, anthropology and philosophy.

**Blair Davis** is an Assistant Professor of Media and Cinema Studies in the College of Communication at DePaul University in Chicago, USA.

**Robert Anderson** is Professor of Communication at Simon Fraser University in Vancouver, Canada.

**Jan Walls** is a Professor Emeritus in the Humanities Department at Simon Fraser University in Vancouver, Canada.

# Routledge Advances in Film Studies

# Rashomon Effects

Kurosawa, *Rashomon* and their legacies

**Edited by Blair Davis, Robert Anderson
and Jan Walls**

LONDON AND NEW YORK

First published 2016
by Routledge
2 Park Square, Milton Park, Abingdon, Oxon OX14 4RN

and by Routledge
711 Third Avenue, New York, NY 10017

*Routledge is an imprint of the Taylor & Francis Group, an informa business*

*British Library Cataloguing in Publication Data*
A catalogue record for this book is available from the British Library

*Library of Congress Cataloguing in Publication Data*
  Rashomon effects: Kurosawa, *Rashomon* and their legacies / edited by
  Blair Davis, Robert Anderson and Jan Walls.
    pages  cm. – (Routledge advances in film studies; 44)
  Includes bibliographical references and index.
  1. Rashomon (Motion picture)  2. Kurosawa, Akira, 1910–1998–Criticism
  and interpretation.  3. Kurosawa, Akira, 1910–1998–Influence.  I. Davis,
  Blair, editor.  II. Anderson, Robert, editor.  III. Walls, Jan, editor.
  PN1997.R244R38 2015
  791.43'72–dc23      2015019880

ISBN: 978-1-138-82709-7 (hbk)
ISBN: 978-1-315-73874-1 (ebk)

Typeset in Times New Roman
by Out of House Publishing

Dedicated to the memory of Donald Richie (1924–2013)

# Contents

# Illustrations

**Figure**

**Photos**

**Boxes**

# Contributors

**Robert Anderson** is Professor of Communication at Simon Fraser University, Burnaby, BC, Canada, where he teaches a course on dialogue and negotiation in conflict situations. He became interested in the Rashomon effect in 1966 as a graduate student in anthropology, and this concept became a core resource in his thinking and teaching. He is also a historian of the environment and international nuclear relations. His most recent book is *Nucleus and Nation: Scientists, International Networks, and Power in India* (2010) Chicago: University of Chicago Press.

**Jef Burnham** holds an MA in Media and Cinema Studies from DePaul University, Chicago, Illinois. He currently teaches in the Communication Department at DePaul and has taught cinema studies courses at Columbia College Chicago and Facets Multimedia. He has co-authored essays featured in *Reading Mystery Science Theater 3000* (2013) Lanham, MD: Scarecrow Press, and *Remake Television: Reboot, Reuse, Recycle* (2014) Lanham, MD: Lexington Books, and contributed a chapter to *Sherlock Holmes and Philosophy* (2011) Chicago: Open Court.

**Blair Davis** is an Assistant Professor of Media and Cinema Studies with the College of Communication at DePaul University in Chicago, Illinois. He is the author of *The Battle for the Bs: 1950s Hollywood and the Rebirth of Low-Budget Cinema* (2012) New Brunswick, NJ: Rutgers University Press, and has had several essays featured in the *Historical Journal of Film, Radio and Television* and the *Canadian Journal of Film Studies*. He has also written numerous chapters for such anthologies as *Reel Food: Essays on Film and Food* (2004) London: Routledge, and *American Horror Film: The Genre at the Turn of the Millennium* (2010) Jackson, MS: University of Mississippi Press. Blair Davis has a PhD in Communication Studies from McGill University, Montreal, Canada.

**Andrew Horvat** had a twenty-five-year career as a Tokyo-based correspondent reporting for the Associated Press, Southam News, the *Los Angeles Times*, *The Independent* and Public Radio International. He later served as Japan representative of The Asia Foundation, and as director of Stanford University's overseas studies program in Kyoto. At present he is visiting professor and vice-director of the Global College program at Josai International University. He is a translator of works by the novelist Kobo Abe, co-editor with Gebhard Hielscher of *Sharing the Burden of the Past: Legacies of War in Europe, America and Asia* (2003) The Asia Foundation & Friedrich Ebert Stiftung, and author of *Japanese Beyond Words* (2008) 2nd edn, Albany, CA: Stone Bridge Press. Horvat completed his Masters in Asian Studies at the University of British Columbia.

**Janice Matsumura** is Associate Professor of History at Simon Fraser University, Burnaby, BC, Canada, specializing in modern Japanese history. She is the author of *More Than a Momentary Nightmare: The Yokohama Incident and Wartime Japan* (1998) Ithaca, NY: Cornell East Asia, and has contributed to such journals as *Gender & History*, *Modern Asia Studies*, *Canadian Journal of History* and the *Bulletin of the History of Medicine*. The focus of her past research has been on the Asia-Pacific War (1931–45), including the relationship between state propaganda and medical policies. She is currently conducting a study of Japanese colonial psychiatry.

**Teruyo Nogami** was Kurosawa's principal assistant from 1947, beginning at age twenty. She worked with the director for fifty years, and still lives and writes in Tokyo. This chapter about *Rashomon* is reprinted from her *Waiting on the Weather: Making Movies with Kurosawa* (2006) (trans.) Berkeley, CA: Stonebridge Press.

**Stephen Prince** is Professor of Cinema at Virginia Tech, Blacksburg, USA, and former president of the Society for Cinema and Media Studies. He is the author of *The Warrior's Camera: The Cinema of Akira Kurosawa* (1999) Princeton, NJ: Princeton University Press, as well numerous other books. He has also provided audio commentaries for many DVD and Blu-ray editions of Kurosawa's films, including *Yojimbo*, *Seven Samurai*, *Ikiru*, *The Hidden Fortress* and *Ran*.

**Donald Richie** was a distinguished writer and columnist on art and culture for the *Japan Times*, who resided mostly in Tokyo from 1947 until his death in 2013. Richie is credited with having introduced to foreign audiences the works of not only Akira Kurosawa but such other major Japanese film directors as Yasujiro Ozu, Kenji Mizoguchi and Mikio Naruse. Starting in 1959 with *The Japanese Film: Art and Industry*

(1959) North Clarendon, VT: Tuttle, Richie wrote more than a dozen books on Japanese films, including *The Films of Akira Kurosawa* (1996) 3rd edn, Berkeley, CA: University of California Press, and *A Hundred Years of Japanese Film* (2005) Tokyo: Kodansha. Richie's insights into Kurosawa and his films have long helped Western scholars and audiences alike gain a better understanding of the director, his country and its film industry. This book is intended as an homage to Richie's generous outlook and encouragement of all scholars, including the editors and writers of this collection of essays.

**Jan Walls** is Professor Emeritus in the Humanities Department at Simon Fraser University, Burnaby, BC, Canada. His BA, MA and PhD degrees were all in Chinese and Japanese languages, literatures and folklore; he majored in Chinese and minored in Japanese. Before retiring from the university in 2006, he taught Chinese courses and developed Asian Studies programs for thirty-six years in three British Columbia universities. He is co-editor of *East-West Identities: Globalization, Localization, and Hybridization* (2007) Leiden, Boston and Tokyo: Brill Academic Publishers, and co-author of *Using Chinese* (2009) New York: Cambridge University Press.

**Nur Yalman** is Professor of Social Anthropology and Middle Eastern Studies, Emeritus, and Senior Fellow of the Society of Fellows at Harvard University, Cambridge, USA. He has served as the Director for the Center for Middle Eastern Studies both at the University of Chicago and also at Harvard University. He is the author of *Under the Bo Tree: Studies in Caste, Kinship, and Marriage in the Interior of Ceylon* (1967) Berkley, CA: University of California Press, and co-author of *A Passage to Peace: Global Solutions from East to West* (2008) New York: Macmillan, and has contributed numerous articles to major scholarly journals. He has done fieldwork in Sri Lanka, India, Iran and Turkey. He has a PhD from Cambridge University where he studied under Edmund Leach, and is currently a Trustee of Koc University in Turkey, and a Member of the American Academy of Arts and Sciences.

# Acknowledgments

The editors would all like to thank Donald Richie for his continuing and generous-hearted support for this project until shortly before his death in 2013. We acknowledge and thank the David See-Chai Lam Centre for International Communication, and the School of Communication at Simon Fraser University for organizing and sponsoring the conference whose presentations and dialogues led to the production of this book.

Marty Gross skillfully negotiated the rights to the images used, as well to reprint the chapter and sketch from *Waiting on the Weather* included herein. We are grateful to Kodakawa-Daiei for permission to publish images associated with the film *Rashomon*. Our thanks to Teruyo Nogami for granting her permission to reprint this chapter and to Juliet Carpenter for granting her translation rights, as well as to Peter Goodman of Stone Bridge Press who originally published the English translation of Nogami's book.

We are grateful to the libraries and librarians of Simon Fraser University in Vancouver and DePaul University in Chicago. DePaul's University Research Council generously provided grant funding for image and reprint permissions, while the Simon Fraser University Publication Fund provided funding for the editing of this book. Careful readers of final drafts and others who gave excellent assistance included Terry Neiman, Jennifer Bednard and Satomi Ichikawa. We also are grateful for the very skilled assistance of our copy-editor and indexer in Vancouver, Margaret Manery, our patient and far-sighted editor at Routledge in London, Stephanie Rogers, and her steadfast assistants, Rebecca Lawrence and Hannah Mack, before her.

We also thank the critical reviewers who wrote thoughtful assessments of this book before it was published. Mindful of the toll extracted from our dear and good-humored partners, we offer a Rashomon-esque variety of explanations and ask forgiveness, yet again.

[*A note re: the images*: The photos used in this book are publicity stills from Kadokawa-Daiei which were shot during the film's production. The limited range of images available for purchase included only three of the film's actors, and only in poses from the scenes in the forest grove. Several attempts were made to acquire the rights to images representing the key moments under the gate, but we were repeatedly refused the right to pay even for DVD frame-grabs of the scenes reflecting some of the most vital examples of the Rashomon effect in the film. Mindful of the Kodakawa Corporation's position on the use of their films, we have foregone including these additional images.]

# Chronology

| | |
|---|---|
| 1892 | Ryonosuke Akutagawa born; |
| 1910 | Akira Kurosawa born; |
| 1915 | Akutagawa publishes *Rashomon*; |
| 1922 | Akutagawa publishes *In a Grove / Yabu no naka* and *Autumn Mountain / Akiyama*; |
| 1927 | Akutagawa dies in Tokyo, by taking poison; |
| 1930 | Kurosawa deemed physically unfit to serve in Japanese military; |
| 1936 | Kurosawa begins to work as assistant director; |
| 1941 | December, Pacific War begins with Japan's attack on Pearl Harbor; |
| 1943 | Kurosawa directs his first film (*Sugata Sanshiro*) under Japanese government censorship; |
| 1945 | after Japanese surrender, SCAP (the Supreme Commander for the Allied Powers) oversees Japanese government operations, censors' criticism of US Occupation; Hashimoto begins to write film scripts while recovering from tuberculosis; |
| 1946 | May, first portrayal of a kiss in a Japanese film; |
| 1946 | June, Kurosawa lobbies with producers successfully on behalf of Toshiro Mifune, who is hired at Toho in spite of having failed his job interview; |
| 1948–9 | Kurosawa meets Hashimoto, reads *Rashomon* script, decides to complete it himself, then to direct it; |
| 1950 | May, US Occupation orders purge of Communist elements from Kyoto/Tokyo film studios; |
| 1950 | June, Kurosawa meets cameraman Kazuo Miyagawa on set of *Rashomon* and begins long collaboration with him; |
| 1950 | July–August, shooting completed in forty days near Kyoto and Nara; film nearly destroyed by fire; |
| 1950 | August–September, *Rashomon* first screened at Imperial Theater in Tokyo; |
| 1951 | summer, Giuliana Stramigioli, Tokyo-based Japan scholar and film importer, enters *Rashomon* in Venice Film Festival over objections of Daiei President Masaichi Nagata. Stramigioli provides subtitling and covers cost of transport of film to Venice; |
| 1951 | film chosen for competition at Venice Film Festival, though Kurosawa not informed; |

1951        September, Kurosawa and *Rashomon* win top prize at Venice; Japanese
            critics begin to debate the significance of *Rashomon*, at home and abroad;
1951        December, *Rashomon* screened in New York;
1952        March, Kurosawa wins special honorary Oscar at Academy Awards in
            Los Angeles.

# Front cover image

Publicity still featuring Machiko Kyo. The samurai's wife clutching her dagger, which comes to play an important role in the Rashomon effect. The American censors of Japanese films such as *Rashomon* made in 1950 expected directors to portray women in strong and self-confident roles. Kyo was a former dancer and had not acted before Kurosawa cast her for this film, but in her pivotal role she achieved an unusual dramatic range from childish whining to adult rage and scorn, and her performance was a hit with international audiences. (Courtesy of Kadokawa Corporation)

# 1 Introduction

*Blair Davis, Robert Anderson and Jan Walls*

Since Akira Kurosawa's death in 1998, a process of reflection has begun about his life's work as whole and its legacy to the cinema and its global audiences. There are already magisterial books on the works of Kurosawa, including some by authors featured in this volume. Our objective is to explore a core part of Kurosawa's legacy by using his most famous film, *Rashomon*, as the primary reference. First screened in August 1950, and winner of the 1951 Venice Film Festival prize, *Rashomon* has arguably become the best-known Japanese film, ever. After this, his twelfth film, Kurosawa's reputation was firmly established in international cinema, and *Rashomon* continues to be discussed and imitated more than sixty years after its first screening. Our bibliography includes the essential sources on cinematic history about Kurosawa, including Donald Richie's early seminal book in 1972: *Focus on Rashomon*.

Legacies are not simply intentional: Kurosawa often deflected questions about his intention. Legacies are not necessarily recognizable to those in whose name they emerge, but the legacies discussed here testify to the polyvalence of the work and its creator.

This collection of studies is entitled *Rashomon Effects: Kurosawa, Rashomon and Their Legacies*. We use the plural form intentionally because the essays in this volume address issues beyond the realm of *Rashomon* within film studies and center around the Rashomon effect, which itself has become a widely recognized English term referring to significantly different perspectives on and interpretations of the same dramatic event by different eyewitnesses. The dual figures of ripples and circles comprise the organizing image and principle of this book. The ripples represent the creative energy caused by each new iteration of the Rashomon principle, namely that any event or process usually involves more than one take, and indeed at times multiple, inconsistent and even conflicting takes. In this book, we describe the continuing and spreading results of an event or action as ripples. Like the ever-expanding ripples moving across water when an object is dropped into it, a ripple effect occurs when there is incremental movement outward from an initial state. This image has also been applied in financial markets to describe the impact of an event and how it circulates through the players in the industry and its effect on stock price and stock coverage. While the movement of the ripples represents the continuing and vibrant influence of Rashomon effects into the twenty-first century, the circles represent specific events, such as the publication of a new script, a particular production or a remake.

The ripples formed by dropping a small object into still water naturally form an expanding system of concentric circles. In our envisioning of the spread of awareness of Rashomon effects, its development has occurred in three significant stages – the boundaries of which we see as three time–space circles. In the innermost circle lies the origins of Kurosawa's Rashomon narrative, its literary archaeology from the seminal version found in the centuries-old *Konjaku Monogatari*, through Akutagawa's 1922 *Yabu no naka* to Hashimoto and Kurosawa's final screenplay entitled *Rashomon* in 1950. Then appears the larger middle circle, involving the production, circulation, translations and receptions (domestic and international) of the finished film. Third, we envision an outer circle that includes all of *Rashomon*'s subsequent transcultural, transdisciplinary and cross-media influences, all of which generate ripples that influence other iterations.

This fluid pattern of expanding ripples and geo-cultural circles describes the organization and structure of the book. In the twentieth century, light was discovered to consist of both particles and waves, and the tension between those two interpretations of the same phenomenon led to enormous creativity in science. Similarly, it is the vibrant and creative interaction between the kinetic energy of the ripples moving ever outward and the limits of each circle that this collection of essays captures.

Thus, this concentric and interactive structure of ripples and circles explains why different perspectives occur throughout this work. While there may be reasons to take a more unitary and singular approach to this complex phenomenon, we, on the contrary, feel that the strength and reach of this book lies in highlighting and emphasizing the number of possible interpretations of Rashomon effects, thus confirming and applying our underlying thesis, and producing our very own Rashomon effect.

All of us are limited by our different takes or spins on what we perceive to be reality or truth. The Rashomon effect is quite likely to have a permanent role in culture because it provides the perfect name for something that we cannot easily put a name to, because the film dramatizes and contains so much of our common experience. The appearance of a film's title in the language of our everyday life, for example, is consistent with our experience. It is quite common to hear people describe an intense sight, event or experience as like in a movie. Millions around the world have sat spellbound in darkness seeing films, thus establishing a cognitive link from cultures to the real world. Even the huge everyday presence of the movie industry, its stars, hype and money, does not diminish the cinema's effect in our imaginative worlds. Some describe even their most unusual experience as 'just like in a movie' – and this includes witness accounts of the sight of the airplanes crashing into the World Trade Center towers in New York in

September 2001. In part this infusion might derive from the representation on screen of things not seen previously, where the screen foreshadows in imagination something that comes later in life. Also in part this infusion constitutes a natural cognitive bridge. Given this dual power of the cinema in our ordinary and imaginative worlds, is the cinema not also bound to appear in language?

But we are suggesting that the relation of *Rashomon* and life is a little different from the common description. Spellbound by Kurosawa's art, viewers widely report that *Rashomon* represents and frames common everyday experience. They find a powerful connection between the way the film does not explain or close in on itself, and their own remembered and perplexing experience. They know intimately the ambiguity that *Rashomon* leaves in a new audience, because it is their ambiguity too. Therefore saying 'like in *Rashomon*' is consistent with the appearance of film in the language of everyday life, but moves it away from unusual experience and in the direction of usual experience. This is why it makes sense to speak of the Rashomon effect. Moreover, films seem at first glance to be easier than other media to understand, after all we see the same images, so brilliant in the darkness, therefore the experience must be shared. But is this so? Is it true, as D.P. Martinez asks in *Remaking Kurosawa*, that films are seen and believed to be fundamentally translatable as visual texts, that humans share a way of seeing? She also suggests audiences take for granted that the experience of being in the world is somehow shared. Is this true or is it an important fallacy (Martinez 2009:15)? This book tests the responses to *Rashomon* against that question.

This circular path – from an assessment of the work of an individual film-maker who began in a restrictive working environment, through a consideration of his impact during his long life and then to the legacy of his films far beyond his country and language – takes us back to Kurosawa as an individual genius. This circular path engages us in the inner life of an individual artist and his immediate social context in Japan, constantly enlarging the context along with Kurosawa's effort, so that from its furthest circumference, we must continue to put the artist and his legacy near the center. We become curious about something that has reached us by transcending its origins – how could this be achieved, we wonder? – and we are taken back to Kurosawa's original circumstances. Mindful of these origins, each author in this book adds something for a new generation so that it may more deeply appreciate Kurosawa's exceptional contributions and influence. The contributions glide from the early work of an individual artist (and viewers of his films) at the center of this enlarging circle to its furthest circumference – the legacies, the implications, the enduring puzzles. There are a variety of approaches to our subject that befit Kurosawa and *Rashomon*.

Much ink has been spilt on the issue of the non-Japaneseness of *Rashomon*, regardless of the surface manifestations of traditional Japanese setting, costume, architecture and language. This only became an issue after the film began winning prizes overseas, and the implication of the criticism clearly was that Kurosawa had intentionally pandered to Western audiences, thus exceeding the boundaries that define a Japanese film. In the field of boundary studies, a crucial distinction is made between people whose identity is marked by thick boundaries and those marked by thin boundaries. What we are calling circles in this book could also be called boundaries; particularly the circle that divides Japanese ripples from international ripples.

You will find here concise summaries of information on *Rashomon* from different authors, presented from different scholarly and critical perspectives. This is in keeping with the spirit of the film in that each variation presented is given its own distinct consideration, but without creating the conflicting representations that give rise to the Rashomon effect. There is also an unspoken intent in this book, and that is the wish of contributors not to subtract from the unique experience that first-time viewers have with *Rashomon*. Instead we think that when new audiences encounter this film and others by Kurosawa, there is a great satisfaction and reward in de-constructing their rich potential. As a young Canadian wrote recently, 'You avoided telling me why you asked me to see this film. Having seen *Rashomon* I find it now comes back to me, again and again. I cannot avoid the Rashomon effect. It was there all the time' (personal communication, November 2012).

Not only does Kurosawa's influence pertain to the cinematic imagery of future generations of filmmakers, but through films such as *Rashomon* the director has succeeded in overcoming essentialist notions of how cultural products are to be understood. That *Rashomon* has acquired its international reputation is testament to how the film simultaneously communicates with both Japanese and world audiences. Kurosawa himself writes: 'I decided to use the Akutagawa, *In a Grove* story, which goes into the depths of the human heart as if with a surgeon's scalpel, laying bare its dark complexities and bizarre twists' (1983: 135). He also writes that '... the human animal suffers from the trait of instinctive self-aggrandizement' (1983: 140). Both of these statements reflect his concern, not with Japanese characteristics, but with human characteristics. Kurosawa and screenwriter Hashimoto had steeped themselves in the literary, cinematic and artistic traditions around them, and in so doing were in a position to innovate. *Rashomon* was also subject, however, to specific challenges during its creation, as well as subsequent opportunities after its release, and these small details must be remembered when considering if and how an artistic creation is able to transcend its origins. Kurosawa's legacies are multifold: not only cinematic and artistic, but also cultural and cognitive, which the following chapters demonstrate from different perspectives.

## Outline of the chapters

This book asks broad historic questions, namely: What were the literary antecedents of the screenplay that began with Hashimoto's first effort to rewrite

Akutagawa's short story into a feature film; where did Akutagawa get the idea of presenting three irreconcilable self-exonerating testimonies recounting the circumstances of a death; how did the details of his biography influence the paths taken by the director; how did he seize creative opportunities and fuse them into a work of enduring value; was he much influenced by the work of other filmmakers; how does *Rashomon* fit into his view of his own work; what was the evolution of the characteristic Kurosawa aesthetic; how was *Rashomon* received critically at the time; how did *Rashomon* make its way to the Venice International Film Festival without the director himself even knowing about the submission; and as the ripples expanded, what did this film mean to others far removed in space and time from its origin?

In Chapter 2, Jan Walls explores the literary genealogy of the plot in which mutually irreconcilable self-exonerating testimonies are presented by partici-pants in or observers of a dramatic incident. This is essential information for the full appreciation of the film, but should be absorbed only after the viewer has first seen it. This contextual information was part of Kurosawa's own socially and culturally embedded awareness, but may need to be made explicit for a non-Japanese viewer.

Teruyo Nogami was twenty-two years old when she was handed the screen-play of *Rashomon* and told that she would work as the director's assistant. Chapter 3 recounts that experience, distilled much later through her memory of working with Kurosawa firsthand.

Donald Richie reflects on the production history of the film in Chapter 4, offering insights into the aesthetic and thematic reasons for Kurosawa's cre-ative choices on the set while filming in Nara and Kyoto.

In Chapter 5, Andrew Horvat investigates the circumstances that led from the first screening in Tokyo at the Imperial Theater to being short-listed and ultimately chosen for the top prize at the Venice International Film Festival in 1951. The way the choice was made by the jury, and reverberations in the Tokyo film and critical communities are remarkable for their diversity and disagreement.

In Chapter 6, Janice Matsumura examines some of the historical origins of attitudes and behavioral standards depicted in the film. She discusses their significance in light of Kurosawa's belief that historical authenticity must be maintained in pictures made entirely for a contemporary audi-ence. Matsumura discusses the Rashomon effect as an allegorical critique on human behavior in light of the (then) recent war crime trials in postwar occupied Japan.

Beginning the part of the book that focuses on the third circle of ripples, outward beyond Japan and beyond cinema, Robert Anderson explores in Chapter 7 what the Rashomon effect is, and what it is not. He identifies a more complex constellation of elements, a new paradigm that constitutes the Rashomon effect as found in many disciplines (including the courts). He con-trasts this complex paradigm with the simplified convenience of the popular understanding of it being about differences in perspective.

In Chapter 8, Nur Yalman explores the role of the Rashomon effect in anthropological thinking – where anthropologists have to understand the purposes and intentions of the actors yet recognize that due to their privacy and cultural complexity these intentions are not easily known. The Rashomon effect thus challenges the work of all social scientists, and so demands a high degree of self-awareness. Doing existential anthropology requires us to contain or even suspend our selves, and Yalman suggests that Kurosawa is working like an anthropologist, knitting the different pieces together.

In Chapter 9, Blair Davis and Jef Burnham examine the ways in which the director negotiates with screen audiences, and how audiences are enticed to negotiate with *Rashomon*. The film challenges the audience's expectations about narrative logic, and shows other directors a new way of storytelling. Davis and Burnham place *Rashomon* in its historical context regarding the use of narrative and structural elements in creating a nonlinear film.

In Chapter 10, Richie considers the reception that *Rashomon* encountered from audiences and critics upon release, concluding that the film not only shows us that which is typically Japanese, it also shows us that which is typically ourselves. He considers Kurosawa in the context of Japanese culture of the time, also examining the director's reputation after his death in regard to his legacy. Kurosawa sought in particular to have his greatest impact with younger audiences, wanting to teach them moral lessons through his films, but found little reception for this in his later years.

Stephen Prince describes, in Chapter 11, the vast international legacy rippling outward from Kurosawa's early work and its ongoing influence, reminding us that directors have to negotiate with an industry that survives by making profits, not art. Here is the long bridge between Japan and Hollywood and other film centers, where editors and directors first spoke and speak of a Kurosawa effect.

In the closing Chapter 12, Donald Richie and Stephen Prince sustained a dialogue from 2000 almost until Richie's death in 2013; this chapter compares the interesting differences between their own judgments on *Rashomon*. Here, the two scholars consider Kurosawa's role in Japanese history (both national and cinematic), as well as his own self-reflexivity. Despite the inward-turned quality of many of his films, Kurosawa remained an obtuse figure throughout his career, typically unwilling to discuss any questions of meaning in his films. However, as Stephen Prince notes, film directors around the world, working in very different genres and other film traditions, continued to cite Kurosawa as an inspiration.

## Writing about *Rashomon* and Kurosawa

Those of us who do not speak or read Japanese have found a window into *Rashomon* and its place in Kurosawa's world – in the unusual person of Donald Richie. While living in Tokyo from 1947, Richie was probably the first writer in English to look for and gather evaluations and criticisms of *Rashomon*, beginning with his *Rashomon: A Film by Akira Kurosawa* (1969). In that 1969 book he collected essays on *Rashomon* by a number of authors, beginning in 1952, and he also included his own essay published in 1965. Soon after that, while he was a Curator of Film at the Museum of Modern Art in New York in 1971–72, Richie followed up as editor of a second work, *Focus on Rashomon* (1972). Here he collected more reviews, commentaries and essays going back to 1952 and 1953. His own long essay for that book, titled simply 'Rashomon', was extracted from his first major book, *The Films of Akira Kurosawa*, in 1965. This is how, between 1965 and 1972, he began publicly to frame this film as worthy of intellectual analysis from diverse points of view. His prolific writing on other Japanese films and directors ran in parallel, and he sometimes said that the film that most intrigued him was *Rashomon*. As early as 1991, Stephen Prince said 'when one thinks of Kurosawa … one also thinks of Richie' (1991: xiv).

A series of major studies then opened *Rashomon* to careful scrutiny, and deepened our understanding of the director's life – much beyond his own rather circumspect 1982 book which he admitted was something like an auto-biography. The first major work was Stephen Prince's initial contribution in 1991, and drew on a wide grasp of aesthetic, filmic and conceptual history. *The Warrior's Camera* was so successful that an enlarged edition appeared eight years later, in 1999.

In his major study published in 2000, Mitsuhiro Yoshimoto decided to analyze each of Kurosawa's films separately, by itself, in sequence of completion by the director. Addressing *Rashomon*, and quoting Akutagawa, he conducted a careful analysis of its formal organization, and how the narratives are framed but left incompatible (2000: 182–9).

In 2001 Stuart Galbraith wrote a large biography of the lives and films of Kurosawa and his favorite actor Toshiro Mifune, with a wealth of detail gathered from interviews among Japan's film community (in English and in translation).

D.P. Martinez, an anthropologist of Japanese society in London, took a slightly more social approach in 2009 to *Rashomon*, in the context of Japanese understandings of that film, and then moved to the global permutated understandings of Kurosawa's work. These permutations are very like the ripples outward from Akutagawa and Kurosawa which we are exploring in this book.

More recently two monumental projects appeared, one in DVD form and one in the form of a beautifully illustrated book. The DVD project, assisted in part by the Toronto filmmaker Marty Gross, was the new re-mastered and re-translated Criterion edition of the film itself, and appeared in 2002. And the 2010 book by Peter Cowie has the written engagement of both Donald Richie and Martin Scorsese, and includes the drawing and script-notes of Teruyo Nogami (whose Chapter 3 appears in this book). Seeing Richie's role through this long period, his willingness to assist others, and his own evolving thoughts about this film – all of these suggest why we consider this work to be a kind of homage to this generous person.

## The effects of *Rashomon*

One of the earliest examples of the film's adaptation and transcendence into the realm of international art is that of a 1959 stage play of *Rashomon* by Fay and Michael Kanin in New York. In a trade publication advertisement running in *The Hollywood Reporter* in February 1959, several quotes from theater critics were offered in praise of the play, including:

> A beautiful and haunting setting
> Picturesquely exotic
> Out of a legend it conjures a mood
> Delicate and dynamic, sensitive and savage …
> Dozens of exotic images …
> Alive with scorn, full of laughs
> Nothing on Broadway is better acted, prettier to look at or
> more rewarding to think about.
>
> (*Hollywood Reporter* 1959: 18)

The rhetoric of these quotes is striking because they are a pioneering example of *Rashomon*'s move, like ripples, from one circle – its own cinematic production and reception – into another circle, that of international adaptation for live theater. Together these two circles should be seen as concentric. Although the focus on the exotic and the savage nature of the play in the above quotes might seem a typical example of a Western fascination with the charming qualities of an oriental Other, they are in fact signifiers of a larger process through which Kurosawa's *Rashomon* was able to have such widespread effects in international artistic and cultural circles. One of the advertisement's quotes goes on to state, 'No one can despair of a commercial theatre that can deal in elusive materials with so much delicacy, expertness and charm' (1959: 18). While the play's charming aspects may indeed have enticed viewers, the play, the film and their literary origins actually deal with moral and philosophical questions that are indeed complex – elusive perhaps – and certainly rewarding to think about. As such, by way of adapting Japanese source material to American commercial theater, a cross-cultural transfer was occurring in 1959, allowing Kurosawa's *Rashomon* influence to extend outward far beyond its original cinematic audience.

This rippling process would be repeated in numerous media forms and genres in the decades that followed, and *Rashomon*'s effects began to multiply as its legacy grew. At the same time, its legacy attained an intellectual currency when different figures in a variety of institutional contexts began to apply the film and its ideas to a wider and wider range of social and cultural phenomena as a way of trying to understand such elusive concepts as truth, reality and objectivity.

Examples of its continuing trans-media influence are too numerous to catalogue here, but a few examples will suffice for our present purpose: In 1959, the Kanins' stage play *Rashomon* ran for six months on Broadway; in 1973, the famous Thai writer and politician Kukrit Pramoj wrote a play called *Rashomon*, based on Kurosawa's film; in 1996, Argentine composer Alejandro Viñao created an English-language chamber opera called *Rashomon*; in 2005, the animated feature film *Hoodwinked* had Red Puckett, Granny Puckett, the Wolf and the Woodsman each tell the police their dramatically different versions of what really happened; in 2013, the Prithvi Theatre in Mumbai presented a Hindi-language musical called *Rashomon Blues*, based on Kurosawa's story; and in April 2014, Britain's National Youth Dance Company performed a dance entitled *The Rashomon Effect* at Sadler's Wells. In this way, *Rashomon*'s legacy continues to extend outward, moving from one concentric circle into another. It is this legacy and its effects that our contributors explore in this book.

---

Akira Kurosawa describing the struggles to get *Rashomon* made, and the creative inspiration for the Rashomon gate:

The Daiei management was not very happy with the project. They said the content was difficult and the title had no appeal. They were reluctant to let the shooting begin. Day by day, as I waited, I walked around Kyoto and the still more ancient capital of Nara a few miles away, studying the classical architecture. The more I saw, the larger the image of the Rashomon gate became in my mind.

(Kurosawa 1983: 133)

Publicity still featuring Machiko Kyo as the samurai's wife and Toshiro Mifune as the bandit. According to one of the narratives the samurai's wife pushes the bandit to kill her husband, but the bandit's expression betrays a range of emotions beyond the proud bravado seen in his own account of the events. When he is eventually captured at the riverbank, having fallen from his horse, the bandit is taken to a court where he explains his role in killing the samurai with his sword, and then the other participants recount their versions of the truth concerning the same death. (Courtesy of Marty Gross and Teruyo Nogami)

# 2 From Konjaku and Bierce to Akutagawa to Kurosawa

## Ripples and the evolution of *Rashomon*

*Jan Walls*

This chapter reflects the belief that knowledge of the story's evolution will enhance the viewer's understanding and appreciation of the ripple effect that gave rise to Kurosawa's cinematic masterpiece and, through the ripples created by its international circulation and acclaim, produced many other films and dramas based on the phenomenon now known as the Rashomon effect.

The historical background to the creation of the film starts with two anonymous short stories in the twelfth-century anthology called *Konjaku Monogatari* (Ury 1979). As mentioned in the Introduction, Rashomon effects are best understood through the ripple effect of something tossed into an existing pool. These ripples, or expanding circles, begin with the inner, or domestic Japanese, circle, which already showed us an example of trans-media ripple effects, as the Kurosawa-Hashimoto screenplay was an adaptation of two short stories written by Ryunosuke Akutagawa (1952), each of which was itself a vernacular elaboration of two twelfth-century Japanese anonymous tales. Akutagawa elaborated and expanded using techniques absorbed from reading such Western authors as Ambrose Bierce[1] and Robert Browning.[2] For example, in writing *In a Grove / Yabu no naka*, he borrowed the most important structural component from Ambrose Bierce's short story entitled *The Moonlit Road* (1918/2012) about three different deposition-like statements recounting the circumstances of a murder, one of which is the murder victim's spirit speaking through the voice of a medium. This is clearly the source of Akutagawa's and later Hashimoto's insertion of testimonies from the three involved parties, including that of the slain husband through the mouth of a *miko* medium.

Robert Browning's influence would have been through his four-volume dramatic narrative poem, *The Ring and the Book* (2001), which itself was based upon written records of a real-life case – written testimonies from a 1698 murder investigation in Italy – which he discovered while browsing in a Florence flea market in 1860 (Hodell 1908).

The influence of Bierce on Akutagawa has been stated by scholars in refereed journals. For example, in their Introduction to *Kirishitan Stories by Akutagawa Ryūnosuke*, Yoshiko and Andrew Dykstra state:

Akutagawa mentions in one essay that he admires Ambrose Bierce most among Western writers. The stories published here reveal Akutagawa's aversion of stupidity, greed, and hypocrisy, as well as a tendency to non-conformism as if to emulate Ambrose Bierce, the master satirist of the late 19th century.

(Akutagawa 2006: 23)

Renowned Akutagawa scholar Dr. Kinya Tsuruta stated in an article published in *Monumenta Serica*, one of the most respected journals in Japanese Studies:

A voracious reader, he discovered in many Western writers a rich source of literary inspiration both in form and subject matter. Prosper Merimee, Anatole France, Oscar Wilde, Edgar Allan Poe, to mention a few, exerted a considerable influence upon Akutagawa, and he is credited with introducing Ambrose Bierce to Japan.

(Tsuruta 1970: 14)

I maintain that the connection with Bierce's *The Moonlit Road* is much stronger than mere influence. The original Konjaku tale only told of a man joining a husband and wife on a country road, then luring the husband into a thicket with the pretense of showing him valuable hidden artifacts, then tying him up, raping his wife and running off with their horse. To this medieval Japanese core, Akutagawa added the story structure of Ambrose Bierce's *The Moonlit Road*: (1) detailed statements by (2) the main participants, (3) recounting the sequence of events leading to (4) a murder, (5) one of which statements was made by the murder victim (6) speaking through a medium. We could express this by a simple formula: $K + B = A$, where $K =$ the Konjaku tale, $B =$ Bierce's *The Moonlit Road* and $A =$ Akutagawa's *In a Grove*.

There are, however, at least two very significant innovations which Akutagawa added to the Konjaku tale that were not derived from Bierce: the addition of testimonies by people uninvolved with the three main participants (the woodcutter, the Buddhist priest, the wife's mother, the arresting policeman and the unseen judge-prosecutor who asks the questions that are answered in the testimonies) and the all-important element of irreconcilable self-exonerating differences in the testimonies of the three principal characters, leaving the reader unable to deduce who was most responsible for the husband's death, and feeling unsettled over being shown the darker side of decent people and the almost decent side of an infamous bandit.

When we finish reading *The Moonlit Road*, we not only know that the murderer was the husband, but we even know that he had suspected his wife of being unfaithful, and upon returning home in the dark of night he mistook his glimpse of a fleeing figure to be that of his wife's lover, and strangled her in his rage. The murder was based upon a misinterpretation of reality – mystery solved! Thus, in the genealogy of the all-important Rashomon effect, the lion's share of credit must go to Mr. Akutagawa.

The second *Rashomon* ripple effect, as cited in the Introduction above, is the production, circulation, translations and receptions (domestic and international) of the finished film. The third circle, which came as an unintended by-product of international film distribution, involves similar approaches (multiple irreconcilable self-exonerating perspectives) applied to creative works in different language-cultures around the world, resulting in the framing and naming of a universal social experience with human cognitive roots, now widely known as the Rashomon effect. The ripples from *Konjaku* and *The Moonlit Road* combined to create a bigger ripple with the publication of *Yabu no naka*, and its bigger literary ripple in Japan inspired Hashimoto's screenplay, which inspired Kurosawa to expand it into a larger screenplay called *Rashomon*, whose ripples have expanded to inspire audiences around the world so profoundly that the term Rashomon effect has now become familiar to people who have never even viewed the film itself.

## The associations of *Rashomon*'s title

An interweaving of titles and tales: the screenplay for *Rashomon* was co-written by Kurosawa and Shinobu Hashimoto. The latter had begun his screenwriting career by mailing handwritten scenarios to master filmmaker Mansaku Itami for criticism and guidance. One day, while reading the works of Ryunosuke Akutagawa, and realizing that none of them had ever been adapted into a screenplay, he decided to work on *Yabu no naka / In a Grove*. He originally entitled his screenplay *Male Female / Otoko-onna*, a Japanese term which is also used to describe effeminate men and masculine women. Kurosawa liked the script, but found it too short for a feature film. Knowing that it was based upon Akutagawa's *Yabu no naka*, Kurosawa decided to add the recollections of two trial witnesses plus the skeptical townsman while taking shelter from the rain at the Rashomon gate, which was inspired by another of Akutagawa's short stories, *Rashomon* (1983).

Akutagawa's short story entitled *Rashomon*, truth be told, is just a slight elaboration of the Konjaku Monogatari tale entitled *How a Thief Climbed to the Upper Story of Rajomon Gate and Saw a Corpse*, with no significant new elements added to the plot, except for some dialogue between the two figures, and the thief's explaining his own justification for stealing the old hag's clothes after listening to her justification for stealing her dead mistress' hair. Akutagawa does, however, intensify the feeling of moral decay, and the selection of Rashomon gate sets the moral tone for the irreconcilable and self-exonerating testimonies of the four versions of what happened in a grove.

This is, in fact, the essence of both of Akutagawa's short stories – *Rashomon* and *In a Grove*. In the former, the old hag stealing hair from her former mistress' corpse, and the fired servant stealing clothes from the old hag, both portray themselves as having just cause for stealing. *In a Grove* has each participant – the robber, the wife and the husband – put a different spin on the sequence of events that lead to the husband's death, each intended to exonerate the narrator.

Akutagawa's short story *Rashomon* provided Kurosawa with a setting: a crumbling old city gate inhabited only by crows and abandoned corpses, heavy rainfall, and a central focus on ethics. In Akutagawa's short story, a man ducks into the Rashomon gate seeking shelter from the relentless rain. For the past few years, the city (Kyoto) had been devastated by a series of calamities, and people were dying of hunger and poverty. This man is a servant who has just been fired by a master who could no longer afford to keep him. He begins to think that he, too, is destined to starve if he doesn't resort to robbery. When, after hearing a noise from above, he climbs up the dark stairway into the gate tower, he finds an old woman moving around in the darkness with a torch. She seems to be pulling out hair from the head of a female corpse. Watching such immoral behavior, he becomes indignant. Angrily he draws his sword and confronts the trembling old woman. She explains that she is pulling out her late mistress' hair to make wigs, adding that the woman from whom she was stealing hair also did immoral things to survive, so the corpse would understand that her immoral behavior, too, is unavoidable. 'Well, in that case then, it's okay if I rob you too', the man concludes, and runs off with the old woman's clothes (Akutagawa 1952: 40).

Kurosawa's film begins under the same Rashomon gate with people seeking shelter from the relentless heavy rain, a scene taken straight from Akutagawa's short story; the film ends not only back at Rashomon gate, but also with the townsman's stealing of clothes (this time from an abandoned baby), with the self-exonerating claim: 'What's wrong with that? Dogs are better off [than people] in this world. If you're not selfish, you can't survive' (1952: 40). This is followed by the woodcutter's remark: 'Damn it. Everyone is selfish and dishonest. Making excuses … even you!' (1952: 40). The townsman then quickly points out that the woodcutter has no right to lecture him about morality, because it's pretty obvious that he stole the valuable pearl-handled knife the woman had pulled out when she discovered that Tajomaru had tied up her husband. This revelation stuns the woodsman into the realization that all of them except the monk are motivated by greed and self-exoneration (Richie 1987).

But unlike the two Konjaku tales and Akutagawa's two short stories, the film doesn't end on this dismal note. In the final minutes, as the rain subsides and the sun appears, the woodsman decides to take the abandoned baby home and raise it along with his six other children since, after all, one more mouth to feed won't make that much difference. He walks out of Rashomon gate into the sunshine with an optimistic and benign smile on his face, having seen the error of his ways. The monk, too, has had his faith restored in the existence of good in this dirty world (1987).

**What's in a name?**

The name of the south gate in the external city wall was Rajōmon (literally, net city wall-gate or web city wall-gate), meaning the gate through the external city wall that surrounds the internal city wall. Akutagawa changed the name to Rashōmon (net life-gate or web life-gate), perhaps to symbolize the issues of life, death and ethics. Web life recalls the web of dharma (cosmic law), which in the Buddhist worldview enmeshes or catches all sinners, as the fisherman's net catches fish. Add 'gate' to this verb-object compound and we have the gate of netted lives, or the gate of enmeshed lives.

The literal title has other connotations in the context of the story and the film. Life here refers not just to any and all living things, but specifically to each of the characters involved in the incident around which the whole story unfolds, for each character has a selfish angle or take on what was happening, and each must share at least some of the guilt for the whole outrageous incident. There is a Buddhist angle here: For Buddhists, the self is believed to be an artifact created by the interplay of illusory forces (*maya*), and therefore essentially unstable and transient – something to be transcended and ultimately shed, so as to enable the unfiltered, direct experience of truth.

While Kurosawa clearly takes the dilemma of different selves very seriously, a Buddhist perspective would say that this further underscores the seriousness of the basic problem itself; perspectives on truth are limited by the boundaries of the illusory self, reinforcing the argument that self with its socially constructed boundaries is something that must be transcended to perceive greater truths.

Another more basic Buddhist take on the story is that all suffering is rooted in selfish desire. The conflict in the story begins with Tajomaru's desire to steal other peoples' possessions, and his desire to have the beautiful woman. Had the husband's desire not been stirred by the promise of hidden treasures, he would not have followed Tajomaru into the woods, and all the suffering could have been avoided.

Interestingly, the film's title was at first to be rendered in English as *The Gate of Hell*, which is an imaginative cross-cultural rendering as it embraces the karmic idea of accountability for sins committed during one's life and fits nicely with the recollection of the trial, whose proceedings structure the film's discourse: The story unfolds as a by-product of the quest for truth and justice, through which process the guilty will have hell to pay. Unfortunately, however, *The Gate of Hell* is the literal translation of the title of another Japanese feature film, *Jikoku no mon* (1953) directed by Teinosuke Kinugasa, so perhaps the best way to deal with the title *Rashomon* is to leave it alone, leave it untranslated.

If an English speaker wishes to discuss the film with a Japanese friend or colleague, *Rashomon* is more likely to be recognized, than any English translation of the title, which would probably require much explanation before it would be identified as referring to Akutagawa and Kurosawa's masterpieces.

Tajomaru is branded a bandit. It matters who is called a bandit, and when. Freedom fighters in Chechnya have been called criminal bandits by the Russian military that were fighting them. Soldiers and fighters at war in Afghanistan in 2001 were soon re-classified as bandits in 2002, depending upon whose side they elected to support in their guerrilla warfare and robbery. In medieval China, Song Jiang and his band of rebels became heroes in the tales of the *Water Margin*, just as Robin Hood and his Merry Men were seen as outlaws by the medieval English establishment, but regarded as heroes in popular lore.

We are lucky to have a useful source on the lives of bandits, noblemen and warlords in medieval Japan in the work of Pierre Francois Souryi (2001).[3] He portrays a world upside down, held there by the weakness and chaos of Kyoto and the ambitions of Kamakura.

This is medieval Japan, the era portrayed in the Konjaku tales, from which Akutagawa drew much of his inspiration, where bandits moved in pairs or groups committing robbery, assault, poaching and contract intimidation. However some bandits also cut hay in the spring and harvested rice along with the peasants, often in their hometown areas. Many bandits preferred to work alone, but groups of them could grow large enough to challenge the authorities and resist taxation. Some bandits actually came from local ruling groups, including warriors and estate managers. A monk from Mount Hiei led a group of a hundred bandits, who did battle with the governor's troops. Bandits also targeted toll barriers, gates, markets and sites linked to trade activities (2001). Beside affiliation with certain monks, some bandits cultivated an association with *yamabushi*, mountain priests, who were thought to be sorcerers dealing with mountain demons and ghosts.

In the original Konjaku tale, the anonymous man who joins the husband and wife on the country road is never referred to as a bandit, and after he lures the husband into the woods with the promise of showing him hidden treasures, ties him to a tree and rapes his wife, 'the man arose, dressed himself as before, strapped the quiver on his back and the sword to his waist and, bow in hand, hoisted himself onto the horse. To the woman he said, "… I'm sorry, but I must go away. I have no choice. As a favor to you I'll spare your husband's life. I'm taking the horse so I can make a quick escape"' (Ury1979: 185). And he galloped away, no one knows where. He is portrayed as a robber-rapist with a conscience. In Akutagawa's much expanded version, the same robber-rapist is referred to by the arresting policeman as 'a notorious brigand called Tajomaru' (1979: 4), but in his own testimony, Tajomaru says that he had no intention of killing the husband, but was forced to when the wife decided that she would go with the one who survived their fight to the death. In the Kurosawa-Hashimoto version, Tajomaru (by his own testimony) is also forced to do battle with the husband when the wife tells him: 'Either you or he must die. To be doubly disgraced, disgraced before two men, is more than I can bear … I will belong to whoever kills the other' (Richie 1987: 57). In a sense, especially when compared to the defiled wife and the cold-hearted husband, Tajomaru does not come across as a mere bandit, but more like an outlaw with a sense of honor. Everything depends upon the spin imposed by the speaker.

## *Rashomon* in translation

It is appropriate to give some attention to the matter of *Rashomon* in translated subtitles, for the vast majority of non-Japanese viewers (including most of the Academy members who voted for it to receive an Oscar as Best Foreign Film) follow the story only through its translated subtitles.

If you can understand colloquial Japanese, and you sit down and watch *Rashomon* with one eye on the English subtitles, the other on the main screen, and both ears listening to the Japanese sound track, you find that the subtitles reflect what is spoken on the Japanese sound track quite accurately. The noticeable differences between the English subtitles and the Japanese sound track are mainly in stylistic or connotative equivalence. The written English subtitles for Tajomaru's utterances, for example, are not as vulgarly colloquial as Mifune's spoken Japanese – but to the English reader/viewer/listener, Tajomaru's vulgarity can't be missed as it comes through unmistakably in his facial expressions and in the gruffness of his voice. On the other hand, Masago, the bride, tells Tajomaru rather abruptly in the English subtitles 'Kill him! Kill him!' while her Japanese line is the much more formal and dignified '*Sono hito wo kuroshite kudasai! Sono hito wo kuroshite kudasai!*' ('Kill that person, please! Kill that person, please!').[4] But we can imagine that, even there, the effect of surprise on the Japanese listener and the English-speaking viewer is probably about the same. The English subtitles for *Rashomon* must be considered highly effective overall, although sadly I cannot locate the name of the skillful translator.

In 2002, further attention was paid to the film's subtitles, when the Criterion Collection released a new DVD of *Rashomon*. The disc features (along with an excellent audio commentary by Donald Richie) new translated subtitles – one example of which proves to be particularly intriguing. At the end of the film when the priest and the woodcutter discuss the newfound baby's fate, the woodcutter says in the standard translation, 'I'm the one who should be ashamed. I don't know why I did that' – a line that some have interpreted as a confession of guilt over his behavior after he discovered the corpse. The newly translated subtitles offer the following variation, adding further mystery to the woodcutter's motives: 'I'm the one who should be ashamed. I don't understand my own soul'.[5]

## Notes

1 Ambrose Bierce (1842–ca. 1914) was a famous American journalist and short story writer whose stories are considered among the best of the nineteenth century.
2 Robert Browning (1812–1889) was one of the foremost poets of the Victorian era, best known for his dramatic verse and especially for his dramatic monologues.

3  I am grateful to Robert Anderson for bringing this to my attention.
4  In Richie (1987) 'The Continuity Script', shot #177, the English translation is 'Wait. Stop. One of you must die. Either you or my husband', but the English subtitle on the film reads 'Kill him! Kill him!'
5  *Rashomon* (2002) Criterion Collection DVD, 1:25:29) [1 hr, 25 min, 29 sec into the film].

---

Akira Kurosawa on the ways in which *Rashomon* was inspired by silent cinema:

Since the advent of the talkies in the 1930's, I felt, we had misplaced and forgotten what was so wonderful about the old silent movies. I was aware of the esthetic loss as a constant irritation. I sensed a need to go back to the origins of the motion picture to find this peculiar beauty again; I had to go back into the past. In particular, I believed that there was something to be learned from the spirit of the French avant-garde films of the 1920's.

(Kurosawa 1983: 134–5)

# 3 'Smiled on by Lady Luck: *Rashomon*' (2006)

## *Waiting on the Weather: Making Movies with Akira Kurosawa* (English translation by Juliet Carpenter)

*Teruyo Nogami*

### Akira Kurosawa arrives

In 1946, the year that Mansaku Itami died, producer Seiichiro Eida arranged for everyone in Tokyo with some connection to the man to get together in a pub and drink to his memory. Together we formed a society called The Itaman Club. Members included haiku poet Kusatao Nakamura, whom Itami had called Basho reincarnate; Kiyoshi Saeki, Itami's chief assistant director; fledgling scriptwriter Shinobu Hashimoto; and many others.

A strange series of circumstances led Hashimoto, who was born in 1918 in Hyogo Prefecture, to embark on the career of scriptwriter under Itami's tutelage. As a young man, he had such radiant good looks that Mrs. Itami tells me his nickname was 'shining prince Genji', after the title character of the Heian-era novel. Nonetheless, he had been sickly from childhood. Having suffered from pulmonary tuberculosis, intestinal blockage, diseases of the kidney, pancreas and liver, and even bone fractures, he had been through major surgery time and again. Virtually no part of his body was left untouched – yet after each bout of sickness he made a full recovery, with all the resilience of a Rasputin.

Had he never come down with tuberculosis (TB), however, Hashimoto might never have become the great scriptwriter that he is today. Indeed, the motion picture *Rashomon* might never have existed, either.

Among Itami's unfinished scenarios was one entitled *If*. In it, a samurai on a journey rushes to a ferry crossing but arrives a second too late, so the ferry leaves without him. The story develops from there, showing what would have happened if he had caught it in time. As that storyline showed, sometimes luck truly plays havoc with people's lives.

Hashimoto was drafted into the Tottori Fortieth Regiment during the war, but he soon came down with TB and was sent to the Disabled Veterans Sanatorium in Okayama, where tubercular members of the military were housed. He was put in a middle bed in a six-man ward. One day the soldier next to him handed him a magazine, saying, 'If you're bored, try reading this.' The magazine was *Nihon Eiga* (*Japanese Movies*), published by the Great

Japan Motion Picture Association. In the back was a scenario. Hashimoto read it through and said to himself, 'I could write one of these.' Turning back to his neighbor, he asked who the top scriptwriter in Japan was, and was told, Mansaku Itami. His roommate must have been an avid movie fan.

Transferred to a new ward, Hashimoto decided to write a scenario, but he had no idea what to write or how to begin. He went ahead and bought some writing paper, and at the top of the first page he wrote in bold letters, Scene 1, followed by the name of the sanatorium, which was known informally as the mountain sanatorium. He decided to do a portrait of the soldiers who came there, calling it *Mountain Soldiers*.

When he had finished, he sent it off to Itami in Tokyo. The reply he received came from Kyoto, however, to where Itami had retired after leaving Toho upon contracting TB himself. This was in 1941.

In his letter, Itami wrote frankly, 'Your style is immature, and I see no sign of a gift for writing.' But he added, 'Yet there is something beyond these flaws.' Hashimoto says he suspected that Itami's interest lay less in the scenario itself than in the new treatment for tuberculosis it described. Still, he was thrilled to have heard from Itami at all. He went to show the letter to his former roommate, only to find that he had already been released and sent home to Matsue. When he telephoned his home, he was told that the soldier had died three months before. The man who opened a door that fatefully changed Hashimoto's life never lived to see the outcome of his chance remark.

Hashimoto kept on writing scenarios and sending them to Itami for advice. His health gradually improved, and after the war he got a job working as an accountant for a bicycle company in Himeji. One day, having injured his back, he stayed home from his job and read works of the brilliant short story writer Ryunosuke Akutagawa. Realizing that none of them had ever been made into a film, he decided to try adapting *In a Grove* (*Yabu no naka*) for the screen.

He put his desk out on the veranda and began writing with such absorption that he never even noticed when it began to snow. In three days he was finished. He titled his script *Male and Female* (*Shiyu*). It was very short, only ninety-three pages of half-size writing paper.

Unfortunately, by this time Itami, too, had passed away. When Hashimoto went to Kyoto to attend a memorial service for his mentor, Mrs. Itami introduced him to Kiyoshi Saeki and told him that from now on, this was the person to whom he should send his scripts. Accordingly, he later sent a packet of them, including *Male and Female*, to Saeki in Tokyo.

Born in 1914 in Matsuyama, Kiyoshi Saeki attended Matsuyama Middle School, as did Daisuke Ito and Mansaku Itami. This connection led to his becoming Itami's assistant director. After Itami's retirement, Saeki stayed on at Toho as chief assistant director for Hisatora Kumagai and Yasujiro Shimazu. He also became friends with Akira Kurosawa, who was then chief assistant for Kajiro Yamamoto.

In 1941, Saeki was dispatched to Borneo as a member of the navy press corps, and he remained away from Japan until April 1945. In the interim, Kurosawa achieved great success with his directorial debut, *Sanshiro Sugata* (*Sugata Sanshiro*, 1943), a film whose reputation reached even Saeki overseas. When Saeki came back to Toho just before the end of the war, Kurosawa wrote a script for him called *Bravo! Tasuke Isshin* (*Appare Isshin Tasuke*) to demonstrate support for his friend's debut as director. But Saeki left Toho, which was beset by postwar labor strife, to join the breakaway Shin Toho Company, and Kurosawa made *The Quiet Duel* (*Shizukanaru Ketto*, 1949) at Daiei.

After the two men went their different ways, in another trick of fate, they suddenly met again one day in front of the fountain at Toho studios. Kurosawa mentioned to his old friend that there was talk at Daiei of doing a period piece, and asked if he knew of any likely stories. When Saeki mentioned the Hashimoto script, Kurosawa expressed immediate interest. The two men set off right away, walking over to Saeki's house. Kurosawa skimmed the script and asked if he could borrow it for a while. It was a tad short, he said, but it might have possibilities. Saeki agreed, and said that if the script seemed usable to let him know and he would have the author come up from Himeji.

In the course of time, Hashimoto received a postcard from producer Sojiro Motoki and made the trip to Tokyo. He stayed in Saeki's house and traveled to and from Kurosawa's house in Komae to work on the scenario. This is how Kurosawa met the man who would go on to write the scripts for masterpieces such as *Ikiru* and *Seven Samurai*.

To lengthen his script, Hashimoto tried combining the story with another Akutagawa work called *Rashomon*, but the result was too long and less interesting than before. On top of that, Hashimoto's back pain returned, rendering him immobile, so in the end Kurosawa did the rewriting himself.

In 1950, the Daiei Kyoto Studios were abuzz with the news: Akira Kurosawa was coming. *Stray Dog* (*Nora Inu*, 1949) had just been released. With his regular entourage in tow, including producer Sojiro Motoki and actors Toshiro Mifune, Takashi Shimura and others, Kurosawa swept into the studios with all the grandeur of the rising sun.

In our excitement, we rushed to the window, making comments like, 'Look, it's really Akira Kurosawa!' and 'I can't believe how tall he is!' as we watched him stroll around the lot with Mifune and the rest. Just walking around, he and the others exuded a kind of overawing vitality.

## Dancing on Mount Wakakusa

I wrote earlier about being cheated out of good money we paid for Lucky Strike cigarettes – an episode that underscores how popular Western cigarettes were back then. Here is director Yoshitaro Nomura talking in 1974 about the filming of *Scandal* (*Sukyandaru*, 1950):

I was quite impressed that while our maestros [at Shochiku] all smoked Western cigarettes, director Kurosawa puffed away on a Japanese brand. [*laughter*] Then, after a while, Kurosawa turned to me and said he had run out of smokes, and did I know of any place nearby that sold Western cigarettes? [*laughter*]

(Akira Kurosawa Dokyumento 1974)

I have a personal recollection in the same vein from the shooting of *Rashomon*. For location shots in Nara, we stayed in an inn at the foot of Mount Wakakusa. Directly above the assistant directors' room was the banquet room where the crew and actors all ate dinner. I was in the assistant directors' room for a meeting, and heard waves of laughter from overhead. Then we saw a cigarette come tumbling down; clearly, someone upstairs had stubbed it out and pitched it out the window. The misshapen butt landed on a stone in the garden, where it continued to emit a steady stream of thin smoke. Tokuzo Tanaka, the third assistant, looked at it and commented wryly, 'Looks like upstairs they're smoking Western cigarettes. See, it doesn't go out.'

The chief assistant then was Tai Kato, and second assistant was Mitsuo Wakasugi, who later joined the theater group Mingei. Later, each of the three men would go on to become a film director with a unique style of his own. Kato, then thirty-three years old, was the nephew of the famous director Sadao Yamanaka. He joined the Toho studios in Kinuta through his uncle's good offices and would go on to direct many superb yakuza movies; despite his undeniable talent, however, for some reason he and Kurosawa did not get along.

Before shooting began, the three of them called on Kurosawa, told him they found the script impenetrable, and asked him to explain it. Kurosawa answered by telling them that the script was about the very impenetrability of the human heart. From that point on, Kato began to drag his feet. He would show up late for a shoot or stand looking from a distance, a pipe in his mouth and a critical look in his eye. Still, it was he who affectionately bestowed on me my nickname, Non-chan. It happened like this.

One day before shooting began, Kurosawa was playing a game of catch with Takashi Shimura. As I walked by, the ball came rolling right up to my feet. Wearing a piqué hat, a white T-shirt and jeans, his hand encased in a baseball mitt, Kurosawa waved at me to get my attention. 'That's our ball,' he called, and to Kato, beside him, he said, 'What do you people call her?' I was still a newcomer with no nickname, so Kato was at a loss for a reply. On the spur of the moment, he mumbled, 'Er, Non-chan. That's Non-chan.' Lacking the strength to throw the ball from a distance, I picked it up, went over close to Kurosawa and then tossed it to him a bit shyly. He smiled at me in that charming way of his and said, 'Thanks, Non-chan.'

And from that moment on, Non-chan is what Kurosawa always called me. Peering through the viewfinder, he would call, 'Non-chan, bring me some water,' or 'Non-chan, haven't you got any ice?' My heart beating fast with

ut that a cord
He got teased
at his phobia

sawa and the
usa. At such
:asugi wrote,
t our under-
d down, and

n a circle to
companying

ing. (Later, of course, as my bloom
n! What do you think you're doing!')
summer, and when I took Kurosawa
of sweat and garlic would assail my
/er from the banquet the night before.
called *sanzoku-yaki,* (*mountain bandit*
garlic.

naturally I was not present at the ban-
w, even teetotalers such as cameraman
:en'ichi Okamoto, would join Kurosawa
me a hallowed tradition, partly because,
:nue for directing. Sometimes right in the
he would make an important announce-
ad to be ready.

s person. When he got back to his room
carefully write down all sorts of data and

t

/

that point

pened the lens as much as possible to gauge
n I used eight mirrors (four feet square) to
s and over the cliffs, so that I could clearly
:ting in black-and-white contrast.

(Nogami n.d.)[1]

gin forest of Nara. The movie opens with a
ltter, proceeding deeper and deeper into the
nis shoulder.

spectfully
rs old – it
matically
ise of the
in Kyoto,
*un,* but in
was only
in Kyoto

rk print.
anies to
o, extra
al form.
ne main
o to get

d back
always

rs to reflect sunlight. But because the sun is
sky, the lighting crew had to scout out places
g and lug the heavy mirrors there across the
:e afternoon, Okamoto called up, 'Kameoka,
lair more to the west?' The answer came down,
won't hit it.' The soft drawl of the Kyoto dialect
nyone from Tokyo it sounds slow and happy-go-
aching, the director bellowed in irritation, 'Then
lace where the sun WILL hit it!' His angry words
ncidents help explain why the Kyoto crew com-
ounds too harsh.

looting had mountain leeches, we were told. They
ut could plop down on you from branches over-
lpon hearing this, we were literally shaking in our
ore setting out we smeared our necks and ankles
ver, said cheerfully that he would rather deal with
th snakes. One day as we were preparing to shoot
e stared, pointed and leaped up like a monkey. His

face was ashen. He thought he had seen a snake, but it turned
dropped by the lighting crew had come sliding down the path.
for being afraid of an electric cord, but there was no doubting th
was real.

At night, when the reveling reached its peak, oftentimes Kuro
rest would dash outside and race each other up Mount Wakak
times I would join in, puffing along behind them. Mitsuo Wa
'There was one time Tokuzo Tanaka and I raced in nothing bu
wear. Yelling "Return to the wild!" or some such thing, he stripp
I rashly followed suit' (Akira Kurosawa Dokyumento, 1974).

When we had all reached the top of the mountain, we'd get
sing the folk song *Tankobushi* (*Coal Miner's Song*) and do the ac
dance in the moonlight.

| | |
|---|---|
| *Tsuki ga deta deta* | The moon is out |
| *Tsuki ga deta* | The moon is out |
| *Miike tanko no ue ni deta* | Over Miike coal mine |
| *Anmari entotsu ga takai no de* | The chimney is so tall tha |
| *Sazoya otsukisan kemutakaro* | The moon must be smoky |

That far, we danced in the style of the summer Bon dance, but from
on we shifted to an energetic digging motion, like coal miners.

Everyone was young. Kurosawa himself was barely 40.

## The camera work is one hundred plus!

At the Kyoto studios, it was customary to address the director re
as *Sensei*. It might be his first picture, he might be only twenty yea
didn't matter. As soon as someone became a director, he was aut
given this title of respect. One day, however, Kurosawa banned the
word, insisting that he be called by his name. Conventions die hard
and at first people found it awkward to address him as *Kurosawa-s*
time they got used to it and even felt closer to him because of it. This
the first of many revolutionary changes he brought about at Daiei
during the filming of *Rashomon*.

One such change I have touched on already: the editing of the wo
In those days it was customary not only at Daiei but at most comp
pre-edit the negative. The daily rushes were rough cut, but even
material had been snipped away, and what we saw was close to fin
I assumed that this was the proper way to edit a film. Undoubtedly, t
reason for doing it that way was to save money on work prints, and al
a sense of the overall length of the film.

After filming on location in Nara, the crew of *Rashomon* all troop
to the studios in Kyoto. The first dailies after a location shoot are

awaited with a special mixture of anticipation and trepidation. Cameraman Kazuo Miyagawa, who would be seeing the dailies alongside Kurosawa for the first time, must have really been on tenterhooks, as if awaiting judgment. But all of us were feeling nervous as we showed up in the preview room.

As it turned out, that day's viewing ended unlike any other. No sooner were the lights back on than Kurosawa tore outside and began lambasting producer Sojiro Motoki. Editor Shigeo Nishida, a good-natured elderly man, stood off at a little distance, listening with an air of anxiety. The rest of us filed outside, looking uncertain. Kurosawa was walking along, still giving Motoki a piece of his mind. Perplexed, I caught up with them, and heard the director say, 'I never shot the scenes that way!' He was clearly upset. Turning around, he told me, 'Print up the whole thing again, just the way we shot it.'

The editor had simply trimmed the shots and assembled them in order as usual, but in so doing he had apparently altered them somehow. Kurosawa fumed, 'Showing me something like that throws me all off!' He formally notified the company that from then on the dailies should be made without any changes and the editing be left entirely to him.

The location shots in Nara were the important scene where Takashi Shimura's woodman proceeds deeper and deeper into the forest, a sequence of shots whose rhythm was particularly difficult to establish. Subsequently Kurosawa re-edited the scene and finally pronounced himself satisfied. Today, editing the work print, rather than the negative, is universal standard practice.

Amid all this hoopla Miyagawa never got to ask what Kurosawa thought of his camera work. Kurosawa for his part had meant to praise the cinematography, but forgot to do so. Hearing from Shimura that Miyagawa was worried about it, he hastily declared, 'One hundred percent. The camera work is one hundred! One hundred plus!' (Kurosawa 1984).

Another change he brought about had to do with sound recording on location. In those days, location shots were always silent, with no recorded sound. Even the camera they used on location was a primitive, hand-wound contraption; you could almost hear the cameraman protesting, 'Who wants to lug a heavy battery so far? I'll just crank the darn thing myself.' An assistant cameraman would attach a measure and crank to the motor, and then keep an eye on the gauge while turning the crank at the rate of twenty-four frames per second. If the shot lasted ten or twelve seconds that was one thing, but if it went over three minutes the assistant would be pouring sweat, his body bent double from exertion as he cranked along.

This crank-style camera was used on location for *Rashomon*, too – until Kurosawa banned it, saying he found it disagreeable. Of course, he had personal experience operating such a camera. In the dream sequence of *Drunken Angel* (*Yoidore Tenshi*, 1948), at one point Toshiro Mifune is given chase by his own ghost. While Kurosawa was shooting the open sea in the background, some good waves appeared, and with no assistant cameraman around, he took it upon himself to turn the crank – only to find it was extremely difficult to maintain a constant speed. Fluctuations in his feelings were conveyed straight to his hand, creating unevenness in the speed of the film. At the time, he declared himself pleased with the irregularity, but whether those shots made the final cut, I never knew.

To record sound on location, far from a hand-cranked camera, we needed a crystal motor to synchronize the image and sound. Even if the two were recorded simultaneously, little of the original sound was ultimately usable, and generally much of the dialogue would be replaced later. This procedure is still followed today, and it is quite practical. Until it was adopted, the recording crew was never taken on location. It created a stir when we first did it, but the company allowed it because the request came from Kurosawa.

The third technical revolution also had to do with sound recording. Back then the lowliest recording technician of them all was Ken'ichi Benitani. Today he is a superlative master of his craft, but then he was just a kid in a sweaty T-shirt, lugging a heavy battery. I always called him *Beniyan*. Whenever he and I get together, we share endless memories of *Rashomon*, and one of the most notable has to do with the outdoor post-recording of additional dialogue.

Generally, any sound recording done after filming takes place in a recording studio, while the edited film is being projected. But Kurosawa declared that for voices heard from a distance, or loud shouts, you couldn't convey the proper sense of distance in a studio, and so we would have to do it outdoors. It sounded reasonable, but no one had ever done such a thing before. Confronted with this challenge, recording technician Iwao Otani wailed, 'This is cruel!' Beniyan has vivid memories of the experience.

They erected a sort of screen in an empty lot out in back of the recording studio, and reflected the image from the projector on it using two mirrors. The mirrors were big ones we had used frequently during filming. One was fastened to the right side of the projector, and the other was set in the doorway of the projector room so that the image flashed from mirror to mirror and onto the outdoor screen.

'That was a real first', says Beniyan. 'I'll never forget it. But in the daytime it was so noisy outside we couldn't do it. The trains on the Arashiyama Line made a lot of noise. So we had to wait till the middle of the night, after the trains stopped running, to get started.'

That's right. His words brought it all back – the sight of Mifune and Shimura standing outside in the middle of the night, watching that screen and whooping back and forth.

Of the original *Rashomon* crew, few of us are left now. Beniyan suggested the other day that we all get together someday with Kurosawa to share our memories. Now that would truly be a gathering of war veterans.

## Shooting the sun

It should surprise no one if I say that Akira Kurosawa knew all about movie cameras. He would consult with his cameraman and decide the structure of every shot himself, peering through the viewfinder and even selecting the proper lens. As a result, he always knew the precise limits of the frame, and had no trouble telling what was in the picture and what was not.

If we were shooting on a snowy day, for example, the rest of us would tiptoe around, careful not to make footprints in pristine snow, but he would stride fearlessly in front of the camera. Seeing the horrified looks on our faces as we gaped at the big footprints he had made, he would reassure us confidently, 'Don't worry, this is all outside the frame.' You had to marvel at the accuracy of his eye.

Perhaps because he had this reputation, people assumed that he loved cameras in general, and often – particularly when he traveled overseas – he would be presented with first-rate still cameras. But he had no interest in them. Kurosawa was something of an anomaly in that way, a modern man who never in his life clicked a shutter.

Later in his career, from *Seven Samurai* on, he became famous for shooting with multiple cameras, but in the beginning he used only one. *Rashomon* was shot with a single camera.

Cameraman Kazuo Miyagawa was another one who stayed glued to the finder from the time his camera was set up. Kurosawa would come and sit down alongside him, and from then on one or the other of them was always looking through it. Hei-san (Heizo Kondo), an assistant cameraman, used to complain, 'When do I ever get a turn?'

To the end, Kurosawa would insist that his assistants look through the camera. 'Come see!' he would yell. 'Why put passersby over there when they won't be in the frame? It's a waste!' Certainly the assistants did look through the camera, but it was no easy matter to develop an eye as unerring as Kurosawa's.

All of this is meant as prologue to a discussion of *Rashomon*. I think the beauty of *Rashomon* stems from the simplicity of its compositions and the exquisite sense of light and shadow it maintains. In an early scene the bandit, played by Toshiro Mifune, lies asleep under a large tree and awakens – when a gust of wind shifts the shadows of the overhead foliage – to see a woman passing by on horseback. (If only it had not arisen, none of the rest of the action would have occurred.) The shadows play across his chest as he pursues her with his eyes. The scene is beautiful, and ominous.

There is also the beauty of the scene where a beam of light falls on the woman as she rests her white horse in a ravine, waiting alone by the stream for the return of her husband. That scene was shot early in the morning, after Kurosawa happened to notice the ravine when we passed by.

Then the bandit returns, tells her that her husband has been bitten by a snake, takes her hand, and pulls her along as they hurry through the forest. On they rush, through the shadow and light of the surrounding trees. Usually this kind of shot is done with a dolly, the camera on wheels, all of us scurrying along trying to keep up. But Kurosawa rejected that approach because it wasn't fast enough. He insisted that the scene would work only as a panning shot. So he set up the camera, drew a circle around it, and had the actors tear around while the camera panned a full 360 degrees.

The completed scene shows the pair running at full tilt through the forest. Since Miss Kyo's feet did not show, he had her wear sneakers. The combination of sneakers with that ancient costume of hers was hilarious.

Akira Kurosawa loved the sun, and in his autobiography he discusses the role of the sun in *Rashomon*:

> One of my major concerns in filming *Rashomon* was how to capture the sun itself. This was necessary because the light and shadows of the forest would form the keynote of the entire film. I decided to resolve the problem by photographing the sun directly.
>
> (Kurosawa 1984)

At that time, cameramen were still afraid to film the sun straight on, fearing that the sun's rays might destroy the film in the camera. Miyagawa, however, boldly turned his camera up toward the sun, capturing wonderful images of sunlight filtering through the treetops.

The famous scene where the bandit grabs the lady and kisses her against her will was shot from many angles, including one from below showing the sun through the treetops in the background. To do the scene, the actors had to get up on something called an *intore-dai*. This is an easily assembled raised platform named after D.W. Griffith's 1916 film *Intolerance*, where it was first used.

The first Japanese film with a kissing scene was the Daiei production *One Night's Kiss* (*Aru Yoru no Seppun*), directed by Yasuki Chiba in 1946. Back then, that one scene was enough to pull in huge crowds, but since then the novelty of simple kissing scenes had worn off. Even so, Mifune appeared quite tense. He refrained from eating garlic the night before, gargled before the shooting began, and generally tried to be as considerate as possible. When the time came for him to plant his lips on hers, he first said, 'Please forgive me,' with an air of embarrassment.

When it was time to record her reactions, the camera had to be mounted on the *intore-dai* in order to capture her facial expressions from above. I remember Kurosawa standing up there and saying over and over, 'Kyo-chan, open your eyes, keep them open wide!'

As the pair embraced, dappled shadows of leaves played on the sweaty shoulders of the bandit. So that the shadows would stand out clearly, members of the lighting crew stood with tree branches in their hands, waving them in front of the lights. For larger shadows they spread a net overhead, piled it with branches, and then swayed it gently. Mifune's sweat was the work of the makeup crew, who scooped up water in their hands and splashed it on him.

The thicket where all of this took place – i.e. the scene of the rape-murder – was behind the temple Komyo-ji, near the Katsura Detached Palace in Kyoto. It started out as a small clearing surrounded by woods, but as the crew moved in with camera and lights, it was slowly transformed into a movie set. At first the crew would hesitantly ask permission every time they needed to lop off a branch or cut down a tree, but they soon went about their work in a matter-of-fact way, and eventually the clearing became a usable set. The temple's abbot was taken aback; he'd never before realized how much effort went into making a movie, he said. He gave the director a fan on which he had written the words 'Benefit all living beings.'

Shooting went remarkably fast, lasting from 7 July to 17 August 1950, or just forty-two days. When the weather was sunny we went to Komyo-ji, and when it was overcast we worked at the open set of the Rashomon gate at the Daiei studios. Records indicate the reconstructed gate was some 33 meters (98 feet) wide, 22 meters (72 feet) in depth, and 20 meters (65 feet) high, and covered 1,980 square meters (2,368 square yards) on the ground. I can vouch that it was really huge – so big that if we had built the whole roof, the pillars could not have borne the weight. And so we destroyed half of the roof, which also helped bring about the desired effect of ruination. Standing under that gate, you could always get a cool breeze, even on a hot midsummer's day. During lunch breaks the carpenters used to nap under it in a row, like a fisherman's catch laid out on the beach.

For the scenes with the Rashomon gate, Kurosawa wanted to create a downpour through which the gate would loom dimly in the mist, so three fire engines were kept stationed nearby to douse it with spray. No one foresaw how providential this would be.

## The negative, get the negative!

Looking back, it seems unbelievable: despite experiencing two major fires during production, we managed by some miracle to finish *Rashomon* on time. The official history of Daiei describes it this way:

> Moreover, on the evening of 21 August, just before completion of the film, unfortunately a fire broke out on the second stage of the Kyoto Studios, casting doubt on the scheduled release, but the crew members came together and worked so hard that the picture came out as planned. It premiered on 25 August at the Imperial Theater, sponsored by the *Yomiuri Shinbun* as a benefit for the Yukawa Foundation, and went on to be shown at Daiei theaters nationwide from the next day with overwhelming box office results. The fighting spirit shown by all concerned is a source of pride at Daiei.
>
> (*Daiei Junenshi* 1951)

As noted here, the premiere took place only days after a major fire. Not only that, the picture premiered at the most glamorous venue in Tokyo. During the intervening three days, although it is not mentioned in this account, there was in fact another, smaller fire as well. Despite this spate of bad luck, we were able to scramble to meet the deadline. Perhaps our never-say-die determination harked back somehow to the spirit of the final days of the war, when everyone was supposed to be ready to drive the enemy from our shores. In any case, we somehow did the impossible.

A short circuit, we were told, caused the fire on the second stage where director Kimiyoshi Yasuda had been shooting *The Mendicant Monk Mansion* (*Komuso Yashiki*). Filming of *Rashomon* had wrapped the week before, and we were busy with the editing and synchronization of the music, sound effects and dialogue. I have no memory of just when or how I heard the cry of 'Fire!' but I do remember the editing room quickly turning into a madhouse.

The reason is plain: people were editing the negative, with piles of it lying everywhere. In those days, we used nitrate film stock, which was flammable, so the whole room was a virtual tinderbox waiting to explode. And the tenement-style wooden structure we were in, with a series of long, narrow rooms connected by a squeaky wooden corridor, was itself just so much kindling.

The spirit of cooperation was strong in the motion picture industry of those days, and as news of the fire spread, people from the nearby Tokyo Film Company (later Toei) came running. They dashed into the chaos of the editing room and swiftly helped carry out the precious film. In the midst of all this confusion, as people ran around like chickens with their heads cut off, I can remember Kurosawa himself towering over everyone else and bellowing, 'The negative! Get the negative!'

Fire engines tore to the studios along the same route they had traveled so often before, this time with sirens wailing. The water tank on the open set was still full, and soon jets of water from the hoses were crisscrossing over the roof at full blast, just as they had during shooting. Once the film had all been carried out, we sat around at a safe distance and watched as the billowing white smoke and leaping red flames gradually subsided. Some girl assistants were crying hysterically.

Later, Kurosawa told me that at the height of the confusion he spotted a bit of negative on the floor, rolled it up and stuck it in his pocket. Then a security guard came along with the news that cameraman Miyagawa had collapsed at the gate. Kurosawa barked, 'What do you mean, he's collapsed? Don't leave him there, get him to the infirmary!' When he reached the gate, Miyagawa was going on distractedly about a missing segment of negative. Kurosawa produced the rolled-up bit from his pocket, and Miyagawa exclaimed with delight, 'That's it!'

Tokuzo Tanaka, then assistant director, has another story to tell. As he was running around in the aftermath of the fire he bumped into director Kurosawa, who abruptly said, with a strangely satisfied look on his face, 'Well, there's no way we'll make the release date now.' Having come from the Toho studios, he underestimated the determination of Daiei not to let a little snag like this interfere with a deadline. Soon he had to eat his words.

*Rashomon* was safe. Second assistant Mitsuo Wakasugi told me that he loaded the cans of negative on the back of his bicycle, went out to an empty field in front of the set, and watched the firefighting efforts. Kurosawa soon came walking along, looking glum. Wakasugi reached over wordlessly and tapped the cans behind his bicycle to indicate that all was well. Understanding, Kurosawa gave him a delighted smile of relief.

'The next step was harder,' Wakasugi remembers. 'Straightening it all out again.' All the different batches of film in the room had been grabbed up and thrown in together, so everything had to be sorted out. 'Mixed up with *Rashomon* was part of a movie called *Raccoon Dog Palace* (*Tanuki Goten*),' he recalls with a chuckle.

I was put to work alongside the assistant editors in the hunt for a missing piece of sound negative containing a bit of Toshiro Mifune's dialogue. It was the part where his character, the bandit Tajomaru, says, 'I've never met such a tough woman.' The search was complicated because unlike camera negative, sound negative gives you no visual clue – nothing but a pattern of stripes, like a bar code, so there's no way to tell what you may have without putting it into the Moviola Editing Machine and listening. Anyway, there we were with the premiere breathing down our necks, and we just couldn't find it. In the end, we had to have Mifune make a special trip back from Tokyo just to dub that one line.

Several years ago I spoke over the phone with Iwao Ohashi, the recording engineer for *Rashomon*. His voice sounding exactly the same, he marveled that our filming had been so many decades ago. The recording room had been just off the second stage, the source of the fire, he told me, so when the fire started he got flustered and threw the recording equipment out the door, smashing it in pieces. As a result, for dubbing he was stuck with an older model that was usually reserved for working outdoors. He lamented that the process didn't work very well. 'No use whining,' he told me, 'but I wish it had come out better.'

Whatever he may say, in my opinion the dubbing came out beautifully, a testament to hard work and dedication. Ken'ichi Benitani, a recording assistant at the time, recalls that the night before the dubbing they had an expert from Tokyo Film Company come over and work with them all night as they tried to put the smashed machine back together, to no avail.

With no time to catch our breaths, the day after the big fire we were back at work, rushing to get the film dubbed, when yet another fire broke out. Suddenly the picture on the screen froze; evidently the film was stuck in the projector. The next thing we knew, the center of the projected film frame began to turn black, a hole opened in it, and then it was in flames. All of this showed on the projection screen. 'Another fire!' we shouted, and scrambled outside. Smoke billowed from the projection room.

As before, everyone scurried around, carrying bits of the film to safety. Benitani and some others, feeling like old pros, formed a bucket brigade to throw water inside the burning room, but this turned out to be a mistake: the nitrate film stock then released a poisonous gas, filling the room instantly with clouds of noxious smoke. Otani and Benitani both had tears streaming from their eyes and saliva drooling from their mouths, and suddenly they fell down, unconscious. When they came to, they were lying on straw mats outside the infirmary, along with many others.

There was nothing to do but start the dubbing all over again. Back then there was no tape, so all the music was recorded live as the picture was projected. If anything went wrong, it meant starting again from the top. The famous segment reminiscent of *Bolero* went on for a whole ten minutes. I can remember looking at the backs of director Kurosawa and composer Fumio Hayasaka as they sat and listened without stirring. When it was finally done, Kurosawa looked at Hayasaka with apparent satisfaction. By then, it was already morning.

## Lady Luck

Today's youngsters will unfortunately never know the thrills we experienced dubbing movies in the era of *Rashomon*. Time spent recording the music was filled with special intensity: a mistake by one person meant starting all over again from the top, or just gritting your teeth and letting it go. Today you can say, 'Okay, we'll take it from a few bars back. Connect it where the drum comes in,' but not back then. Nowadays editors use tape with abandon, cutting and splicing all they please. Do they have any idea how lucky they are, I wonder? The difference between having and not having tape is about as dramatic as the difference between before and after the light bulb.

Nowadays a two-inch tape has twenty-four tracks, divided by instrument, so with a flick of the finger you can adjust the sound any way you want, increasing the volume of the chorus, say, or eliminating the piano. All of the orchestra members don't even have to show up at the same time. If people's schedules don't match, there's no reason different parts can't do their recordings on different days.

Back in the old days, all of the musicians had to show up at once. As the scene requiring music was shown on a big screen, the conductor kept watch, synchronizing the movements of his baton with what was unfolding before him. Since the musicians had their eyes on the conductor, naturally they were sitting with their backs to the picture. When a love scene came on, those with nothing to do at that moment would twist around in their chairs to watch.

Bear in mind, this was an age when each company put out four motion pictures a month. The musicians worked for different companies simultaneously, wandering from place to place with their instruments in hand, and often working nights at a cabaret to boot. Many were old foxes who gambled on cards and horses when no one was looking.

They held Hayasaka in awe, however. Once, during the recording, one musician asked him, 'Isn't there something wrong with this part?' Hayasaka retorted, 'No, there's something wrong with your head.'

Once the recording for *Rashomon* was done, everyone stepped out of the room, rubbing their bleary eyes and saying, 'Look, it's morning.' I went outside and found Hayasaka sitting in the coolness of the summer dawn, smoking a cigarette with evident enjoyment. Going over to him, I had the boldness to say, 'Listening to that Bolero music, it sounds as if the woman is being held in contempt' – as if I knew what I was talking about. He listened and said only, 'Is that so,' with what actually seemed to be a contented smile.

At the time, I was immensely drawn to Hayasaka, which is probably what led me to say such a thing. 'Is that so' was a pet expression of his, and even when some busybody went and told him I had a crush on him, that was all he said. Unfortunately, I was quite beneath his notice.

As I mentioned earlier, one segment of dialogue by the bandit Tajomaru was mislaid in the confusion caused by the fire, and actor Toshiro Mifune had to make an emergency trip back to Kyoto. His whiskers now gone, he showed up at the dubbing room looking dapper, and said sympathetically, 'Well, you've had quite a time of it, haven't you?' According to recording engineer Iwao Otani, his line, 'I've never met such a tough woman,' was added during the recording of the music, using a separate microphone. That's how desperate a state we were in.

Although the 25 August premiere at Tokyo's Imperial Theater loomed dead ahead, the fire on 21 August paralyzed the studio. Then on 22 August we experienced the smaller fire in the projection room in which Otani and his assistant Ken'ichi Benitani were knocked senseless by poison fumes. It really seemed as if God was testing our endurance.

Today I wonder: How on earth could we have made the release deadline? Did we force Otani and Benitani to revive, and then start dubbing that very night? Even assuming we set to work on the morning of 23 August and worked straight through the night, it would have taken at least until noon of the following day to record all the music. A car must have been parked idling outside the recording room, ready to take off at an instant's notice for the processing room. As soon as the shout went up, 'Here it is!' the courier must have grabbed it, yelled, 'Okay, I'm off!' and torn off posthaste for the darkroom.

The first print was ready at around seven that night, I believe, but for the life of me, I cannot remember sitting down to preview it with the director and staff. After working around the clock for the better part of a week, I must have been pretty woozy. In any case, there was nothing for it but to send that print off to Tokyo overnight. The job fell to assistant director Tokuzo Tanaka, who boarded the last night train and headed for Tokyo with a fresh print in his lap. If it had been a movie, music would have swelled up, overlapping with the train whistle as he departed.

Early on the morning of 25 August, Tanaka arrived in Tokyo and went straight to the Daiei studios, where President Masaichi Nagata and other executives were waiting. An immediate prescreening was held. Later, Tanaka described the scene this way:

After the pre-screening, the lights came back on, and nobody said a word. Usually this was when somebody would say, "This picture'll do well," or "It'll be a hard sell," or that sort of thing. Not this time. The room was hushed, all of the executives trying anxiously to read the boss's face. After a while, he opined, "Well, I don't get it ... but it certainly is a high-toned picture." Just like that, the screening room filled with its normal buzz and chatter.

(Tanaka 1996)

And so, one hour after its preview at the home studio, having been completed as if by a miracle, *Rashomon* premiered at the Imperial Theater in Tokyo and was released nationwide the following day.

Reviews were not favorable, however, and it looked as if the movie was destined to create only a brief stir before fading into oblivion. That might well have happened had not the Japan representative of Italiafilm, Giuliana Stramigioli, chanced to see it. Thanks to her enthusiastic endorsement, in September 1951 *Rashomon* was entered in the twelfth Venice Film Festival, where it won the Grand Prix. This electrifying news provided inestimable encouragement and inspiration to Japanese in the postwar era.

It is well known that Daiei president Nagata, on being informed of the picture's success, said wonderingly, 'What's a Grand Prix?' He wasn't alone; nobody knew. Kurosawa himself never even knew that his film was in competition until it won. His next picture, *The Idiot* (*Hakuchi*, 1951), shot at Shochiku, had been so badly received that Daiei rescinded permission for him to shoot his next picture with them. Kurosawa, full of bitter disappointment, decided to go fishing, but the first time he tried to cast his line it caught on something and snapped. Feeling like the whole world was against him, he went home in a dark mood. When he opened the door, his wife said, 'Congratulations!' and told him the news about the Grand Prix.

He commented, 'Thanks to that award, I was spared from having to eat cold rice [i.e. be shunted aside].'

Not everyone connected with the picture basked in its glory. Some, such as assistant director Mitsuo Wakasugi, went into limbo. Just after the release of *Rashomon*, Wakasugi was forced out of the film company in a red purge, and expelled from the labor union as well. Just as colleagues were distancing themselves from him and he found himself suffering in isolation, he received a postcard from Kurosawa:

It said, 'This is the perfect chance, so write a scenario. Don't be afraid of failure.' I was so happy; I broke down and cried like a baby. I thought, I'm still in the movie business. In that trying time, he was the only one in the movie business who gave me any encouragement.

(Akira Kurosawa Dokyumento 1974)

Wakasugi's purge must have struck a chord of sympathy with Kurosawa, himself a survivor of the labor strife at Toho.

After winning the Grand Prix, Kurosawa was in demand from all sides. The following year, in 1952, he went back to Toho for the first time in four years to make *Ikiru.*

### Farewell to Kyoto

The year 1950 was a tumultuous one in the Japanese movie industry. It was also, of course, the year of the outbreak of the Korean War.

In May, Toho dismissed 1,300 people from its payroll. General MacArthur's official notice of a purge of Communist elements quickly took effect nationwide, and in September, Daiei also sent out pink slips to thirty people. Meanwhile, another twenty-nine members of the film industry previously purged as war criminals were now happily de-purged, and they returned to work one after another. It was interesting to see the two groups switch places.

The official history of Daiei contains the following description:

> Our company quickly published the names on the 25th, and except for those involved in filming, from that day on their access to the studio was denied. From then on Daiei faithfully kept its pledge, not allowing the invasion of any destructive elements, and cooperating internally as well.
>
> (Akira Kurosawa Dokyumento 1974)

I'll never forget a scene I saw then, exactly like something from a movie. On either side of the tightly closed main gate, people who had been work colleagues the day before stood with their arms reaching out, grasping and thrusting, jostling and tussling with each other. I walked by at a distance, pretending not to see, but deep down the sight left a lasting sense of shame.

After *Rashomon,* the next movie I worked on that year was Taizo Fuyushima's *Demon Azami.* This was the seventh picture made at Daiei by actor Kazuo Hasegawa, who had joined Daiei the previous year on the picture *Koga Mansion,* with the rest of the Shin Engiza people.

Fuyushima started out as a scriptwriter, and he apparently wrote a lot of scripts for Hasegawa when he was still a budding actor known as Chojiro Hayashi. He knew a lot about Kabuki theater. He could only have been fifty or so, but to me he seemed like an old man. He walked with a shuffle, and his voice was weak. With skin as fair as a Caucasian's, thick hair and lustrous black eyes, he was handsome, but there was something gloomy about him. Cameraman Kohei Sugiyama, on the other hand, was stylish and cheerful. While testing his panning shots on location, he would say, 'After all their practicing, suppose they do the scene and finally get an OK on it, and then I tell them, "Oops, forgot to turn the camera!" That would be just great, wouldn't it?'

In those days, shooting with a Mitchell camera was tricky. After looking through the viewfinder lens, you had to slide the camera body laterally back in front of the shooting lens, or nothing would be filmed.

From the first of the following year, 1951, I began working on Issei Mori's *Ashura Hangan*. Mori was from Matsuyama, and so sometimes when we happened to meet in the studio we'd chat about Mansaku Itami and one thing or another. Mori was a big bear of a man; I remember fondly how he used to come lumbering down the corridor. Though you'd never have guessed it from the size of him, he was actually quite shy. Whenever we talked he had a habit of blinking and pursing his lips. 'When I got accepted into Kyoto University, I came in number two. Number two, you got that?' he would say, and then add with that shy laugh of his, 'Of course, that year there were just two of us in aesthetics.'

When it came to making a movie, though, he was a different man, quick thinking and decisive. He had a knack for shooting a movie quickly. To save time, he would do all the shots with the same background at once, so he easily managed fifty shots a day.

'Ready, action. OK. Skip the next scene. Ready, action. OK. What? It's all right, it's all right. Skip the next two. Ready, action. OK. Now a long shot. Next. Ready, action. OK.' He kept up such a fast pace, there was barely time to change the numbers on the clapperboard. Since I was from Tokyo, sometimes he would tease me by deliberately adding a little Tokyo flavor to his speech as he went along.

*Ashura Hangan*, based on Eiji Yoshikawa's novel *Ooka Echizen*, about a famous judge, featured three major stars: Denjiro Okochi in the title role, Kazuo Hasegawa as the shogun Yoshimune, and Takako Irie. In the course of the movie, there was a love scene between Denjiro Okochi and Takako Irie. Some love scene – it consisted of no more than Okochi lying down beside Miss Irie. Even so, Okochi was hugely embarrassed. As soon as the director called, 'Cut,' he jumped up and gasped, 'What took so long!' The entire crew burst out laughing.

Not long after that, Daiei was shaken awake by a huge piece of news. On 12 September 1951, every newspaper in Japan carried the flash that *Rashomon* had been awarded the Grand Prix overseas. Here is an excerpt from the write-up in the evening edition of the *Mainichi Shinbun*:

> The Japanese film *Rashomon* (a Daiei film directed by Akira Kurosawa), which was entered in an international film festival currently being held in Venice, received the Grand Prix (the highest award) on the 10th ... *Rashomon* was released on 2 August. Former British Prime Minister Winston Churchill put in an appearance at this event while on vacation, and is said to have praised *Rashomon* lavishly.
>
> (UP Report 1951)

The studio was in an uproar. Even a nobody like me was showered with congratulations by everyone I met: 'Good for you!' 'What a terrific prize!' 'How wonderful!'

Orders for *Rashomon* came pouring in to Daiei from far and wide, and soon it became necessary to do a special dubbing for an overseas edition. We were set to re-record the music at the Daiei Tamagawa Studio, and for that I would have to go to Tokyo.

One other factor contributed to my decision to go back to Tokyo. Around that time my colleagues had been cautioning me against crossing any forbidden boundaries with Issei Mori, whose wife was a former script girl and our senior. Never do anything to upset her, they stressed.

When I told Mori that I would be returning to Tokyo, he stared at me and said he was going there, too. He would be shooting *Vendetta of Samurai* (*Ketto Kagiya no Tsuji*, 1952), with screenplay by Akira Kurosawa, for Toho. 'It's all settled,' he told me.

Later I, too, joined Toho, but I never worked with Mori again.

In 1951, young master Juzo had gone home to Matsuyama, entering Matsuyama East High School. His fellow alumnus, writer and Nobel laureate Kenzaburo Oe, once gave me this description of his friend during his schooldays: 'He always wore a short cloak, and looked like [French actor] Gerard Philipe.' It gives me pleasure to imagine what a dashing figure he must have cut.

Just before New Year's 1952, I left Kyoto.

And so I bade farewell to Uzumasa, the neighborhood of the Daiei Kyoto Studios. Looking back now, I feel warm nostalgia for all the people I worked with there.

## Notes

1 Nogami citing *Satsuei Oboegaki* (Miyagawa's 'Cinematography Notes').

Figure 1 Sketch by Teruyo Nogami depicting Kurosawa as he directs *Rashomon*. (Courtesy of Marty Gross and Teruyo Nogami)

# 4   The production history of *Rashomon*

*Donald Richie*

At the heart of the Rashomon effect is the ambiguity the film instills in the viewer. When we see the film, it opens up as the short story *Rashomon* opens up – in the rain with the spokesmen, one of whom is the woodcutter. The woodcutter's story is the one that Kurosawa took probably the most care with when it came to scripting because I think he wanted to conserve the ambiguity in the story, and for that reason put a hole in its center. What he wanted to do – although Kurosawa has never said anything about this – was to ensure that everybody had an agenda. He suggests in the film that the woodcutter also had an agenda: the dagger. Where is it? Who took it? By providing everyone with an agenda, the film becomes comparable to an Agatha Christie story. Everybody has a reason for killing the person who was murdered, and by so doing Kurosawa has hopefully made a level playing ground.

On the other hand, there are many people who believe that the version told by the woodcutter is the definitive version. In fact, one of the generally accepted accounts of *Rashomon* is that all the other people had agendas that motivated them to lie, but that the woodcutter didn't have any reason to do so. They believe he was a good man anyway, because he took the baby. However, there is another school that says the woodcutter took the baby out of contrition for having murdered the nobleman. This web of life is something that Kurosawa and Hashimoto purposefully wove, in order to keep the ambiguity in the story, which is what Kurosawa would have considered one of the most precious things about it.

At the end of the script, Kurosawa particularly thought that something was necessary to create a kind of a closure and to make more of a definite ending – which would be otherwise unrelieved, and philosophically anarchical. The morality in the film is that there really isn't any, since morality is presumably based on some sort of truth, and truth itself as the film has demonstrated is divisive. At this point comes the notorious baby. The baby does not figure into any of the material that they were working with. At the end of the film, however, the priest describes how men cannot be much better than animals if they do not respect human life, as indeed the film has been suggesting. Sure enough, at that point they manage to save the baby, with the woodcutter doing the noble thing and taking the baby home with him. The sun comes out and the rain stops, creating an example of the pathetic fallacy at work.

This scenario suggests a happy ending, but it is a happy ending at an entirely different level than the film itself has been operating on. In other words, the metaphysical concerns that the picture has been engaged with have been transferred at the end to completely emotional – sentimental, as you would have it – irrelevant concerns. This works toward the film's power very well, because we realize that questions have not been answered, and something has been fobbed off on us. I do not think that Kurosawa intended this, but as a matter of fact it benefits the film considerably.

Of particular interest about the script's adaptation is the presentation of the trial in the film. As presented on screen, the trial in *Rashomon* was viewed as theater in Japan. Everything that is said by the characters during the trial is theatrically recounted, presented, dramatized. Japanese audiences in 1950 were familiar with the conventions from the original story, which was extremely famous. This is not representational cinema, it is presentational cinema, and the conventions of the theater – even classical theater – have this idea of the presentational. In other words, we are looking at a series of performances, at least as far as the trial in the film goes. Even the dialogue does not acknowledge that there are judges present. The woodcutter says things such as 'Yes, that's right, I was the one who found the body,' 'What? Did I see a sword or something?' and 'That was all I found, yes'.[1] In other words, you do not hear the questions. All you hear is the repetition that the woodcutter gives, with the judges being implied.[2]

This format occurs several times in the film. When the bandit is busy scratching himself and laughing at the judges, you do not hear what the judge has said to bring forth this laughter. Rather, all you hear is the response. Stylistically, this is a brilliant device, because just as in the written story, you only see the separate facets of something that might or might not be the truth. You also do not hear anything except the characters' explanations of how this occurs. The people whom we are looking at on-screen control all of the other voices, and this increases the feeling of their separateness.

Once the script had been completed, the next task was finding a place to make the film. Even in 1950 Japan, finding a dense forest was extremely difficult. They finally found such a one in the old capital of Nara, and went through the negotiations that are always necessary with the owner of anything. The land was owned by a temple, and so negotiations were made with the head priest. He agreed to the filming, but soon discovered that the crew were cutting down trees in order to improve camera angles. The priest remonstrated at this, until they paid him some money, which allowed them to continue to cut down trees. So in this way, little by little, the forest scenes were filmed.

The cast and crew were living on location very near the temple, and for recreation in the evenings they would often look at movies. They had a 16-millimeter projector with which they would show movies at the temple itself. The films that Kurosawa ordered for showing could be considered rather strange in that they were mainly animal films. Martin and Osa Johnson were explorers who made several animal documentaries in the 1930s, and Kurosawa ordered three or four of them to show. During the films, when a black panther came slinking on screen, Kurosawa turned to lead actress Machiko Kyo and said, 'Now, this is the way you do it'. Then when a lion came on, he turned to Toshiro Mifune and said, 'This is your model for the role' (Kurosawa and Cardullo 2008: 10). He said it half playfully, but these people were used to working with Kurosawa, and they knew what to take seriously or not.

Accordingly, when you look at the scenes in the forest in *Rashomon*, you see the animality that everybody mentions. Of course, you would naturally see the animality of human beings in that situation, but there is also the animality of animals present. While the actors do not do animal imitations, nonetheless everybody has sort of taken Kurosawa's advice, and this indeed has ended up in distinguishing the acting in this film.

The acting base, of course, is not classical; it is not the Noh, nor the Kabuki, nor the Bunraku. It is very close to Shingeki, which is what passes for modern theater in Japan, but is Shingeki-plus whereby it becomes expressionist acting, just as the film itself is expressionist in style. When you look at Kazuo Miyagawa's photography, do remember expressionist cinema. In viewing the first scenes of the walk in the forest, the critics suddenly remembered Fritz Lang's *Siegfried* (1924), and they were on the right track. Kurosawa had seen *Siegfried*, and so had his cameraman, and while they were not concerned at all with the principles of expressionism, they were in a way making an expressionist document.

The producer, Mr. Nagata, walked out of the screening in the middle, saying *Sappari wakarimahen*, which is Osaka dialect for, I don't understand a single thing I'm being shown. Nevertheless, he did not forbid it. He thought it was a kind of novelty picture, and that is why he let it go through. Although critics in the West have long wanted to believe that the film was very unsuccessful (and that it was only its discovery by the West that saved Kurosawa's skin), this is not true. The film was among the ten highest grossing films in Japanese theaters in 1950. Hence a lot of Japanese saw the film, and a lot of Japanese thought well of it. What criticism there was denounced the acting. Poor Mifune was always hauled off to one side and told he didn't know how to act. Someone else said that Machiko Kyo was being excessive, criticizing that a court lady would never be that vulgar.

On the whole, however, the film was very widely accepted in Japan – accepted and forgotten. Then what seemed like all of a sudden, the Venice prize descended and the film made its reputation in the world, surprising everyone in the process. Kurosawa was extremely surprised at its international reception. He simply had not thought that it would ever be shown abroad, since this did not happen to Japanese films. He certainly did not think that it would be accepted abroad, not realizing at that point – although he would realize later on – that his vision, his metaphysics, transcended his own Japaneseness, and spoke in a lingua franca, which all of us understand.

In a way, I think that all Kurosawa scholarship is because of *Rashomon*. It was the first Japanese film that commanded the attention of the West. It was not the first Japanese film ever shown in the West, however, as that film was a Naruse picture that ran in New York under the title of *Kimiko* in 1934 and played for a couple of weeks at the Fifth Avenue cinema. This was not enough, however, to give anybody much of an idea about what Japanese cinema was like. In 1951, when *Rashomon* was shown at the Venice Film Festival, it opened everybody's eyes not only because people hadn't known that Japan even had a cinema, but also because the film itself was so extraordinary, and for its time so demanding, that it at first baffled people. I remember that when it first came out people were going around scratching their heads and saying: What on earth could it be about? It was originally known as a puzzle picture, like *Last Year at Marianbad* (1961) the following decade, whereby audiences reveled in speculating about what it all meant. But then little by little, ripple by ripple, the film became influential. It was the tip-of-the-iceberg portent of what we hadn't seen before, and opened a whole new world of Japanese film to those abroad.

## Notes

1 Kurosawa 1950: 0:01:15:15.
2 Kurosawa's debt to Akutagawa should be acknowledged here, because the one-way dialogue with an implicitly present magistrate was his creation in the short story *In a Grove*.

---

Akira Kurosawa on Akutagawa's short story *In a Grove*:

[It] goes into the depths of the human heart as if with a surgeon's scalpel, laying bare its dark complexities and bizarre twists. These strange impulses of the human heart would be expressed through the use of an elaborately fashioned play of light and shadow.

(Kurosawa 1983: 135)

---

Akira Kurosawa on adapting *In a Grove*:

There were only eight characters, but the story was both complex and deep. The script was done as straightforwardly and briefly as possible, so I felt I should be able to create a rich and expansive visual image in turning it into a film.

(Kurosawa 1983: 135)

# 5 *Rashomon* perceived

The challenge of forging a transnationally
shared view of Kurosawa's legacy

*Andrew Horvat*

Humans have shared stories across boundaries of language and culture
since time immemorial. The field of literary translation exists today because
speakers of different languages have wished to benefit from the creative efforts
of all humankind in spite of the vagaries of international politics. From
time to time, however, it happens that a work of art is valued significantly
more highly in a culture other than the artist's own. The awarding in 1951
of the Venice Film Festival's grand prize, the Golden Lion, to director Akira
Kurosawa's *Rashomon* is one example of this phenomenon.[1]

Heated debate about the disconnect between European and American
evaluations of *Rashomon* on the one hand and appraisal by Japanese critics
of the film's worth on the other has continued for more than half a century,
spilling over into national identity discourse and leading ultimately (at least
in Japanese eyes) to the question of who has the right to define the value
of a cultural product made in Japan: foreigners or Japanese. As we examine
the comments of a number of Japanese critics, we shall see that the particular Japaneseness – as vague and indefinable as that concept may be – of a
work of art is the primary concern of most domestic critics. Foreign critics
seem to have been more attracted by the moral-philosophical questions raised
through the telling of conflicting versions of the same story from different
perspectives.

Tadao Sato, Japan's pre-eminent film critic, author of more than one hundred books mostly about cinema, is openly dismissive of the view that this
moral-philosophical question is the central theme of the film. Sato writes:

> In foreign countries ... the word '*Rashomon*' came to be synonymous
> with several parties to an incident giving conflicting versions of events.
> Because the word was bandied about in that sort of way, the generally
> accepted view of this movie [abroad] is that its main theme is skepticism.
>
> (2002: 131)

Unfortunately, the condescension that oozes from Sato's pen cannot
be easily conveyed in English. That is because Sato chooses *katakana* (the
syllabary used to write words of foreign origin) to spell *Rashomon*, a title

normally written with Chinese characters. In other words, what Sato is say-ing is that a moral-philosophical interpretation of *Rashomon* is not the one that we Japanese know but some outlandish thing that has been concocted by others, or perhaps more precisely the Other. His choice of a verb inflection *tari* that can have a pejorative connotation (meaning sort of), which I trans-lated as bandied about, should also indicate Sato's generally low opinion of non-Japanese visions of *Rashomon*.

So what is the correct vision of *Rashomon*, that which foreigners can-not understand? According to Sato, the director's true intent was to offer a criticism of the immorality of the immediate postwar period. Sato writes that even though Toshiro Mifune was playing the role of a character of a thousand years earlier, Kurosawa had intended for him to represent 'reck-less youth born of the moral collapse of defeat' (2002: 132). It may be useful to recall that *Rashomon* was filmed and released during the American-led Occupation of Japan. One does not have to have an advanced degree in international relations to be able to read anti-American sentiment between Sato's lines.

In fairness to Sato, it is good to remember that, at the time when he was writing, Americans and Japanese understood very little about each other's culture and American critics commenting on Kurosawa made some rather outlandish statements. For example, Joan Mellen, a critic who visited Japan for a few weeks in the early 1970s, places *Seven Samurai* in the 1600s. Anyone familiar with Japanese history will know that Mellen was off by at least one century. By the 1600s the Tokugawa Shogunate had unified the country. The kind of banditry portrayed in *Seven Samurai* would have been typical of earl-ier times. In other words, Sato is not completely unjustified in feeling uncom-fortable with foreign evaluations of Kurosawa. But one can also sympathize with Mellen when she declares in her 1975 book *Voices from the Japanese Cinema* referring to a verbal confrontation with Sato, 'I had the feeling that whatever I said he would say the opposite. He didn't want to occupy the same cultural space' (1975: 51).

Japanese commentary on *Rashomon* – no matter what the logic – would seem to have a single particular aim, namely to draw a line between Japan and the West, a line that was crossed when *Rashomon* was chosen at Venice uni-laterally by foreigners to become transnationally shared cultural property. To re-establish the proper order of things, *Rashomon* and Kurosawa needed to be placed firmly on either one side or the other of the thick boundary that distin-guishes typically Japanese from un-Japanese. One such approach has been to suggest that Kurosawa is popular with foreigners because he is not typically Japanese. This kind of thinking means that a ripple cannot flow beyond the circle of what is perceived to be truly Japanese.

Asked in a filmed interview to account for Kurosawa's greater popular-ity outside Japan than at home, the film critic Nagaharu Yodogawa gave the example of the use of dialogue in the films of Yasujiro Ozu, a director whose works are regarded in Japan as quintessentially Japanese. Yodogawa stated that Ozu's dialogue is slow paced whereas in Kurosawa's films the exchanges are fast like in foreign films: 'Ozu's films sound like a *shamisen* and Kurosawa's sound like a violin and a piano' (2008).[2] This argument assumes that one has to be Japanese to appreciate Ozu and a foreigner to like Kurosawa. Yodogawa's explanation is essentialistic in its logic: Ozu is Japanese so he is a *shamisen*, a Japanese musical instrument, and Kurosawa is Western in his artistic style so he is a piano. We can detect an undercurrent of cultural nationalism – perhaps even a kind of apartheid – by which Japanese and foreigners must occupy either one side of a cultural boundary or another, and hence must be labeled as either Japanese or foreign. It is for this reason that, after Venice, Kurosawa came to be referred in the media as *Sekai no* Kurosawa, meaning Kurosawa of the world, i.e. the world outside Japan.

In this case, Kurosawa is placed across the foreign-Japanese dividing line by having his name spelled not as 黒澤 in Chinese characters as is the custom for a Japanese citizen but as クロサワ in *katakana*, the syllabary used to write the names of all foreigners (except ethnic Chinese). This is the same practice as was mentioned above in regard to the dismissal of the foreign view of *Rashomon* by Sato, who intentionally spelled the title of the film in *katakana*. The Kurosawa of the world epithet – associated exclusively with Kurosawa and no other Japanese film director – identifies him as someone entirely unique, a Japanese who is no longer completely Japanese by virtue of being liked by foreigners. Incidentally, ethnic Japanese who are citizens of other countries, such as the Canadian scientist and media personality David Suzuki or the American historian Francis Fukuyama, also have their names written in *katakana* to indicate that they are not Japanese. The major difference, however, is that Kurosawa was born in Japan to Japanese parents and educated in the same school system as millions of other Japanese. Perhaps the finest example of this kind of essentialistic treatment can be seen in an interview with director Nagisa Oshima (*The Realm of the Senses*, 1976) which starts with Oshima asking Kurosawa if he had any foreign relatives or ancestors given the fact that his films, his behavior and even his large body size are so un-Japanese. Apparently quite used to such a question, Kurosawa answers, 'It is quite possible. I come from the Northeast and there may be some Russians in our family' (2013: n.p.).[3] Kurosawa makes it clear however that this is just speculation.

Another technique utilized by critics to regain ownership of Kurosawa is to argue that it was not so much *Rashomon* that was singled out for praise at Venice but rather that Kurosawa's Golden Lion was intended to be an affirmation by Europeans of the high quality of Japanese film artistry as a whole. For example, Yuichiro Nishimura, a prolific film critic, writes of *Rashomon*'s 1951 Venice Film Festival prize: 'As the Soviet-American Cold War worsened and people no longer knew what to believe in, this film, produced by an insignificant country of the Far East forced the world to take notice' (2000: 68). What Nishimura is saying is that *Rashomon* is not the product of the creative genius of an individual Kurosawa who happens to be Japanese but that of his nation as a whole. It is almost as if Kurosawa were an Olympic gold med-alist sent out as the representative of his country's national team to bring fame and glory to his people. With this sentence Nishimura appropriates Kurosawa's Golden Lion in the name of the nation. The only problem with this view is that the choice of *Rashomon* as an entry in Venice was made by a foreigner, Giuliana Stramigioli, over the vociferous objections of Masaichi Nagata, president of Daiei Films at whose studios *Rashomon* was made. Far from having been sent out to represent his country at an international event, Kurosawa at this stage of his career had been written off by Daiei as a fail-ure. Moreover, it is well documented that Nagata saw no value in *Rashomon* whatsoever, having walked out of its screening with the single word, *wakaran*, a rude expression meaning incomprehensible.

Not surprisingly, Sato totally concurs with Nishimura's position that the Golden Lion was an honor conferred on Japanese films as a whole: '*Rashomon* wins the Grand Prix at Venice thereby making the world aware of the high quality of Japanese films. *Rashomon* should be celebrated as the first Japanese film to do so' (1969: 146). Another writer goes one step farther by likening Kurosawa's triumph in Venice to the impact on Asian people of Japan's 1905 victory over Russia, a European imperial power. The writer, Ryuza Mikuni, states:

> Rashomon proved to Asians that an Asian too could make a world-class film and in that sense Rashomon had a social and humanistic influence. Kurosawa had an especially powerful impact on India's future directors. Having been the first (to be appreciated in the West), Kurosawa paved the way for the popularity of films from Asia, Africa and the Middle East.
>
> (1998: 110)

Not to be outdone, Sato writes of *Rashomon*'s Venice prize as 'having shown to Asians that they too can make a film as great as any produced by European people' (2002: 413).

But perhaps the meanest form of Kurosawa-bashing after Venice was to deny his films the domestic recognition that they should have received. Although *Rashomon* was ranked number five in 1950 in the popular film magazine *Kinema Junpo*'s annual Best Ten list, films made by Kurosawa prior to Venice such as *Drunken Angel* (1948), *No Regrets for Our Youth* (1946) and *Stray Dog* (1949) garnered first, second and third place, respectively, on that same list. There is more than just a kernel of truth to the suggestion that after Venice some Japanese film critics went out of their way to punish Kurosawa for the overseas success of *Rashomon* and subsequent films.

For example, between 1952 and 1966, the years when Kurosawa produced such classics as *Ikiru, Seven Samurai, Throne of Blood, Hidden Fortress, High and Low, Yojimbo, Tsubaki Sanjuro* and *Red Beard*, the film critics of the three national dailies, the *Asahi, Mainichi* and *Yomiuri*, adjudicators of the Blue Ribbon Prize, found only two Kurosawa films worthy of being rated the best that year. The two were *Hidden Fortress* and *Red Beard*, good movies but hardly masterpieces compared with *Ikiru*, ranked by the domestic critics as number eight; *Seven Samurai*, number three; and *Yojimbo*, an incredible number ten. To add insult to injury, the Blue Ribbon prize for best actor did go to Mifune, star of *Yojimbo*, but not for his role in the Kurosawa film. It should be noted that the above papers had (and still have) a combined daily circulation in excess of twenty million. In other words, their writers can be described to be representative of popular thinking of the time.[4] Incidentally, *Yojimbo*, which hardly made the rankings in Japan, was turned by Italian film director Sergio Leone into *Fistful of Dollars*[5] catapulting Clint Eastwood's career.

But it was not merely resentment of Kurosawa's overseas success that denied the director the recognition that he might otherwise have had at home. There was a genuine disconnect between the worldview of the Japanese during the postwar period and that of Europeans as well as Americans. The failure of *Seven Samurai*, among Kurosawa's very best films, to obtain first place in a major domestic list of top movies for 1954 had to do with the simultaneous release of Keisuke Kinoshita's *Twenty-Four Eyes*, the sentimental story of a young female teacher assigned to a school on a small, impoverished island in the Inland Sea during the dark years leading up to World War II. Virtually forgotten outside Japan, *Twenty-Four Eyes* was probably the single most popular Japanese movie of the postwar period.[6] The contrast between it and *Rashomon* reveals some radical differences between Japanese and European perceptions of a difficult past.

As has been already mentioned in this book (see also Matsumura, Chapter 6), *Rashomon*, though not a film specifically about World War II, is very much a product of it. Shot within two years of the conclusion of the Tokyo War Crimes trials, *Rashomon* focuses on the reluctance of protagonists in a crime to take responsibility for their actions. For all that, however, the film ends on a positive, existentialist note, with the woodcutter who, though tainted with guilt, takes on the task of adopting an abandoned child. Although Kurosawa has been criticized for adding the final scene in which the priest responds to the woodcutter's altruism with the words, 'You have restored my faith in humanity',[7] for Europeans who had come out of the same devastating conflict on the other side of the globe, the moral-philosophical message modulated by the positive final scene must have reverberated very strongly indeed.

As stated earlier, the choice to send *Rashomon* as a Japanese entry to Venice was made by expatriate Italian film importer and academic Giuliana Stramigioli. Thanks to the publication of a collection of essays in memory of Stramigioli,[8] we have reason to believe that she may have had some personal reasons for choosing *Rashomon*. A brilliant translator and scholar of medieval Japanese literature,[9] Stramigioli had been a member of the Fascist Party of Italy. An active propagandist for Japan's wartime aims, she had posed for a photograph that appeared in a Japanese newspaper during the early days of

World War II showing her in a kimono holding a Japanese sword under the headline, 'Now is the time to come to the aid of the motherland'. In the late 1930s and early 1940s Stramigioli had written widely in support of the actions of Japan's military on the Asian mainland. Tainted by association with a lost cause, Stramigioli sensed that she would have great difficulty finding employment with any government-affiliated organization in Italy and therefore chose to live in self-imposed exile in Japan where she augmented a meager salary as a professor of Italian at a Japanese university by importing neorealist films from Italy. It was in that capacity that she chose to enter *Rashomon* in the festival at Venice. It should be mentioned that when Daiei's Nagata rebuffed Stramigioli's request for cooperation, Stramigioli arranged for subtitling and transportation of the film by air to Italy.

Stramigioli must have understood well the moral ambiguities that characterize so much of human behavior and which Kurosawa did such a brilliant job of portraying in *Rashomon*. We should also remember that Kurosawa made no secret of his regret at having gone along with his country's war aims, ingratiating himself with the authorities when it was expedient to do so and offering no resistance.[10] After Japan's defeat he came to the conclusion that individual action by citizens based on their moral beliefs was absolutely necessary in order to prevent the recurrence of war. It is in this context that the decisive behavior of the woodcutter, the bravery of bureaucrat Watanabe in the face of intimidation by gangsters in *Ikiru*, and the white knight heroics of the masterless samurai played by Toshiro Mifune should be seen.

We should also keep in mind that 1951, the year that Stramigioli chose to send *Rashomon* to Venice, was also the year that the Treaty of Paris establishing the European Coal and Steel Community was signed. Calling for the pooling of both resources and sovereignty, its preamble contains some of the most beautiful language to be found in any international agreement. The signatories – including Stramigioli's Italy – agreed to put past conflict behind them and to lay the foundations for a 'destiny henceforward shared'.[11] The 1951 document served as the first step toward the establishment of the European Union. The atmosphere in Europe at the time of *Rashomon*'s arrival was idealism tinged with memories of recent horrors. The same period in Japan (as Matsumura describes in Chapter 6) was quite the opposite: It was a time when war criminals were being paroled early, and when the United States funneled tens of millions of dollars through various foundations, including one set up by the CIA, into programs hastily aimed at US-Japan reconciliation so as to mobilize Japanese support for the Western camp in the Cold War.[12] Kinoshita's *Twenty-Four Eyes* captured the mood of the times in Japan far better than *Rashomon*. The work portrays the fate of twelve schoolchildren (hence twenty-four eyes) unfortunate to be just at the age when they will suffer the most during World War II. Three of the protagonist's male pupils are killed in action and one comes home from the front blinded. Film critic Sato is as acerbic about *Twenty-Four Eyes* as he was about foreign opinion of *Rashomon*. He writes that the schoolteacher remembers a former student killed in the war:

> as an innocent, smiling schoolboy, a particularly moving image to a Japanese audience, as if the boy had been killed in all his purity. However it does not take much imagination to suppose that these innocent school-boys went to their deaths fighting. One wonders how many enemy sol-diers they might have killed, whether they committed any atrocities or engaged in rape or pillage ...

(Orr 2001: 115)

Sato labels *Twenty-Four Eyes* a tear-jerker. This, however, did not stop the film from winning the number one spot in the *Kinema Junpo* Best Ten list as well as most other domestic film prizes in 1954.

In other words, the gap between Japanese and foreign perceptions of *Rashomon* and its creator is not confined to public intellectuals but represents the views of Japanese audiences. It is good to keep in mind that until the late 1950s most Japanese had no television sets; going to the movies was their main form of entertainment. The Japanese film industry was prolific, releas-ing ten new features each week. Japan's films catered to a mass market and most of its products were forgotten within weeks of their release. *Rashomon* was produced by such an industry and aimed for a mass market. But the film festival to which it was sent catered to an audience that considered films to be an art form. Kurosawa was unique in that he took pride in satisfying the tastes of both types of audiences, highbrow and low.

It should not come as a surprise that in Japan Kurosawa is remembered far more as an entertainer than as a great artist. Although *Rashomon* ranks twenty-second on the UK's *Empire* film magazine's list of one hundred best films of world cinema, in Japan the customer poll at *Tsutaya*, the coun-try's largest chain of DVD rental stores, gives the film a rating of 3.5 out of 5. Many *Tsutaya* outlets do not even have a copy of *Rashomon* to rent. During one recent visit, clerks asked: Who is the director? and How do you spell *Rashomon*? While *Rashomon* is consistently included in the sylla-buses of film appreciation courses at universities in North America, films are not objects of academic study at most Japanese universities. But anyone in Japan who can still remember seeing a Kurosawa film (they are shown only rarely) can choose to relive the atmosphere of *Yojimbo* or *Red Beard* at one of four Kurosawa theme restaurants in Tokyo. Plans for a Kurosawa museum were recently shelved but had the project succeeded a gift shop would have offered a range of Kurosawa goods such as key chains and other memorabilia.

To be sure, there have been similar transnational disconnects between domestic and foreign evaluations of an artist's work. A case in point is the leg-acy of American comedian Jerry Lewis, who in his sixty-year film career never once received a work-related Academy Award,[13] but who has been lionized in France where leading intellectuals claim to see genius in Lewis's humor. Of course, not all Americans dismiss Lewis as a superficial slapstick comedian. But in contrast with the outbursts of Japanese critics confronted with foreign praise for *Rashomon* or Kurosawa, we see no such resentment in the occasional displays of American amusement over French paeans to Lewis.[14] A similar example of acceptance of transnationally conflicting evaluations of a work of literature can be seen in the contrast between the mass following in Japan of the juvenile novel *Anne of Green Gables* and the far more qualified praise Canadian literary critics have given to the output of Anne's creator, Prince Edward Island author Lucy Maude Montgomery. A major collection of essays on Anne and her author includes contributions from not only Canadian but also American and Japanese academics and public intellectuals (Gammel and Epperly 1999). In other words, there is no resistance among Canadians to sharing a cultural icon.

Perhaps the best example of a case similar to that of *Rashomon* is the hostile reaction among leading members of the Hungarian literary establishment triggered by the awarding of the 2002 Nobel Prize in Literature to Holocaust writer Imre Kertész. In the highly emotional and nationalistic reaction to Kertész's Nobel Prize, we can observe the same kind of rejectionist and essentialistic criticism in the Hungarian media as has flowed from the pen of Tadao Sato.[15] Some obvious parallels exist in the case of the Kurosawa and Kertész awards: both the Venice Film Festival and the Nobel Prize Committee are foreign and make their decisions based on their own criteria, not on those of the artist's home country. Cultural nationalism is the norm in both Hungary and Japan. One commentator urging restraint and introspection after the disappointment that a real Hungarian had not been chosen (Kertész is Jewish and lives in Germany), cautioned that Nobel Prizes are not the same as Olympic medals. They do not raise national flags and play national anthems when Nobel Prizes are awarded.[16] One suspects the same is true at film festivals. But perhaps more germane to these two cases is the shared experience of defeat in war and occupation by foreign powers, a fate in the collective memories of Japanese as well as Hungarians. No wonder that in both Hungary and Japan the self-appointed guardians of national identity – public intellectuals writing and speaking in various media – would feel the urge to draw more clearly the border lines of their nation's cultural essence should they perceive these to have been blurred as a result of foreign intervention.

The ferociousness of some of the statements regarding *Rashomon*'s triumph in Venice provides us with a unique opportunity to eavesdrop on a domestic conversation about national identity. (The examples quoted in this article are but the tip of an iceberg.) This discussion should be of interest not only to aficionados of Japanese films but also to students of Japanese intellectual history. As the anthropologist Harumi Befu has noted, in the postwar period culture replaced the usual symbols of Japanese national identity such as monarch, flag and anthem since these had been discredited through defeat.[17]

Kristin Surak in her recent book, *Making Tea, Making Japan*, homes in on aspects of cultural nationalism to be found in the Japanese tea ceremony, which 'is all but universally recognized as a defining constituent of Japanese culture … peculiarly characteristic of the nation …' (2013: 1). James Orr mines novels and films in search of the postwar Japanese transformation of defeat into victimhood because: 'While education curricula reflect the consciously sanctioned national heritage, it is in popular culture that one typically encounters less self-consciously propagated mythologies' (2001: 106).

Our examination of the pronouncements of public intellectuals on the true meaning of *Rashomon*, as opposed to whatever foreign critics may have alleged, brings us in contact with some of these less self-consciously propagated national myths. These include, among others, the alleged role of *Rashomon* in re-establishing national pride after World War II. As Hiromichi Horikawa, who worked as assistant director on a number of Kurosawa films writes, 'Nowadays there are hundreds of international film festivals. Back in 1950 there were only two major ones, Venice and Cannes but at the time all but a very few Japanese were totally ignorant of their existence' (Horikawa 2000: 146). The question therefore arises: How could victory at Venice, a festival hardly known in Japan, suddenly raise the spirits of the average Japanese? The answer is that nothing of the sort happened. The story of *Rashomon*'s triumph shares much with the theme of *Rashomon* the film itself: It is a story that emerged to fill a need. While it is true that *Rashomon* was greatly admired abroad, it was only much later that Kurosawa's success was interpreted in the media as a triumph to be shared by the entire nation. In September 1951 when news of *Rashomon*'s award at Venice was transmitted to Japan, it merited five lines in the inside pages of Japanese newspapers.

Among other myths that emerged was the one that *Rashomon* appealed to foreigners because of its exotic setting.[18] This myth has become widely accepted as fact in Japan. But Gian Luigi Rondi, a member of the Venice Film Festival jury in 1951, writing in the above-mentioned collection of essays in honor of Stramigioli gives an entirely different and far more nuanced account of how *Rashomon* was chosen. Rondi recalled:

In 1951, I was a member of the jury at the Venice Film Festival. At that time I was also a good friend of the [festival's] director, Antonio Pedrucci, who often consulted me on his programs. Already at the time when films to be shown had been selected, Pedrucci told me about an Italian woman who was very knowledgeable about Japan and who had alerted Pedrucci about the work of a Japanese director, Akira Kurosawa, already well established in Japan but not known outside his country. She had sent the movie *Rashomon* and we watched it together. It was of particular interest to me because a director working in the Far East seemed to be familiar with our culture, Pirandello in particular. The movie *Rashomon* was accepted as an entry in the festival at the very last moment.

(Maurizi and Ciapparoni La Rocca 2012: 222)

The reference by Rondi to Pirandello would seem to indicate that this critic, who later went on to be a prize-winning scenario writer, was pleasantly surprised not by the exotic but by the familiar, namely the similarity between *Rashomon* and the work of Italian novelist and playwright Luigi Pirandello, whose works were widely regarded as precursors of the postwar Theatre of the Absurd. Rondi recalled that two strong candidates emerged for the Golden Lion: Robert Bresson's *Diary of a Country Priest* and Elia Kazan's *A Streetcar Named Desire*.

As Rondi put it,

> Neither side was willing to give in to the other. I was not yet thirty and as such the youngest member of the jury but I could see that there was an impasse. So I put forward the case for Kurosawa, recalling Rashomon's great value including that of the happy meeting in it of Japanese and European culture. The other jury members agreed and we were able to award the Golden Lion to Rashomon.
>
> (Maurizi and Ciapparoni La Rocca 2012: 223)

Rondi's comments reveal perhaps the greatest gap between Japanese and foreign evaluations of *Rashomon*: the absence of person-to-person exchanges between Japanese and foreign critics. While Japanese critics often display a sophisticated understanding of Western culture, many of their conclusions reveal preconceived notions about the ways of thinking of foreign people that point to a fairly obvious absence of personal acquaintance with individual foreigners. Perhaps the clearest indication of the lack of real-life, day-to-day contact between Japanese film people and their foreign counterparts is the total absence of any surviving Japanese media portrait of Stramigioli, the individual most responsible for assuring that *Rashomon* and its director received the international recognition they deserved. This hiatus is all the more intriguing given that Professor Stramigioli spent half of her adult life in Japan, spoke Japanese, and remained in Tokyo for fifteen years after the triumph of *Rashomon* in Venice. Had Japanese film critics bothered to seek her out, they would have been able to understand why a European intellectual with a complicated political past might have lobbied so aggressively and with so little thought of personal gain to make the moral message of *Rashomon* part of an internationally shared cultural legacy. It is tempting to speculate how Japanese-foreign cultural exchanges might have progressed had Stramigioli and Japanese film critics met and perhaps even sat down for a few meals together. But there seems to be no record of any of them ever having done so and that fact speaks volumes about the sharing of artistic legacies in an era of cultural nationalism.

# Notes

1 The author would like to thank Mr. Fernando Mezzetti, an authority on the history of fascism in Italy and a former correspondent in Tokyo, Beijing and Moscow for Italian newspapers, for translating the comments of Venice Film Festival jury member Gian Luigi Rondi at the end of this chapter, and for valuable information and advice on the early life and career of the Italian academic Giuliana Stramigioli. The translations from Japanese in this chapter, unless otherwise stated, are the author's.

2 The *shamisen*, mentioned by Yodogawa, is a three-stringed, banjo-like instrument often used to accompany traditional singing. Yodogawa refers to it in order to contrast its sound with that of the violin and piano, instruments for playing Western classical music.

3 The word Oshima uses for un-Japanese is *nihonjinbanare*, literally: departing from Japanese. The expression is used to describe someone who is Japanese but looks or behaves like a foreigner.

4 To be sure, the three films were ranked higher on other domestic lists but the contrast between the domestic and foreign reception of these Kurosawa works is still notable: *Ikiru* won the top award at the Berlin Film Festival, is number forty-four on the British *Empire* film magazine's 2010 list of Best One Hundred Films ever made and is at number twelve on the International Movie Database list of 250 Top Films, *Seven Samurai* is the highest-rated Japanese film on the list; *Yojimbo* garnered several prizes for Mifune in Venice and a nomination for best director for Kurosawa.

5 Kurosawa sued Leone for making what was an unauthorized copy of *Yojimbo*; the suit was settled out of court very much in Kurosawa's favor.

6 James Orr, writing in *The Victim as Hero: Ideologies of Peace and National Identity in Postwar Japan*, quotes film critic Tadao Sato as saying, '[*Twenty-Four Eyes*] has probably wrung more tears out of Japanese audiences than any other postwar film' (2001: 110).

7 *Rashomon* (1950) DVD, Akira Kurosawa (dir.), Tokyo: Daiei, 0:01:55:51) [= one hour, 55 minutes and 51 seconds into the film.]

8 Titled *La figlia occidentale di Edo / The European Daughter of Edo*, the work is a Festschrift consisting of essays and reminiscences in honor of Professor Stramigioli by former colleagues and students at the University of Rome and the Tokyo University of Foreign Studies, the two institutions where she spent the major part of her career (Maurizi and Ciapparoni La Rocca 2012).

9 The Wikipedia site on *Rashomon* incorrectly identifies Stramigioli as an Italian language teacher. While it is true that she taught Italian language and literature at the Tokyo University of Foreign Studies, at the time she chose to send *Rashomon* to Venice she was concurrently the representative of the Italian film industry in Japan and in that capacity was responsible for importing most of the early postwar Italian neorealist films.

10 In *Something Like an Autobiography*, translated by Audie Bock, he writes, 'I am ashamed of this, but I must be honest about it' (Kurosawa 1983: 145).

11 The relevant passage from the Treaty of Paris (1951) is: 'Resolved to substitute for age-old rivalries the merging of their essential interests; to create, by establishing an economic community, the basis for a broader and deeper community among peoples long divided by bloody conflicts, and to lay the foundations for institutions which will give direction to a destiny henceforward shared ...' (Fassbender 2004: 860).

12 For a detailed description of how the US government supported the work of US foundations in early postwar Japan, see Ashizawa Gould 2006: 101–33.

13 Lewis did receive an Academy Award in 2009 but it was not for acting or directing. His Oscar, officially known as the Jean Hersholt Humanitarian Award, is given to actors who work on behalf of charitable causes; Lewis helps raise funds for research to find a cure for muscular dystrophy.
14 It has been common practice in the past to poke fun at the French for awarding Jerry Lewis not one but two Legion d'Honneur prizes. For a recently published serious work by an eminent American film critic, see Fujiwara 2009. Fujiwara is at present the artistic director of the Edinburgh Film Festival.
15 'The reception of Kertész's work in his native and "literary" country, Hungary, in contrast to his position and reception where he feels at home intellectually, namely Germany, contextualizes and locates his own media statements and the public discourse in general in a political and ideological momentum. Kertész, I believe, is a public intellectual ... and thus he is of great significance ... with regard to latent and currently explicit anti-Semitism and ethnic essentialism in Hungary' (Tötösy de Zepetnek 2005: n.p.).
16 Babarczy 2002, originally published as 'Nobel dilemma – itt az alkalom' in *Nepszabadsag* [Hungarian newspaper], 19 October 2002.
17 See Chapter 5 'Symbolic vacuum' (Befu 2001: 86–104).
18 Donald Richie writes in *The Films of Akira Kurosawa*, 'Eventually they [Japanese film critics] decided that [*Rashomon* had won at Venice] because *Rashomon* was exotic and that foreigners like exoticism. Even now it is the rare critic who will admit that *Rashomon* could have had any other appeal in the West' (1996: 80).

---

Akira Kurosawa describing the explanation he gave to his assistant directors on the set of *Rashomon* when they persisted in knowing what the film was about:

Human beings are unable to be honest with themselves about themselves. They cannot talk about themselves without embellishing. This script portrays such human beings – the kind who cannot survive without lies to make them feel they are better people than they really are. It even shows this sinful need for flattering falsehood going beyond the grave – even the character who dies cannot give up his lies when he speaks to the living through a medium. Egoism is a sin the human being carries with him from birth; it is the most difficult to redeem. This film is like a strange picture scroll that is unrolled and displayed by the ego.

(Kurosawa 1983: 135)

Publicity still featuring Machiko Kyo as the samurai's wife and Toshiro Mifune as the bandit. The different versions of the encounter between their two characters depict both a simple assault and a complex negotiation. The balance of power between the wife and the bandit differs greatly in the film's various accounts. This difference in the interpretation of their encounter helps to construct and compound the complexity of the Rashomon Effect. (Courtesy of Kadokawa Corporation)

# 6 *Rashomon* as a twelfth-century period picture and Occupation period social critique

## Janice Matsumura

Stephen Prince observed in 1991 that '*Rashomon* has become an enormously powerful and symbolic cultural entity, which engages, then as now, diverse currents of history, philosophy, and art criticism' (1991: 128). This chapter explores particular aspects of the film's engagement with history, first as a period film and then as a critique of the US-led Allied Occupation of Japan (1945–1952). The transcendence of these origins is a powerful illustration of the Rashomon effects that are the subject of this book.

## As a twelfth-century period picture

Period pictures often arouse debate about historical accuracy, and one may ask how a Japanese film, such as *Rashomon*, fares in terms of knowledge of the twelfth century. There are no doubt inaccuracies and improbabilities that an expert on medieval Japan would more easily catch, but it is hard to believe that historians would react to *Rashomon* in the same way that they have to the Hollywood film *The Last Samurai* (2003).[1] Kurosawa said of himself,

> I am often accused of being too exacting with sets and properties, of having things made, just for the sake of authenticity, that will never appear on camera ... The quality of the set influences the quality of the actors' performances ... For this reason, I have the sets made exactly like the real thing. It restricts the shooting, but encourages that feeling of authenticity.
> (Kurosawa 1983: 197)

He clearly took pains to reconstruct the historical gate, and he has received praise for creating not just the look but also the mood associated with medieval Japan:

> Towards the end of the Heian period [794–1184] and through the tumultuous Kamakura era (1192–1336), Rashomon fell into destruction and disrepair due to wars, earthquakes and other calamities. According to legend, locals often associated Rashomon with death, destruction and

the end of moral truth. Kurosawa's *Rashomon* takes this foreboding background as the setting of its main narrative layer. During the credit scene, the camera pans across the sight revealing the extent of the gate's destruction. The sharp angles of the wooden beams accentuate the themes of confusion and moral destituteness.

(Yamada 2006: n.p.)

Scholars of Japanese intellectual history and religion have argued that the dominant concept among individuals or, at least, the elite of the late Heian (794–1184) and early Kamakura periods (1185–1333) was that society had entered the Buddhist age of *mappō*.[2] During this age of institutional, physical, moral and spiritual corruption, people would be unable to grasp the truths of Buddhism and attain enlightenment.

In choosing Ryunosuke Akutagawa's Rashomon as the site for recollection of the conflicting trial testimonies, Kurosawa thus provides a historical setting and intellectual background to the essential message in his film. In his autobiography, Kurosawa recalled that when his assistant directors expressed confusion about the script, he explained:

Human beings are unable to be honest with themselves about themselves. They cannot talk about themselves without embellishing. This script portrays such human beings – the kind who cannot survive without lies to make them feel they are better people than they really are. It even shows this sinful need for flattering falsehood going beyond the grave – even the character who dies cannot give up his lies when he speaks to the living through a medium. Egoism is a sin the human being carries with him from birth; it is the most difficult to redeem.

(Kurosawa 1983: 183)

Kurosawa does not allow any of the characters in the film to create an attractive persona for themselves, and on the issue of characterization, individuals in Japan who first saw the film in 1950 had complained about its portrayal of a court lady. One critic focused on Machiko Kyo, who had not previously acted but had been a dancer, for being too excessive and vulgar. It is not known what exactly was vulgar about her performance, but the criticism does raise questions concerning the assumptions that individuals in 1950 entertained about Japanese women in earlier periods.

Postwar Occupation reforms to promote gender equality occasionally had the effect of reinforcing the image of Japanese women as powerless prior to 1945. Film historian Kyoko Hirano asserts that American censors initially opposed portrayals of Japanese women outwitting men because it was at odds with their understanding that 'women had been consistently and without exception victimized under the traditional social system' (1992: 72). The reform-promoted image of Japanese women as victims in need of liberation, together with a general tendency to view female empowerment as a modern development, may have made Kurosawa's presentation of a woman who asserts her views seem anachronistic.

However, one can find a basis for different representations of the Machiko Kyo character, Masago. In her own account, Masago presents herself as help-less and subject to the will of men, and there exist similar self-depictions in the works and diaries written by court ladies. Portraying oneself in this way could work to one's benefit. By denying agency, Masago could avoid accusa-tions of adultery and, thus, punishment. The film is set around the city of Kyoto, the seat of the imperial government, and under imperial law at the time, a married woman who had been raped would not be punished, but one who was guilty of adultery could be sentenced to a two-year prison term. The situation changed in later periods, and according to the laws eventually established by the warrior government in Kamakura, even a woman who was raped could be severely punished for having sexual relations with a man other than her husband (Tonomura 1999: 140–2).

Women of the twelfth century enjoyed more social and legal rights than their counterparts in later times. Historians, such as Hitomi Tonomura, have demonstrated that women of the late Heian and early Kamakura peri-ods could inherit and bequeath property, hold office, maintain a greater claim over children and may have been able to initiate divorces.[3] One could conjecture that, given these legal and social rights, they would have been able to be more assertive in dealing with men. Consequently, the accounts of the film's (and the earlier Akutagawa short story's) male characters that present Masago as strong and demanding come across as historically plausible.

As for the male characters, Toshiro Mifune's character is translated and portrayed as a bandit, and the competing visions of Tajomaru (victimizer/ sociopath in the wife's version or victim/upholder of conjugal loyalty in the husband's version) actually fits nicely with research that has raised ques-tions about the identity of medieval bandits. Religious institutions and other groups that were losing or competing for control over land gifted by the court may have tried to defame rivals by accusing them of various illegal acts and calling them *akutō* (literally, evil bands). Consequently, just like Kurosawa with his different depictions of Tajomaru, scholars have argued against a nar-row definition and understanding of *akutō*:

> by treating the acts mentioned in the documents, and not only those allud-ing to *akutō*, with caution and not taking at face value all the claimed murders and acts of arson and plunder, we may also get a step closer to a better understanding of the people … not merely as violent hooli-gans, bloodthirsty villains, or greedy highwaymen, but also as cultivators, estate officials, and smaller land holders trying to improve their lot and protect old rights and privileges in a society undergoing dramatic, eco-nomic, political, and social change.
>
> (Oxenboell 2005: 259)

Still, while a case can be made for the film's portrayal of a court lady and the ambiguity surrounding the role and nature of its bandit, the depiction of a twelfth-century trial is questionable. It is not known what law courts looked like in the late Heian period, and the court in the film seems to be based on what was existent during the much later Tokugawa period (1603–1867). A Tokugawa court had a gravel yard, where the accused would be placed, and a set of tiered wooden platforms, with the most senior or influential officials sitting at the highest levels. But, aside from the incorrect physical configuration of the court, the key and substantive historical inaccuracy about *Rashomon* from a legal standpoint is that there really was no such thing as a trial, as we might understand it, in Japan in times past.[4] One did not have competing stories presented in adversarial terms in a courtroom, as is done modernly.

Even in a mid-twentieth century Japanese courtroom – and this would be true also in Tokugawa Japan – the actual trial was just a recitation, and one never really heard the voices of the people telling their stories. As in so many aspects of Japanese social life, stories were worked out beforehand. The real action, where stories compete, took place somewhere else. In the area of Japanese criminal law, they were worked out in the police station, where there was a confession rate of ninety-nine percent. Hence, there may be emotions of contrition and remorse displayed inside a modern courtroom, but rarely competing stories. This is what is so remarkably and so joyously inaccurate about the film, the way that the voices break through. The trial proceedings in *Rashomon* were, after all, merely elaborations of those presented thirty years earlier in Akutagawa's famous short story, *Yabu no naka*, and a mere recitation in the film would have stripped the story of much of its dramatic power.

Moreover, suppose for a moment that Kurosawa had chosen merely to elaborate and expand upon Akutagawa's own chosen setting for *Yabu no naka*, the trial courtyard itself. Critics have proposed that the addition of the gate and its ramshackle condition at the end of a historical era certainly would have been sufficient to trigger the allegorical association with Japan's immediate postwar situation (Davidson 1954: 497). The gate's shattered appearance may have simply conjured up for many members of the audience in 1950 recent memories of bombed-out buildings at the start of the Allied Occupation. This connection might explain why Kurosawa's film was named after the gate where the story was recounted, and not *In a Grove* where the happenings occurred.

## As Occupation period social critique

As in the film *Rashomon*, in which he presented conflicting accounts of a crime, Kurosawa expressed contradictory opinions about the film. When he was informed in 1951 that it had been awarded the Golden Lion at the Venice Film Festival, he expressed regret that he had not won for a contemporary film. *Rashomon* certainly marked Kurosawa's return to period pictures. His wartime films, *Sugata Sanshiro* and *The Men Who Tread on the Tiger's Tale*, were historical. His immediate postwar films, *No Regrets for Our Youth*, *Drunken Angel*, *Quiet Duel* and *Stray Dog*, were all contemporary. However, as Donald Richie has noted, Kurosawa considered even his historical films to be contemporary as commentary on postwar Japan, a time of competing interpretations, with the American authorities represented by SCAP (Supreme Commander for the Allied Powers, i.e. General Douglas MacArthur) attempting to overturn pre-1945 attitudes and promoting their own views on conditions in Japan. For example, in a meeting with Japanese film company representatives, SCAP officials observed that 'Western morality is based on concepts of good and evil, not feudal loyalty ... The entertainment media and the press should all be used to teach these ideals' (Hirano 1992: 38). Kurosawa contested both the notion of a clear-cut moral dichotomy and criticized the media's supposed promotion of such ideals.

In the very same year that *Rashomon* was produced, Kurosawa made *Scandal*, a film that has received far less attention. In his discussion of this film and its impetus, Kurosawa declared that 'After the Pacific War a great deal of noise began to be made about freedom of speech, and almost immediately abuses and loss of self-control ensued' (1983: 177). *Scandal* concerned a young painter and a popular singer who launch a libel suit against a magazine that has fabricated a story of a secret romance between the two. Kurosawa had witnessed how studio executives during a labor dispute in 1948 could manipulate press coverage to sully the reputation of filmmakers, and he also expressed indignation at fictional-masquerading-as-factual stories in celebrity magazines.

When considering *Rashomon* in connection with Kurosawa's other films, one may arrive at a greater appreciation of the consistency of this director's questioning of his society by relating *Rashomon* to the contemporary films that preceded it. Both *Scandal* and *Rashomon* addressed the subject of truth and, as veiled criticisms of developments in Japan, tested a relaxation of Occupation period censorship. In his autobiography, Kurosawa described American censors as gentlemanly and, unlike their Japanese wartime counterparts, as never treating filmmakers like criminals. Yet, at the same time, he admitted that 'Democracy was glorified; freedom of speech was recovered (within the limitations permitted by General MacArthur's military policies)' (1983: 144).

Kurosawa had confronted these limitations while making earlier films, such as *No Regrets for Our Youth* and *Drunken Angel*. Two political scandals, the Takigawa Incident and the Sorge-Ozaki Incident,[5] were the inspiration for *No Regrets for Our Youth*, Kurosawa's first official postwar film. The 1946 film centered on the character of Yuki, the pampered daughter of a professor persecuted for his liberal beliefs, and the hardships and personal growth that she experiences after she becomes the lover of an anti-war activist. This plot was actually the product of interference from the Toho studios' union, which, like other unions in the country, enjoyed – at least during the first couple of years of the Occupation – the patronage of SCAP officials. According to Kurosawa, 'the unionists and the communists' in the studios' newly established Scenario Review Committee 'forced' him to rewrite his script so that it did not resemble another film inspired by the Sorge-Ozaki Incident (Hirano 1992: 196). Time did not lessen Kurosawa's indignation, and one can sense his feelings of vindication over the unionists when he observed that it was *No Regrets for Our Youth*, and not the other film based on the Sorge-Ozaki Incident, that enjoyed critical acclaim and commercial success.

With *Drunken Angel*, SCAP officials more directly objected to the plot. This 1947 film dealt with a young hoodlum who must contend with his failing health and the return of his old gang boss. Disapproving of the script's scenes of black marketeering, gambling and prostitution, censors had recommended that the film conclude with the police intervening. Kurosawa did not follow such instructions. He nevertheless attempted to placate these officials by replacing the original ending, which showed the body of the dead gangster being carried away, with a more upbeat one of a young and formerly tubercular girl receiving a clean bill of health (1992: 77).

Although SCAP officials in Japan prided themselves on removing the most conspicuous instruments of the prewar thought control system, abolishing the notorious Peace Preservation Law of 1925, they did not allow for complete freedom of expression, artistic or otherwise. At the beginning of the Occupation, censors not only kept a close watch on historical films (known as *jidaigeki*) and plays to ensure that they did not include anything that was supportive of militarism and feudal values, but they also made it known that they were wary of movies that dealt with suicides, murders and rapes. Censors informed producers that they would clamp down on films that showed suicide as a solution to problems or that even showed people attempting to kill themselves. It was also forbidden to depict murders without presenting moral judgments, and, in 1946, Kenji Mizoguchi's historical film *Utamaro and Five Women* came under fire for showing a character killing a romantic rival. Censors warned that rape scenes had to be staged so as not to incite viewers' morbid curiosity and even complained when a female character in a movie who was 'violently seduced' did not, in their opinion, sufficiently resist the advances of her attacker (Hirano 1992: 44–5, 75, 79).

Censorship rules changed as the avowed goals of the Occupation shifted in the late 1940s from democratization and demilitarization to economic stabilization in response to the Cold War. By 1950, it was safer for filmmakers to deal with topics of murder, rape and suicide, and, through the competing versions of the characters' motives in *Rashomon*, Kurosawa defied the earlier demands of SCAP officials that films help to promote Western morality based on concepts of good and evil and avoid expressions of feudal loyalty. *Rashomon* offered no definite moral judgment on the possible rape of Masago and murder of her samurai-husband as it left her violation and the cause of his death open to question. It also gave the dead samurai-husband the opportunity to claim suicide and justify his actions in terms of some feudal warrior code of honor.

However, not all topics became more open for public debate. SCAP officials had been careful in supervising coverage of the Tokyo War Crimes Trial

(1946–8), the prosecution of the country's wartime leadership. Devoting six months to planning the newsreel that would be released when the judgment on the war criminals was handed down, they had ensured that it included no commentary critical of the Occupation or the verdicts (Hirano 1992: 51–2). In 1950, just two years after the conclusion of the Tokyo Trial, Kurosawa would have been wise to avoid antagonizing these authorities by setting his film in the present and making too blatant an analogy to war crimes trials. One can nonetheless discern parallels between the Tokyo Trial and the trial in *Rashomon*, which reflect the biases of the times. Both trials, for instance, privileged the crimes against men.

The Tokyo Trial failed to deal with the issue of comfort women, with Japan's atrocities against women in its colonies such as Korea and Taiwan and in the areas occupied by its military forces such as the Philippines. Writers have attributed this oversight to the Occupation authorities' indifference to victimization of women. Historians such as Yuki Tanaka have not only discussed the Japanese government's establishment of similar comfort stations for US soldiers but have also uncovered numerous instances of American soldiers raping Japanese women during the Occupation (2002). Moreover, in a study of how male writers at the time focused on the rape and prostitution of Japanese women to express their sense of humiliation at the hands of the occupiers, Michael Molasky indicates that rape was only socially significant when it exposed the inability of the men who were supposed to prevent it from occurring (1999).

Kurosawa appears to have shared this attitude toward rape. In *Rashomon*, his focus for the trial is the murder, with the alleged crime against the wife, her rape, treated as incidental to the crime against her husband. In his 1965 Tokugawa period piece, *Red Beard*, Kurosawa also has his eponymous hero, a doctor working among the poor, reject the argument that the murderous impulse of a female patient is the result of her being repeatedly raped as a child. Red Beard insists that others had suffered similar injustices, but have not become dangerous criminals (Prince 1991). A pervasive disregard for the crime of rape, which one can detect even in Kurosawa's films, has a very contemporary significance. As legal historian Stephan Salzberg suggested in 2000, it may account for the continued public tolerance of rape comics, of magazines that offer graphic depictions of sexual violence against women.

Rather than send up a red flag to censors by placing his film in the present, Kurosawa could have delivered more effectively a subversive dig at SCAP officials who were so critical of Japan's artistic traditions by relying on a centuries-old method of evading censorship. Since at least the Tokugawa period playwrights who wished to mock some policy or satisfy their viewers' interest in a scandal had tried to escape official censure by situating their plays in earlier times. Kurosawa may thus have counted on his audience's ability to see beyond the film's historical setting and transpose the story of a twelfth-century trial to a more recent one that, despite all the publicity given to it by SCAP, the majority of people considered irrelevant to their own experience.

The Tokyo Trial was meant to have an educational value for the Japanese people, and scholars on the proceeding, such as Madoka Futamura, have examined the media response to it and what individuals may have taken away from it:

> the long and dry legal procedures seem to have bored even journalists ... after its closure, the Tokyo Trial became much less visible in public discourse ... The coverage dropped drastically in 1949, with only 12 articles published in comparison to 325 in 1948 ... As research examining Japanese sentiments and attitudes at the time illustrates, many people were angry and frustrated towards their wartime government for the hardship and struggle they suffered during and after the war. This created 'victim consciousness' within the Japanese psyche, that is, they were the victims of a war recklessly conducted by their leaders and a military clique.
>
> (2011: n.p.)

If audiences recognized the trial in the film as an allusion to the Tokyo Trial, depending on the identity that they assigned to the characters, they may have found themselves prompted to consider the fate of some convicted former leaders as well as their own role in the war. Viewers could have connected the film's shifting depictions of the wife Masago and the bandit Tajomaru, murderous villains in one version and then as victims or dupes in other versions, to the rapidly changing status of political actors. Kurosawa's audience was witnessing the rehabilitation of war criminals and the persecution of groups that had earlier enjoyed the patronage of Occupation authorities. As early as 1950 – just two years after the judges of the Tokyo Trial had handed down sentences ranging from seven years to death by hanging – some individuals were being paroled. Included among them was former ambassador Shigemitsu Mamoru, who quickly returned to public life.

At the same time, when social critics in Japan were demanding that the people consider their own individual responsibility for the war as a national crime (Futamura 2011), some viewers might have seen themselves in the characters. If they cast themselves and not just their former leaders in the roles of Masago and Tajomaru, who insisted that they were victims or who downplayed their crimes, the woodcutter's response to such arguments, his aside directly to the audience that 'They're all lies! Tajomaru's confession, the woman's story – they're lies!' would be particularly unnerving. A more agreeable identification would be with the woodcutter. Kurosawa does not permit the character to maintain his image as passive witness of the crime, indicating that he may also be guilty of wrongdoing by stealing the dagger of a dead man. Still, he emerges as a benign character, winning the praise of the priest for adopting the abandoned baby.

In drawing an analogy to the trial of war criminals, Kurosawa would anticipate many films that dealt with the war and war crimes. The majority of post-Occupation war crimes films did not deal with the Tokyo Trial or the prosecution of the wartime leadership but instead focused on ordinary soldiers who had been convicted of war crimes by military tribunals outside Japan. Although these films depicted their characters as neither heroes nor villains, they encouraged more sympathy and greater social acceptance for such soldiers. Historian Sandra Wilson has revealed this little-known aspect of Japanese film history, observing that '[d]iscussion of war criminals had naturally been restricted during the Occupation, but after mid-1952, popular movies both contributed to and reflected the changing public mood' (2013: 548–9).

Writing in 1954, two years after the end of the Occupation, James Davidson examined what he believed was the 'outcropping of anti-Americanism in Japan since the end of the Occupation' (1954: 492). A US State Department official who had worked for the Far Eastern Commission, he used *Rashomon* as an example and claimed that a prominent Japanese official agreed that the film reflected current Japanese feelings about the Occupation. Davidson was particularly concerned about the character of Tajomaru and described him as

> a half-clad savage, uncouth, insolent and raucous, who 'capers about the screen' … He appears the least Japanese of all the characters, and a sort of incarnation of the *oni*, or ogre, of Japanese folklore, which has often been interpreted as a representation of the foreigner. His build and movements, even his features, suggest something of the gangling awkwardness that appears in Japanese caricatures of Occidentals. He is alternately terrifying and ridiculous, but always alien to the others …
>
> The scene in which the wife is overcome in a prolonged kiss (in itself still a shocker for Japanese audiences) is more horrifying because her attacker is a sweating, scratching, bug-slapping barbarian … The strong suggestion of cultural difference, verging on the ethnic, gives her ultimate lustful response an additional meaning. The problem is as old as conquest.
>
> (1954: 497–8)

It is nevertheless possible that the character of the bandit was for both Kurosawa and his audiences not, or not just, a reflection of the Other but also a self-reflection. Davidson identifies self-reflective moments in the film, citing the cynical commoner who says to the priest, 'Who is honest nowadays anyway?' 'It is hard to believe,' Davidson noted, 'that a Japanese audience was not being led to refer to their own experience and to see the events of the story accordingly' (1954: 497). Like Tajomaru the bandit, many people, especially during the early Occupation, were breaking the law and being complicit in the theft of goods by participating in the black market. While the majority may have initially acted out of sheer necessity, many may have soon come to enjoy their 'outlaw' activities and been seduced by the opportunities provided by the markets. As one expert has observed,

the black market was not solely the site of hardship and despair, as is
often recalled in historical memory, but was also a place of opportunity
and entrepreneurship, a dynamic space that symbolized the energy of a
people 'living in the turning point' (*fukkanki ni ikiru*).

(Griffiths 2002: 825)

Critics have long positioned the film in the context and outlook of the 1950
Japanese audience. The first instance we have outside Japan (in English) was
by Davidson, making my reflections here part of an over sixty-year-long
debate. In discussing *Rashomon*, which presents conflicting descriptions of a
murder, none of which ultimately achieves primacy over the other, one cannot
help but be aware of the Rashomon nature of one's own interpretation of
the film. The term 'Rashomon' is now a part of the English language as the
Rashomon effect, and books and articles on the meaning of the film will
no doubt continue to appear, both as results of, and as contributors to, the
expanding circle of ripples.

## Notes

1 Historian Marc Dresner describes this film as a historical disaster.
2 For example, see works of Paul Varley and Michele Marra.
3 For example, see Tonomura 1990.
4 There are no sources in English that deal with the actual operation of courts and
   conduct of court procedures in early pre-modern through medieval Japan. However,
   Dan Fenno Henderson's volume 2 (1965), in addition to general description and
   analysis of Tokugawa-era court procedures, contains a lively extended account of
   an actual civil case (with some criminal overtones; there was no strict procedural
   or conceptual distinction made at that time) from the year 1808. The procedures
   reflect the same inquisitorial, authoritarian approach reflected in the film, while
   Henderson's retelling conveys well both the physical setting and emotional atmosphere of the courts at that time.
5 The Takigawa Incident involved legal scholar Takigawa Yukitoki, who was accused
   of promoting leftist thought and forced by political enemies to resign from his position at Kyoto Imperial University in 1933. The Sorge-Ozaki Incident involved the
   wartime arrest and execution of journalists Richard Sorge and Ozaki Hotsumi on
   charges of spying for the Soviet Union.

---

Akira Kurosawa describing a fond memory from the production of
*Rashomon* in a remote area near Mount Wakakusa:

Often after supper we climbed up Mount Wakakusa and formed a
circle to dance in the moonlight. I was still young and the cast members
were even younger and bursting with energy. We carried out our work
with enthusiasm.

(Kurosawa 1983: 136)

# 7 What is the Rashomon effect?

*Robert Anderson*

At the conclusion of *Rashomon* people commonly say that the film is about the differences in perspective found in diverse accounts of a single event. They then call this the Rashomon effect. This chapter examines the common difference-in-perspective version of the Rashomon effect, a version that occurs in cognition, epistemology, anthropology, psychology, sociology, communication and other social sciences, and in legal studies. Because so many viewers miss other key ingredients that contribute equally to the Rashomon effect (arising from the film), I concluded that the effect needs a clearer analysis, one that emerges from the film itself. My purpose here is to remind us of the intellectual complexity which Kurosawa, inspired by Akutagawa, has set before us. Can we see freshly those very ingredients in the film that many of us forget to acknowledge? Can we go beyond popular viewings of *Rashomon* which seem curiously incomplete? And finally, what precisely is the Rashomon effect? This essay addresses these important questions in order to better establish its full power as an intellectual concept.

Over the past ten years I have asked roughly four hundred students (in a university in western Canada) about their reaction to seeing *Rashomon* for the first time, and in speech and writing most of them zoom in on one crucial dimension of the film thus overlooking others. The Rashomon effect, most say when asked immediately after viewing it, is the differences in perspective concerning a single event or process.[1] A few others proposed that the Rashomon effect appears where the facts are not known, and consequently varying (typically called unfactual) versions of events are put into circulation by participants or witnesses. Some of these viewers go so far as to claim that these differences in perspective (and the Rashomon effect) undermine the world of facts. Finally, a considerable number of student viewers' interpretations involve the idea that one of the four main narratives is the truth and the others are therefore lies, and that although one character is not lying, the others are. This prompts a curious search for the most plausible account of the incident. Though not entirely wrongheaded, these common interpretations of *Rashomon* diminish the power of both the film and the Rashomon effect. Moreover, these kinds of response mislead viewers of the film who then forget to acknowledge its most important insight. If we examine some of the film's ingredients that are overlooked, because only when taken together do all these ingredients constitute the effect named after *Rashomon* and allow us to see its most powerful expression, it will thus become clear how the concept of a Rashomon effect entered our language.

At the outset, however, it is crucial to say that there really are at least two Rashomon effects arising in and from the film. The first Rashomon effect, usually forgotten by scholars, is the one experienced by first-time viewers of the film: surrounded by the relentless Bolero music, the sound of heavy rain around the gate, the bright sparkling sunlight and shade in the forest, the sudden and subtle switches in the stories, the power of the superb acting. This is a story grounded in twelfth-century Japan and then filmed and edited for screening in 1950, which is a long way back for twenty-first century viewers. Yet, in terms of technique and engagement, few experiences lasting eighty-eight minutes are as memorable. No amount of post-film theorizing about epistemology diminishes the effect of seeing *Rashomon* for the first time. That is an effect I have seen over and over again in susceptible and attentive audiences. We should try to recall the effect when it was first shown in 1950 in Japan and 1951 in Venice, an aesthetic appreciation which arises again and again more than sixty-five years later.[2]

The second and subsequent Rashomon effect is the one I am focusing on here; it is the naming of an epistemological framework – or ways of thinking, knowing and remembering – required for understanding complex and ambiguous situations on the small and large scale, in both the routines of everyday life and in its extraordinary moments. The second Rashomon effect is probably universal in our experience, and that adds to the globalizing and proliferating tendencies of the term. Of course here I speak of the two effects together because they arise together, but one should remember their distinctiveness. I shall also point out a distinction between a strong version of the effect and a weak version of the effect, thus salvaging some parts of the popular level of the film's reception.

It is intriguing to speculate where the term Rashomon effect originates, though it may be impossible to settle this question to everyone's satisfaction, beyond disagreement. In 1988 anthropologist Karl Heider wrote about a Pacific Islands discussion group called the Rashomon Sessions which he coordinated from 1980 to 1984 at the meetings of the Association for Social Anthropology in Oceania. He refers to a lineage of remarks there about *Rashomon*, some of which had been made in passing by others in 1978 and 1979; those earlier remarks showed him, he said, that there was sufficient interest in inviting people to sessions at anthropological meetings in the following four years. Heider concluded that the Rashomon effect, in that period around 1980, was 'a phrase whose anthropological time has come' (1988: 73). Journalist Valeria Alia reports that she used the phrase in the late 1970s and that it was then incorporated in her 1996 book on journalism ethics and truth telling (Wikipedia 2014). D.P. Martinez seems to have been thinking about the idea while an anthropology student at the University of Chicago in 1982

(2009: xi). My own understanding of its origins arises much earlier, upon hearing my respected teacher, Nur Yalman, say to us in a class in early 1966 at the University of Chicago that 'anthropology's main problem is to deal with the Rashomon effect'. Unlike some graduate students in that room in Chicago, I had seen the film in 1961 or 1962, so this remark crystallized something that had been lurking for five years in my memory, but was still unformed and unnamed: that something was the realization of just how complex my experience of the film's unfolding had been, without me being clear minded about it. I suspect the Rashomon effect has shown up in many historic intellectual undertakings that deal with contested interpretations of events or with disagreements and evidence for them, or with subjectivity/objectivity, memory and perception. A pertinent example is the long poem called *The Ring and the Book* by Robert Browning (published in 1868–9, which he based upon a published copy of official written court testimonies in an Italian murder trial from the seventeenth century); the narrator describes from multiple angles the 1698 murder of an Italian countess and her whole family, and there are other versions of these events from different voices. As Walls does in Chapter 2, I recall Browning to demonstrate that the Rashomon effect is not a modernist conceit and is, in this particular case, over one hundred and forty-five years old.

## What is *Rashomon* all about?

The first ingredient of the film is that there is a fact, namely the body of a man in the forest. This is not just any fact, but a compelling fact. Societies expect answers to the question posed by this kind of fact, if not immediately then certainly in due time. There is pressure for an answer, pressure for closure. In *Rashomon* the fact of the body is so compelling that a witness and all principal participants are brought before a judge, over whose shoulder Kurosawa's camera is watching. This is not just any body, but a noble samurai's body. However, the descriptions of the fact and interpretations of it differ both subtly and systematically. The second ingredient is that these interpretative differences are wrapped in long narratives, each carefully cultivated by the teller to give us his or her version of truth. Each of these four narratives communicates the interests of the teller. But they don't offer us a position from which to negotiate agreement or disagreement with them. Kurosawa and cameraman Kazuo Miyagawa are too economical with the evidence and do not enable the viewer to take any such superior position.

   Kurosawa's film oscillates between dialogue about the incident in the forest, and negotiation among the three actors present at the scene. The dialogue in the rain under the half-destroyed gate among the monk, the woodcutter and the commoner is constructed for three voices: the voice of idealism (high Buddhist culture of compassion, the monk's tale), the voice of an eyewitness (the humble woodcutter's two slightly different tales) and the voice of a skeptical realist (a commoner who also ducks in to escape the rain) who, while he interrupts the others with his questions, keeps himself warm by breaking off parts of the gate and lighting a small fire.[3] The conversation between them is intense but still somewhat detached. This could be an allegorical dialogue that could be taken by audiences to be about issues such as the Japanese decision to go to war with the United States in 1941, the dropping of the Allied atomic bombs on Japan in 1945, the rightness of US-imposed reforms in 1946–9 in Japan, or even the removal of clothing from an abandoned baby. But on the surface the film is a dialogue about the probable cause and implications of a twelfth-century nobleman's death. It is, after all, a historic period film based on Akutagawa's stories, in turn based on twelfth-century stories from the famous Konjaku anthology. As both Richie and Matsumura show in their chapters above, the 1950 Japanese audience would have understood these meta-level allegories, and twenty-first century viewers will supply their own references even if they are unaware of the 1950s context.

On the other hand, the negotiation in the forest is more concrete and not at all detached – 'kill him' the lady urges the bandit in one version, pointing to her husband, then 'kill me' the lady urges the bandit in another. Both the negotiation to pretend to fight and the decision to end the play fight with a duel to the death are reached without words. The power of the film is to show how both dialogue and negotiation work in a dialectic process, and lead the innocent viewer to apprehend the Rashomon effect in the very complexity that the actors/characters themselves experienced it. It is their apprehension that is translated into numerous other (non-film) situations, and that is why the film provides a name for the complex effect which has long been known, but not named until recently.

Each account of the samurai's death is both coherent and plausible; the effect lies in that the death of the nobleman is the responsibility of a different person in each narrative and each account appears equally plausible. Remember that no warning is given to the innocent viewer; nothing is suggested during the woodcutter's first story that there will be other stories, or that there will be reasons to later doubt the woodcutter. Then suddenly, twenty-two minutes later, the viewer is thrust into another version of the same incident. It is important for someone who has seen the film many times to remember that the innocent viewer sees *Rashomon* for the first time only once, and that after that one viewing of the film a naïve reading is no longer available. It is remarkable how much engagement and intrigue are experienced by second- and third-time viewers who have nevertheless lost forever the element of surprise and disturbance that is essential in the first screening.[4]

Though coherent and plausible, each account is different in a crucial sense – the mode of the death. The bandit confesses he finally killed the samurai after a lengthy sword duel. The wife thinks she may have fallen upon her husband's roped body when she fainted in remorse arising from their dishonor. She says to the judge: 'I killed my own husband. I was violated by the robber … Neither conscious nor unconscious … I stabbed the small sword through the lilac-colored kimono into his breast.' The dead man, channeled through a spirit medium, described how he took his own life in dignity, using his wife's jeweled dagger which she dropped, after seeing what he thinks is the infidelity of his very beautiful wife. And the woodcutter describes the bandit suddenly and impulsively killing the nobleman after a playful sword skirmish in front of the woman. Having stabbed the nobleman, the bandit runs after the woman but does not catch her.

Read another way, each tale revolves around the samurai's wife, given that the original first causal move, for the entire set of stories, was how the bandit was awakened in the glade by the play of bright sunlight on his eyes, thus breaking his nap under a tree. As the samurai guided his wife's horse through the forest, a gentle breeze raised the clothing covering her ankles, and the bandit glimpsed a hint of her sensual body and fell under her spell. Everything else followed from that powerful intersection of sunlight, charm and desire. Her disadvantage and vulnerability are the starting premise of each narrative, but evolve differently from there. She is not portrayed as helpless, even though she acts out that condition skillfully. As Martinez suggests, 'the beautiful wife is not silent (a great virtue for Japanese women), and she is possibly not virtuous either' (2009, 39). This is how fact and interpretation are inextricably linked in *Rashomon*.

There is one other fact presented, and that is the bandit's sexual advance to the woman (who is married to the nobleman), but this fact is more equivocal. Most viewers conclude that the sexuality of the two, however interpreted, resonates with the death of the man. This sexual episode, whatever it is called, leads the viewer ineluctably to the body of the dead samurai. What gets frequent attention is the embrace and kiss leading to an advance, an assault or a rape occurring between the lady and the bandit. This set of different scenes is not essential to the Rashomon effect but, if anything, is an example of it. The popular memory of seeing *Rashomon*, constructed mostly by male critics, tends to focus more on the death of the samurai than on the experience of the woman. Viewers see this scene variously as the lady's calculated and brave strategy to prevail over the bandit and limit the risk to her person and/or her husband; as the lady's authentic, personal and spontaneous sexual response to the bandit's advances; as the lady's reluctant submission to the bandit's desire leading to her inability to fight off his assault; or finally as the bandit's forceful assault or rape of the resistant noblewoman. The firmness with which many viewers report that an assault or rape occurred is quite striking, when in fact different versions and interpretations of this encounter are carefully presented by Kurosawa. We do not know enough to say this sexual contact would constitute, in modern terms, second-degree rape or some other type – modern legal rape classification systems hinge on degrees of force used, physical injury experienced, confinement, etc. Kurosawa offers no evidence other than her shame in one or two of the narratives. Feminist legal scholar Orit Kamir wrote about her students who had seen *Rashomon*, and also about her friends 'who resisted the film's invitation ... to see an unconventional gender narrative of excluded voices .... [which appears] when we read the film against itself'.[5] In this book we have Janice Matsumura's observation that very soft sanctions against rape were common in Japan in 1950, noting that it was socially significant only when it exposed and embarrassed the very men who were supposed to prevent it from occurring. Other men, and many women in Japan, appear to have understood sexual assault as a mild aberration of normal female-male relations.

The camera angles, the length of shots, the movement of hands and heads all enable us to draw quite different inferences about this sexual episode in the four narratives. In his 'Film Style and Narration in *Rashomon*', Nick Redfern uses time series and multiple correspondence analyses to prove that the four retellings differ not only in content but in form as well. According to Redfern, shifts in pacing and cinematographic technique between retellings indicate each narrator's relative narrative agency, positioning them as either active or passive participants in the sequence. While he concedes that his analysis 'does not solve the epistemological problem at the core of the film', Redfern's analysis provides new insight into its formal construction, revealing that the film's narrative ambiguities owe much to Kurosawa's nuanced approach to each narrative (n.d.: 12).[6] The Rashomon effect directs an audiences' attention to these subtle differences. In the lady's and woodcutter's versions there is no embrace or kiss. In the husband's version the lady goes off with the bandit willingly, but with no embrace or kiss, but bearing a look of beauty, which greatly disturbed the husband nonetheless. In the bandit's version the kiss is most important. This is an example of the Rashomon effect.

## The Rashomon narratives and doubt

Kurosawa's great skill is that he offers no evidence at all by which the viewer may disqualify any of the narratives. Even the eyewitness, usually a privileged narrator in most societies, is found to be only as plausible as the others. Importantly, a doubt about the woodcutter's story is deliberately introduced, so that this eyewitness version cannot be found superior to the others. And the bandit has proudly confessed to killing the nobleman after a sexual encounter with his wife, mentioning at the same time his numerous other previous crimes.

While there is much else that is important, these are the elements of the film that belong in the usual differences of perspective account of it. Because differences in perspective are ubiquitous, and the Rashomon effect is not, it cannot be these differences alone which establish the Rashomon effect. In contrast, I suggest that it is the conjunction of these elements, plus their strong interaction, that make up the Rashomon effect. That means the Rashomon effect is a combination of a difference of perspective and equally plausible accounts, with the absence of evidence to elevate one above others, with the inability to disqualify any particular version of the truth, all surrounded by the social pressure for closure on the question. This convergence is presented to us through Kurosawa's stark minimalism in the different accounts of the events in the forest glade. It is not simply the viewer's conclusion about this minimalism; it has to be each participant's conclusion too. Although the power of the Rashomon effect is said to hit the observer and bystander strongly, experience of it is not restricted to them. Indeed, it affects the participants in this incident too, revealing itself to them sooner or later, often with great inconvenience to them. This uncertainty is inextricably woven into the certainty of the fact (the man's body, in this case) around which the Rashomon effect usually takes shape.

The conclusion reached by a viewer, if any, must be inconclusive. Except for the persistent fact of the nobleman's body, lying in the forest, punctured by a blade – coupled with the expectation that there will eventually be closure around it – there is nothing more to rely on. The camera sitting over the judge's shoulder reminds us of that. The Rashomon effect draws listeners in, participants and observers alike, and they all slowly discover themselves in it. The absence of forensic evidence to help us assign cause is poignant, as it is in the case of many compelling situations. Although the judgment reached may not be logically satisfactory, it must be socially and legally satisfactory. It must be decisive even if it is not beyond reasonable doubt. Although the bandit's and woodcutter's stories implicate the bandit, the other two accounts do not. The judge must judge among these accounts, even if only to acquit the bandit. But when involved in the murder of a nobleman, a bandit seldom fares well – so there will be a judgment.

All this shows that significant differences occur in the narratives, and that many viewers of the film do not remember these differences when the film is over. This narrowing of focus and forgetting of key ingredients, pointed out by numerous studies of memory by psychologists, are curious in the context of a film that so powerfully opposes narrowing, selective forgetting, and early closure. This common reaction reminds us that those who really experience the Rashomon effect are not necessarily comfortable with its implications. Indeed, as is common in most legal process, they might prefer a method by which to undermine one or more of the accounts, privilege another, and arrive at a more satisfactory conclusion than the one they think the film offered them.

Is there any use waiting for some new evidence to come along to satisfy us and permit satisfactory closure? While it is true we often do wait or should wait for this evidence, in the presence of the Rashomon effect such waiting would be futile, because no more evidence is forthcoming, at least not during this period of pressure for closure. This is why the Rashomon effect enters our ordinary daily lives. We are all faced with puzzling situations where a difference of perspective arises yet the absence of forensic and decisive evidence thwarts a satisfactory conclusion. Something else then emerges, something much less satisfactory. The emergence of differences of perspective alone would not endow the Rashomon effect with such power; after all, aren't differences in perspective quite commonplace? No, it is its conjunction with other ingredients mentioned above, such as pressure for closure, etc., that makes it so powerful. This is one reason that judges say they see the Rashomon effect all the time, namely that the evidence is variable, even when provided by otherwise reliable observers/truth-tellers. They too see the effect without always remembering that they are part of the pressure for closure.[7]

But what is compelling about the facts in *Rashomon*? Ask yourself whether this story would have become legendary if the body in the forest had been the bandit's body? Cinematically this might have been quite effective, but would either of the other two principals (the samurai or his wife) have claimed responsibility for killing him? Would the dead man's spirit accept responsibility for his own death, as the nobleman does speaking through the spirit medium? Socially we know that the judge listens carefully to the testimonies because this nobleman's body is more important than a bandit's. Of course, the bandit's body would have been important to his competitors, and to his loved ones or relatives (he says he is not married), and more probably to his former victims. But socially – in the twelfth century as in the mid-twentieth century when Kurosawa made the film – most bandits commanded more fear than respect. What if the body had been the lady's body? How compelling would that be?

I raise these hypothetical questions to remind us that the Rashomon effect does not occur just anywhere. It is not simply the absence of facts that brings it into being, nor simply the appearance of different versions of the truth. Moreover the absence of facts does not itself produce different versions of the truth. The Rashomon effect occurs where interests, culture and power converge to fix our attention on closure, to propel us to ask for explanations, and to expect to get them, and soon. When elements of authority are involved, such as judges representing the state, these expectations are more tangible. That is what I mean here by compelling. Yet the other ingredients of the effect have to be present, in a strongly interacting relationship.

The appearance of a film's name for a cognitive and cultural phenomenon (the Rashomon effect), known in many cultures for a very long time, is therefore a good measure of the reception and acceptance of Kurosawa's work. Subjects so widely separated as groups in conflict with the state over the consequences of toxic waste buried in a canal in northern New York State and the evolution of Israeli fiction writing have come within the analytic and viewing framework of *Rashomon* (these and other examples are shown in the accompanying Appendix I The Rashomon effect in the social sciences). Kurosawa and his producers, admirers and critics could not have imagined such an influence out of all proportion with the film's original intention, and nor could I.

## How is the Rashomon effect experienced?

In November 2000 I sat in the Supreme Court of British Columbia listening to a case of alleged assault and wrongful dismissal in the workplace. The assault turned out to be mostly pushing and shoving, accompanied by harsh language. The judge, having heard the evidence, asked the prosecutor to sum up the accounts of the two principals (employee and employer). The lawyer for the defence nodded concurrence with this summing up when it was concluded. My notes are verbatim:

> So there are two versions Mr. Watson? Yes My Lady, two versions, only two. And nothing to allow us to confirm either one of them, Mr. Watson? Nothing, apparently, My Lady. Thank you counsel. [Judge shakes her head, and then says, muttering the first sentence in a lower voice.] Just like *Rashomon*. I must rule an acquittal. The case is dismissed.[8]

Notwithstanding this remark, and the presence of Kurosawa's camera looking over the judge-prosecutor's shoulder in the Japanese magistrate's compound, we must avoid the impression that the Rashomon effect appears only in judicial form. As one person, now an accountant, said to me, years after seeing the film for the first time, 'it is everywhere, I just hadn't understood it so clearly'. It may be that many judges also think that their references to *Rashomon* are mainly in memory of the difference-in-perspective interpretation of the film, and that they, too (being closer to it), do not acknowledge the other key ingredients in the evidence before them. This case of wrongful dismissal mentioned above was hardly as pressing as a murder. I mention this to stress that we expect to find the Rashomon effect in many spheres of life, not just juridical, and not just those concerning heavy facts such as a body in a forest. Processes or incidents which arouse little interest other than among immediate participants are nevertheless the sites of the Rashomon effect.

Finally, the Rashomon effect induces doubt, in the first step doubt about one's own judgment. This first step necessarily leads to and hinges on the second step, namely doubt about others. This doubt is not a solipsism arrived at in solitude, but is established socially. That means we think about an incident more or less privately but usually come to terms with it together, through a sociable mixture of dialogue and negotiation. Only recently would people have seen the film alone; in the twentieth century, most of them would have seen it socially, as part of an audience. The Rashomon effect is thus a communicative condition above all; it is about the explanations of an incident offered by three (or more) qualified people, explanations which we find unsatisfactory or unsettling, whether we are parties to this incident or not. So, experiencing the Rashomon effect is a very social process, a very communicative process. Its complexity is produced by the presence of the hearers and/or observers who provide some of the social pressure for closure around the question. The dialogue among these hearers/observers is laced with authority, and conclusions (if not judgments) are expected whether or not there is a judge present. Opinions are formed and minds are made up through this process, only to run up against the inherently ambiguous nature of the situation.

This sociability has consequences, arising from the possibility of getting it wrong, and the Rashomon effect draws us there too, eventually. In a subset of cases there are serious consequences to the social nature of these judgments, where responsibility is assigned in error, as in cases of murder or other major crimes. In all cases we prefer not to be wrong, which is why most of us work hard to convince ourselves that we are right. We usually have an interest in not being out of step with those who seem more clearly to be right. This preference is compounded by the social pressure that drives everyone toward closure. Wrongful conviction is thus not arrived at by mistaken solitary solipsism about an error, but by a very collective social process, a mutual appraisal of interests, all deeply influenced by authoritative opinion, usually addressing a set of facts framed by authorities. Another social process that occurs, at least in North America, is the voluntary (and fictitious or false) confessions of guilt, numbering dozens of such improbable and irrelevant confessions made by uninvolved persons, often in widely publicized cases. But in *Rashomon* Kurosawa does not lead us to think these are voluntary, spurious or fictitious confessions; he shows us real pressure and real conviction about placing and accepting responsibility for the death of the nobleman, but embeds all that in different varieties of the truth.

So cultures and societies seem to move back and forth between the experiences of the Rashomon effect in the wild, in real life, and the depiction of the effect at work in their theatrical and fictitious creations (and re-creations). I want to redirect the idea that this effect is a peculiarly judicial phenomenon, although it is hardly surprising that we dwell there, because the process of calling witnesses and pressure for closure in courts is so crucial. It is not restricted to judicial situations at all; it is far more general and widespread in our experience across what are usually called the humanities and social sciences.

## The Rashomon effect in the 1941 Bohr-Heisenberg conversations in Copenhagen

One particularly effective re-creation in the Rashomon mode concerns a famous conversation grounded in the 1941 experience of two physicists who knew each other well, and for whom (and for the wife of one of them) that famous conversation reverberated for years. A closer analysis of this two-day incident, and the theatrical play based on it, will demonstrate the interplay between the experience of the Rashomon effect in the wild and its dramatic reconstruction and re-creation on the live stage. The fact is that physicists Niels Bohr and Werner Heisenberg, although separated in age by sixteen years, had a long friendship. However, in 1941 something occurred between them that ruptured their relationship in such a way that efforts to restore it were painfully unresolved until their deaths. Frayn's play presents the ambiguity of the fact of that two-day visit, with three different interpretations (Niels Bohr's, Werner Heisenberg's and Margrethe Bohr's), and its implications, which could not be resolved, even until the end of time.[9]

Bohr and Heisenberg's friendship was born out of the admiration of each for the extraordinary capabilities of the other in physics, reinforced by the universal perception among other scientists that they were indeed two super-stars in physics. Years earlier, in late 1926 and early 1927, they jointly talked about a Copenhagen Interpretation which was one of the stable formulations of quantum mechanics at the time, particularly Bohr's idea of complementarity, as linked to causality and wave theory. The work of one depended on the work of the other; they co-evolved as scientists and private men, during which time they led the field of quantum mechanics. The privacy of their family friendship is contrasted with the expansive open communication expected among stars of nuclear physics. Frayn's play examines two personalities, each with its concealments, and a friendship that was not simply a professional camaraderie but one that engaged their private lives, their wives and children for seventeen years before Bohr and Heisenberg were divided by war in 1939. But then the war brought German troops into Denmark to occupy the country in April 1940; Heisenberg had moved quickly to the senior position in the German nuclear program, and Bohr (still directing his Danish institute) began to fear for his half-Jewish status once the German authorities decided to enforce the Nazi anti-Jewish laws. Tipped off about his impending arrest, Bohr escaped by small boat to Sweden in 1943, and then went through the United Kingdom to work on the Manhattan Project in the United States.

In this context, in 1941, Heisenberg came to Copenhagen to meet Bohr to talk with him about the uranium, plutonium, reactor and bomb projects of the Germans and the Allies. To the complexity of their long and intimate friendship, and rivalrous professional physicist relations, was added the new gravitational effect of the war, the German occupation of Denmark, and the distinct possibility of an atomic bomb.

In Frayn's play, these men presented three faces to each other: the face of the physicist engaged in open scientific communication, the face of the friend of the family for almost twenty years, and the face of the custodian of (opposed) state nuclear secrets. The Rashomon effect appeared as they adopted and adapted their new roles as custodians of state secrets. In their interaction they were offering something and withholding something else, and each knew it. In these famous 1941 conversations, mediated by Bohr's observant wife Margrethe, the three faces of each man take the stage. In the play the conversation lasts about two real hours; in history the conversations occurred over two days. None of these three faces could be set aside or subordinated for long. Frayn shows us how they tumbled forth, each face overcoming the others in contrapuntal succession.[10] Like Kurosawa the film director, Frayn the playwright compressed time and constructed an ever-opening space for this kind of struggle with high uncertainty.

Which of these three faces would prevail in certain moments of the conversation? Frayn's play skillfully weaves the uncertainty about which face would prevail in the conversation (remember the uncertainty principle of which Heisenberg too was an author). Each stage in the conversation succeeded only in revealing further uncertainty, not in diminishing it. Bohr's wife is shown as a privileged and astute observer, but one also severely challenged to interpret what is going on since she was not a physicist. She queries Heisenberg's object-ive and motive. In her husband's later struggle to comprehend what took place in 1941, and to express himself in writing to Heisenberg, she played a very significant historic role. Margrethe does not simply take her husband's side in all of this, but provides a third and independent voice. She presses Bohr to consider whether Heisenberg had come to try to uncover what Bohr knew about the progress in the UK-US-Canadian-French bomb project but Bohr does not immediately adopt her skeptical position.

Different versions of that conversation attract different moral interpret-ations: Frayn reminds us, almost as a warning, that after his study of all the versions of the conversation, including a careful reading of numerous drafts of un-posted and rewritten letters that Bohr wrote to Heisenberg until his death in 1962, no definitive judgment is possible about Heisenberg's motiv-ation or intent to come to meet Bohr in 1941. These questions still remain: Did Heisenberg choose to reveal to Albert Speer (minister in charge of his atomic project) the probability that a nuclear reactor could produce plutonium for a bomb, or not? Did his conversation with Bohr build Heisenberg's confidence that a reactor could achieve that end? Did Heisenberg's nuclear team delib-erately miscalculate the critical mass of U235 needed to sustain an effect-ive chain reaction in such a reactor, or not? The evidence available does not put beyond doubt what Bohr thought Heisenberg was doing in Copenhagen in 1941, and shows that Bohr had continuing questions and doubt about what Heisenberg's purpose was in coming, and what he actually did after he returned to Germany after 1941. Did he skillfully delay the official German project even marginally, or significantly?

In the un-posted cumulative letter of 1947 to Heisenberg, Bohr wrote, 'Despite our personal friendship we had to be regarded as representatives of two sides engaged in mortal combat'.[11] We only know for certain that Heisenberg intended to send messages through Bohr to other physicists whom they both knew well, including the enemy state agencies he knew to be in touch with Bohr. We also know that Bohr was evasive, being uncertain of the effects of transmitting such messages. Both later felt the 1941 conversa-tions in Copenhagen ruined their friendship, and both deeply regretted this fact throughout their lives, struggling to reopen the relationship. Two facts converge: first the strategic uncertainty surrounding the outcomes of the con-versation at the time, second that this conversation was agreed to have been the cause of a rift in an important friendship. Frayn implies that Heisenberg worked harder at this repair work than Bohr (trying to see and meet Bohr), but considering how often Bohr sat down to draft his ultimate statement about the 1941 conversation, the loss was evidently and undeniably recipro-cal. Although there is social, political and intellectual pressure to settle the question concerning the 1941 Bohr-Heisenberg conversation, different and equally plausible interpretations have been made. This is a classic illustration of the Rashomon effect, in which it is not possible to settle satisfactorily the key question, despite pressure to do so and to reach closure. This example powerfully illustrates the ripple of the effect of the real life Bohr-Heisenberg conversation to its re-creation fifty-seven years later in Michael Frayn's 1998 hit play.

## An example of the Rashomon effect in the Dziekanski Affair, Vancouver, 2007–15

If the Rashomon effect appears on the level of very private conversations (as in the film), it also appears on more public stages. In the same Supreme Court of British Columbia mentioned above, trials began in 2013 of four police officers from Canada's national police force, the Royal Canadian Mounted Police (RCMP). In October 2007 these RCMP officers had hurriedly arrived, confronted and then caused the sudden death of Robert Dziekanski, a Polish immigrant in the airport at Vancouver. His accidental enclosure in the secure international area of the airport, which lasted from the afternoon into the middle of the night, led to the death of this unnoticed forty-year-old adult man who spoke no English. He was coming to visit his mother, and perhaps stay in Canada to work, passing through the airport like thousands of similar immigrants every year. His sense of being neglected, and being unable to exit, probably led to his agitated movements, occasional shouts in Polish (by that time all the interpreters had gone home), and dramatic and erratic gestures, augmented probably by his inability to smoke, and perhaps dehydration or lack of sleep, or all three. He picked up and brandished a chair; he picked up and waved a stapler. But we shall never know what he was thinking. He died a few minutes later.[12]

This unintended death led to a trail of official police notes, reports and statements, which show inconsistencies and changes over time, ultimately revealing a form of the Rashomon effect. All of this recorded detail and oral communication emerged in a 2008 Commission of Enquiry into this incident, because the death occurred in police custody and was partially caused by use of a conducted electrical weapon, known as a Taser. Those changes and inconsistencies in their narrative accounts were the reason that the Attorney General initiated a series of trials six years after that night, trials based on the charge that these four men had cooperated (colluded) with one another to construct a common narrative which was intended to mislead official enquiries, particularly while they were testifying under oath. If they had done so, the court would decide that they had committed perjury, lying under oath – a serious offence. This enquiring and explaining gave rise to a rippling outward of differing versions of the truth about this brief episode, first on the night of Dziekanski's death and the morning after, second in the routine required investigations and official reports in the following days, third after viewing a short video filmed by a witness on the spot (but released to the public only thirty days afterward), fourth in the stages of an official enquiry into Tasers, fifth in the perjury trials that began in 2013 and continued through 2015. This complexity can be better understood through the frame of the Rashomon effect.

Cut to the Vancouver airport in October 2007; suddenly four policemen arrived and interpreted Dziekanski's movements quickly, in a few seconds, and they said (under oath soon afterwards) that Dziekanski's gestures and intentions when he saw them were menacing or aggressive or combative. Acting as a team, one of them fired an electronic conducted energy weapon, commonly called a stun gun or Taser. Falling to the ground with this shot, Dziekanski struggled while receiving three or four more shots of the Taser; the policemen then wrestled with him and put their weight on him, one using his knee on the back of his neck. Later they all described this as the take-down moment, and a heavy baton was also used as a tool to subdue him. This attack lasted thirty-one seconds, and he was handcuffed and writhing on the floor immediately afterwards, slowly dying. Though they called for paramedics, curiously no CPR was administered by the officers on the spot.

As in *Rashomon*, the body of a man lay dead on the ground. There was pressure for closure because police were directly involved, even though this body was not a high-status body, not like the noble samurai in *Rashomon*. This incident produced great pressure on the RCMP concerning its reputation, and they thus wanted (and yet also did not really want) an investigation which would lead to closure. There was also strong pressure for investigation from the Polish government, and for closure from Canadians of Polish origin.

There were testimonies from each of the four policemen and statements from nine witnesses, contributing to the complexity of the Rashomon effect. And then – entering the twenty-first century – an 8.5 minute video appeared, taken through the huge glass walls enclosing Dziekanski and the policemen – all filmed on his mobile phone by another passenger. The eyewitnesses too, like the woodcutter in *Rashomon*, were not high status – limousine drivers, security guards, airport night staff, etc. There were variations in the police testimony and witness reports, but no disagreement about the fact that the death occurred rapidly in police custody. In contrast to *Rashomon* where each tale implicated the teller, the frame surrounding Dziekanski was that no one accepted responsibility, and each of the four police officers avoided personal liability. Even the Commissioner of the Public Complaints Against the RCMP (a government agency), who is a senior lawyer without police experience, observed in his February 2011 report that 'I do not accept as accurate any of the versions of events presented by the involved members [officers] because I find considerable and significant discrepancies in the depth and accuracy of the recollection of the members when compared against the otherwise uncontroverted video evidence.'[13] But in the perjury trials, which started in 2013, each man once again gradually revealed differences in their perspectives, all under the pressure to explain their role around this unnecessary and futile death.

As if in a *Rashomon* sequence, these four policemen's tales were told and re-told in different hearings. Some witnesses had been hurriedly interviewed just after the death, before they could see the (confiscated) video, which, it was feared by policemen, would influence the witnesses and taint their evidence – thus reducing its value in court. The short yet notorious video was soon seen and re-seen *millions of times* by people around the world. Gradually, a debate over police conduct and inconsistent police explanations appeared in the public sphere, usually linked to the video. Four months later, in February 2008, a Commission of Enquiry was instructed to start work and summon the policemen and all witnesses. It became difficult to think about the Dziekanski affair without referring to the video. One judge warned the court in 2013, 'the video must be viewed with caution ... casting doubt upon the proposition that if something cannot be seen in the video it didn't happen.'[14] Note how that statement contrasts with the Judge Commissioner's 2011 report doubting the policemen's narratives in contrast with the video.

Importantly for our study of Rashomon effects, these four police officers were brought back again to court in a series of four separate trials, commencing in June 2013 and continuing through 2015. The charge in each case was that each policeman cooperated and conspired, or 'colluded', to construct a single line of reasoning about this brief event. This collusion enabled them to adopt a common defence during investigations of their conduct, for which their first line of explanation has always been 'self-defence', thus justifying their use of force, including five rapid shots from the Taser. This charge meant that they had lied about the case in court under oath. The separation of the four trials served to enhance the Rashomon effect because separation increased the disassociation of the narratives: They were being tried separately for conspiring together and colluding. In the first 2013 trial one policeman was found not guilty of perjury, in the second and third trials both were found guilty, and the fourth trial in 2015 concluded with a 'not guilty' judgment. In all trials in 2013–15, there was prolonged questioning about whether and how well these men followed standard police practices (note books, reports, the duty to account, reports to superiors, critical incident debriefings, etc.). This inevitably revealed how this procedural apparatus was inadequate to deal with the Rashomon effect. Perhaps more precisely, standard police practices and record-keeping seem to have served to establish, conserve and even uphold the Rashomon effect, enabling observers to compare and contrast over many years the ambiguous and subtly different versions of the same policemen's testimony about the same brief event.

In one of the trials, the former policeman Kwesi Millington described Dziekanski holding a stapler high in the air as if it might or could become a weapon, or surrendering but not holding his hands 'up high'. Having listened to the disagreement about whether or not Dziekanski complied with instructions (in a language Dziekanski could not understand), the Supreme Court Justice said in early 2015 'This isn't Alice in Wonderland ... I'm suggesting all of us are experts in the English language.'[15] In front of four separate judges, asking different questions about the same charge, the result has been that two policemen were found guilty and two were found not guilty.[16]

The inconsistency is profound: One can see that in the Dziekanski affair the Rashomon effect does not fade away, even with the passage of almost eight years.

In the Dziekanski affair there is a kind of reverse Rashomon effect. The four policemen each expressed a very similar narrative in hearings and enquiries, saying that they apprehended violence from him, and thus they countered resistance with force. The systems of police administration and judiciary have truth constructed and applied a 'difference-in-perspective' model, expecting implicitly that these four people would not and could not achieve a singular account of the incident. These current trials proceeded on the premise that the policemen did not tell the truth in their earlier testimony. The trials were not about the fact that they unnecessarily killed a man in less than a minute, but were instead about their versions of the truth. A separate and consistent perspective is provided by the mobile phone and its video record; observers, some judges and witnesses seem to think that the risk of Dziekanski's menacing resistance was misread and exaggerated.

There was (and remains) an emerging consensus that there should be a singular definition of the truth about this incident, but there were reasonable disagreements as to what that truth is. We should recall a remark by Martinez, that 'It [*Rashomon*] is about the conflicting desires of the human condition; we want a single reality, while holding fast to our subjective interpretations.'[17]

## Conclusion

The Rashomon effect is not just about differences of perspective. It occurs particularly where such differences arise in combination with the absence of evidence to elevate or disqualify any version of the truth, plus the social pressure for closure on the question. The convergence of these three ingredients is sufficient in all cases, but there are stronger and weaker cases of the effect – distinguished by the intensity of the interaction of the three ingredients. It is the conjunction of these elements and their intense interaction that make up the strong cases. Through Kurosawa's starkly minimal treatment of the different narratives of the events in the forest glade, audiences experience the power of the Rashomon effect. This fascinating combination of elements, played through the viewers' increasing doubt, gives the film its philosophical and social force. But there is probably a spectrum at work here from stronger cases to weaker. Put another way, with respect to one discipline, Heider said:

> there is a shared reality but differing truths may indeed be said about it. [However,] the value of thinking about the Rashomon effect goes far beyond the relatively few cases of ethnographic disagreement that we shall be able to turn up. The sorts of influences, biases, or predilections we can examine here are at work in all ethnography, even when it is unchallenged.

(1988: 74)

For greater clarity, we can now say there is a strong Rashomon effect, for example in the Bohr-Heisenberg case mentioned above; it had all the necessary elements in the film just described and also involved three narratives or accounts. But to acknowledge the way this old film has been creeping into common thought and speech (remember the judges quoted above), there is also a weak Rashomon effect, for example in the wrongful dismissal case mentioned above; it had the other necessary elements yet unfolded with only two narratives, two accounts, two plausible and unreconciled explanations.

We can conclude that the Rashomon effect provides us with an epistemology that applies to a special set of situations, tracks how we come to terms with the complex properties of these situations, and suggests how we understand or misunderstand them, depending on our insight. From this epistemology we can see precisely how we know what we think we know, and what we say, about this set of situations. In this limited sense, we can say that people engaged in this process arising out of this set of situations all form a kind of epistemic community of uncertainty. Although it may be transitory, that epistemic community is moving toward a deeper understanding of the very situations in which the Rashomon effect arises. The necessary presence of bystanders, witnesses and official listeners or even judges adds to the uncertainty and complexity of the Rashomon effect. I hope I have persuaded you that though not entirely wrongheaded, many popular interpretations of *Rashomon* limit and diminish the power of both the film and the Rashomon effect. As anyone can see easily through Google, there are now hundreds of references to the Rashomon effect. The *Rashomon* ripples which flow across this book are moving steadily through space and time. This essay is intended partly to give it better shape as it moves on that journey.

The Rashomon effect shows up in many intellectual undertakings that deal with contested interpretations of events or with disagreements and evidence for them, or with subjectivity/objectivity, memory and perception. But *Rashomon* may have found its most fertile ground earlier – first in anthropology and later in sociology, social psychology and communication studies.[18] Eventually it arrived in the conceptual world of jurisprudence, and is now found in the study of epistemology; there we see a debate on how we know what we say we know, how we explain how we know that, how we justify our confidence in our knowledge.

We come to terms with these complex situations through dialogue and negotiation, through communication. The film's greatness arises not just in showing how the effect occurs, though that is a great achievement, but also in asking if we can come to terms with it, particularly without much help from its creator, Mister Kurosawa himself.

# Notes

1 These students lived in western Canada, and were asked to speak and write about *Rashomon* in a class taught by me since 2003. They were generally between the ages of twenty and thirty (though about ten percent were older), and more than half were women. Although about half of them came from households where a language other than English was also spoken, very few students understood Japanese. Remarkably, fewer than five percent had seen the film before. Each person was required to discuss and write about the Rashomon effect, and how their work in negotiation and dialogue was related to it.

2 There is obviously a variant of this first kind of effect, and that is the experience of seeing *Rashomon* year after year; thanks to my colleague Terry Neiman for his insightful reading of a draft of this chapter.

3 Donald Richie often said that only the commoner under the gate had no story, so had no version to tell (1972: 73).

4 When analyzing *Rashomon*, a few students recalled seeing Tom Tykwer's *Run Lola, Run* (1999), which they recognized as an equally precise treatment of alternate narratives and alternative outcomes. The logic of one film stirs their memory of the logic of the other. But we observe important differences between the two films. *Lola* is not, like *Rashomon*, about distinct versions of the same incident, but three sequences with different outcomes, each achieved by small alterations in probability and contingency, repeated over a fast, breathless twenty minutes. Releasing the film, Tykwer talked about

> the way time gets manipulated ... The dramatic principle of creating time is, I feel, one of the most interesting aspects of film-making. You can relate what happens in twenty minutes or in twenty years ... the biggest challenge was to make the leaps ahead in time not appear like breaks in the action, but to make all the transitions flow into each other so that the viewers would move from scene to scene with their emotional commitment unimpaired. The space-time continuum gets taken right off its hinges without anyone really noticing ...
>
> (Tykwer 1999: n.p.)

5 An example of an insightful analysis, Orit Kamir's interpretation is best summed up in the following statement

> let me restate this point. The legal discourse tends to engage itself with specifics and details; the compatibility of witnesses' testimony and the determination of the facts occupy significant portions of the legal world's time, effort and energy. As my reading of *Rashomon* demonstrates, such preoccupation is far from being neutral, objective, or purely professional. It distracts from issues such as underlying social stereotypes, screening mechanisms that preclude illegitimate stories, and the unconscious construction of the judging community as a community of men. It thus acts as a conservative force, discouraging reflection, awareness, and willingness to change ... *Rashomon* is a story of men's weakness, selfishness, and greediness and a woman's courageous resistance and survival against all odds.
>
> (2000: 86–7)

Later Kamir wrote that the film leads viewers 'to arrive at the "legal" conclusion marked and predetermined by the film' (2005: 269). But she seems to refrain from saying what that conclusion is. Kamir later collected these ideas in *Framed: Women in Law and Film* (2006) (Kamir 2000, 2005, 2006).

6 I am grateful to Jef Burnham for this reference.

7 An example of witness variability is given by anthropologist Alan Macfarlane, in the experience of a Cambridge judge trying a case of a daylight armed robbery of a post office in Cambridge, UK. In this trial real-time eye witnesses differed on key issues:

> The uncertainty of people's experience and memory is particularly evident where we would expect it least, that is in the study of legal process. My wife was a magistrate (lay judge), trying an armed robbery case in Cambridge in 2001. There were many witnesses to the daylight raid on the post office. She heard their testimonies and was amazed by the discrepancies. People who were standing only a few yards from the scene described the robbers in totally contrary ways. For some they were tall, dark, bearded, driving a red car; for others they were small, fair, clean-shaven, driving a blue car. And so on. Unlike *Rashomon*, there was no possible reason for these witnesses to lie. All thought they were telling the truth. It was simply that, as cognitive psychologists could no doubt explain, we see what we expect to see. Yet even hardened judges and prosecutors, let alone the general public, forget about this expectation – and the Rashomon effect is a powerful reminder.
>
> (Macfarlane 2004)

8 Also judges in less compelling situations are more and more recognizing and referring to the Rashomon effect, as Justice Finkelstein in the High Court of Queensland, Australia, found in August 2008; unable to decide on the evidence in a dispute between an administrator and a litigious citizen who was using the case as a form of discovery, he charged them both with their costs. His judgment referred explicitly to *Rashomon* (2008).

9 Michael Frayn's 1998 hit play, *Copenhagen: A Play in Two Acts*.

10 A face is like a mask, in Erving Goffman's sense of the presentation of self in everyday life, a thing constructed and sustained by the person behind it to whom it belongs. Each face in a network has a valence, meaning its combining power, its capacity to bond with others, as is meant in physical chemistry. That transition is what we call face work. These multiple faces are not limited to famous physicists, and we all know that this increases the intensity of the Rashomon effect.

11 Un-posted letter quoted by Frayn in the epilogue to the film version (2002) of his play directed by Howard Davies. The whole text released by the Niels Bohr Institute can be seen on its website at www.nbi.ku.dk. Note that Bohr also met Joseph Stalin's and Lavretii Beria's delegate from Moscow in November 1945, but there is less doubt about what occurred in that conversation (Bethe, Gottfried and Sagdeev 1995: 85–90). There are four thoughtful essays on Frayn's treatment of the Bohr-Heisenberg conversation (published in *Forum on Physics and Society*, October 2002, pp.36–42). The Bohr family believed this evidence to be so important that they overturned an agreement with their father and published all these letters in 2002.

12 The Dziekanski affair can be understood through Internet-based documents provided by the 'Commission for Public Complaints Against the RCMP' (December 2007 and 10 February 2011); 'Braidwood Commission of Enquiry' for the Government of British Columbia (hearings in February–March 2010, decision in June 2010); Supreme Court of British Columbia R. v. Bill Bentley (hearings and decision in June–July 2013); also R. v. Millington, R. v. Rundel, R. v. Robinson (2013–15); also pertinent but unavailable are 'RCMP Integrated Homicide Investigation Team Reports' of 2007–8.

13 Commissioner for Public Complaints Against the RCMP, Chair's Final Report [re: Dziekanski], 11 February 2011.

14 Supreme Court of British Columbia 2013: 45.

15 Petrovich 2014: n.p.
16 Keller 2015a: n.p.; 2015b: n.p.; Dhillon and Keller 2015: n.p.
17 Martinez 2009: 40.
18 This work began by recording all evidence regarding *Rashomon* in the social sciences, and further into epistemology. But the volume of citations grew too large. See the list of examples of applications of the Rashomon effect in many fields in the accompanying appendices.

---

Akira Kurosawa describing how the rain effects were created at the gate set during the filming of *Rashomon*:

Because the gate set was so huge, the job of creating rainfall on it was a major operation. We borrowed fire engines and turned on the studio's fire hoses to full capacity. But when the camera was aimed upward at the cloudy sky over the gate, the sprinkle of the rain couldn't be seen against it, so we made rainfall with black ink in it.

(Kurosawa 1983: 137)

# 8 The Rashomon effect

## Considerations for existential anthropology

*Nur Yalman*

In one of his most perceptive essays, Isaiah Berlin writes of Johann Gottfried von Herder as a symptom of the future, 'the albatross before the coming storm' (1998: 434). Much the same can be said of Akira Kurosawa. He too is like the albatross circling the ship in ominous weather, a portent before the second storm, after the war, indicating further troublesome times ahead. Every one of his films leaves one searching for words to comprehend its deep impact. In film after film, *Dodeskaden, Rashomon, Seven Samurai, Dersu Uzala, Dreams, Madadayo* and others, he was able to express the sentiments and anxieties of the generation after World War II who were trying to make sense of recent turmoil that had disrupted so many lives. Creative artists were facing a much more chaotic intellectual and spiritual world than what had gone before.

Though *Rashomon* was first screened in 1950, it hit the ordinary popular cinemas in the West in the early 1950s, when Japanese culture was still strange to outsiders. The film's searching exploration of what is taken to be real and true during an exotic incident in the mountains of medieval Japan, became a suggestive metaphor for the uncertainties facing the generations after the horrendous bloodletting in the war in China and the rest of Asia. *Rashomon* reminded us that what appeared to be realities could be unmasked, and that human action was capable of multiple interpretations. In the way Kurosawa presented the events in that ill-fated forest grove in ancient Japan, there was an almost Buddhist sense of *maya*, reality as illusion. When I saw *Rashomon* for the first time about 1960, I had myself recently returned from years of anthropological fieldwork among Buddhists in Sri Lanka. It soon seemed appropriate to me to express these inchoate sentiments of human ambiguity as the Rashomon effect. Kurosawa's vision of multiple possible realities fitted in with the problems faced by anthropologists when they tried to understand the colorful but alien reality of other cultures and interpret them to Western academic audiences. What was their reality we asked? Could a single account, however authoritative, do justice to the richness and immediacy of their own experiences? What kinds of intellectual presuppositions had already colored the spectacles of the observer? As anthropological accounts of other peoples multiplied, these questions became more troubling and more insistent for the development of an intellectual discipline.

We all can now see that the Rashomon effect, which highlighted the difficulties of understanding events in history and human motivation, fits in well with existentialist philosophy, both of the German kind (Dilthey, Weber, Jaspers) and French kind (Sartre, Merleau-Ponty). There had already been much discussion of the difficulties faced by historians in interpreting the behavior of people caught in the current of their history. Von Ranke and Dilthey writing in Germany had long ago distinguished between the physical sciences (*Naturwissenschaft* / the science of nature) where the process of understanding (*Verstehen*) was relatively direct, in contrast to the human sciences (*Geisteswissenschaft* / the science of the spirit) where the intentions and purposes, the consciousness of individual actors had to be taken into account. As Sartre wrote in his critique of Durkheim, it would be impossible to investigate social facts as if they were physical objects (things), since even things were themselves social facts. Purely objective analysis, he said, would turn out to be a chimera. In other words, there was no way to escape the intermediary role of human consciousness in understanding the world out there. So the myriad problems arising out of the understanding, interpretation and misinterpretation of the consciousness of others necessarily introduced a layer of special complexity in the relations of individuals to one another. In the interpersonal effort to attempt to understand what the other person, or persons, have in mind, Sartre referred to understanding this complexity as dialectical reason.

In his preceding chapter, Robert Anderson refers to the play *Copenhagen* by Michael Frayn, which describes the tragic situation into which two brilliant nuclear physicists, Niels Bohr and Werner Heisenberg, very old friends, find themselves trapped by World War II. The subject of the play is the search for nuclear power, and the fate of nations was at stake. Bohr is Danish with British sympathies, and Heisenberg is German. In that impossible context fraught with such danger, two friends who know and understand one another tried to divine the intentions of the other. No clearer example of the difficulty of the human condition with regards to the uncertainty of understanding each other could be imagined.

All significant human action is purposive action; therefore, intelligibility – the understanding of the intentions and purpose of the other – is always potentially ambiguous. This may not seem too significant for most practical purposes in our ordinary lives, but it can turn into a serious conundrum when ambiguous situations arise – in those cases the intentions of the individuals involved do have to be questioned. That question was the frame of Frayn's play *Copenhagen*.

Action without a purpose is meaningless by definition, and therefore incomprehensible to observers. So comprehensible action has been understood by anthropologists in terms of the purposes and intentions of the actors. However, being internal to the individual, private and perhaps even unconscious, these personal intentions present a real barrier to rational analysis, and hence to anthropology.

Jean-Paul Sartre can be accused of many failings, but it cannot be denied that he had a way of looking into men's and women's souls. Who can forget the intense exploration of human emotion in that brilliant play, *Huis Clos*, which so marked the existentialist episode after the horrors of World War II? Two men and a woman, caught together in a stifling room, explore their emotions toward each other with a pathos and ambivalence which constantly borders on miscomprehension and suspicion. The difficulty of understanding the other person, even a very close and intimate person, was a subject at the center of Sartre's thinking about human action, explored so passionately in his novels and plays. It formed the basis of his existential philosophy, and presented a real challenge to the claims of an objective anthropology.

In his well-known *Search for a Method*, and his remarkable exploration of collective action in his Marxist mode in *Critique de la raison dialectique*, Sartre returned to the question of how to understand the motivations of people not just as individuals but as collectivities. He describes how even ordinary actions are not easily understood: simple acts of behavior may be open to interpretations and those interpretations may thus lead to misunderstandings. To understand someone else's action, even a simple act like opening a window in a stuffy room, one has to infer or surmise the purpose for which the act was committed. And, obviously, the moment that purpose is mentioned, all kinds of ambiguities crowd the scene. The act may well be a simple one, but to uncover the purpose of an act, even of someone well known to us, is no simple matter. So, Sartre argues, if this is true about simple acts, committed by persons well known to us, consider how very much more challenging is the understanding of larger actions, undertaken by collectivities. Then he offered us a complex illustration of this ambiguity;

> A member of the ground crew at an air base on the outskirts of London took a plane and, with no experience as a pilot, flew it across the Channel. He is colored; he is prevented from becoming a member of the flying personnel. This prohibition becomes for him a subjective impoverishment ... This denied future reflects to him the fate of his 'race' and the racism of the English. The general revolt on the part of colored men against colonialists is expressed in him by his particular refusal of this prohibition. He affirms that a future possible for whites is possible for everyone. This political position, of which he doubtless has no clear awareness, he lives as a personal obsession; aviation becomes his possibility as a clandestine future.
>
> (1963: 95–6)

Sartre continues,

> this man did not want to make a political demonstration; he was concerned with his individual destiny. But we know also that what he was doing ... had to be implicitly contained by what he believed himself to

be doing (what, moreover, he was doing, too, for he stole the plane, he piloted it, and he was killed in France).

(1963: 109)

This is how Sartre placed the individual action, conscious or unconscious, in the context of the wider surmised (possibly suspected) circumstances that surround the particular incident. But the full circumstances can only be surmised or suspected – the interpretation reaches its limit.

In other words, how can we understand events in history, even when we know some of the context? If history presents us with major challenges of interpretation with our own past, consider then the problem of anthropological analysis of other peoples in the context of their particular histories. This renders the task of anthropologists even more challenging, beyond all the difficult languages, the challenging customs, the bizarre foods, and all the other features of cultural distance. How do we understand the other?

These matters became the subject of a profound inquiry in the hands of Lévi-Strauss in the last two chapters of his justly celebrated *The Savage Mind*. He writes of the distinction between dialectical reason and analytic reason to claim that, in the last resort, analytic reason has to go beyond the difficulties presented by dialectical reason. Lévi-Strauss was saying that Sartre is right to raise those problems, but we have to move beyond him. Lévi-Strauss at least thought that collective facts can lend themselves to certain kinds of systematic analysis because they are often structured. Structures, in turn, whether in the form of institutions – social, economic, political structures – or communication systems – language, music, myth, art – can be examined as patterns of order. This is without the interference of the ambiguities I just described, namely the ambiguities which surround meaning and purpose.

So the difficulty of penetrating other minds is now clear, but how can one argue that collective forms are more amenable to analysis? What Lévi-Strauss and those who followed him had in mind is that there are large areas of social life that are structured. They are organized in such a way that the kind of ambiguity mentioned above does not arise, and can be analyzed objectively without the interference of individual intentions. The most obvious of these collective structures lies in the realm of language. It is clear that the phonemics, morphemics and grammar of languages are astonishingly ordered. Moreover the intrinsic order is almost completely unconscious to the collective speakers. As we speak, we can communicate because the very sounds we utter are patterned into their most intimate details. These patterns are decoded by the listener since their order or pattern is also in his/her mind. Note here that the very slightest phonemic signal, such as a foreign accent, or the slightest hint of difference is immediately registered. The slightest hint of a difference in accent or the selection of a phrase is noted. Education, high class, low class, region, fluency, etc. all come to attention and are expressed. This is structured experience, and can be analyzed as such. There are other areas of social life – collective rituals, social, political and economic organizations, the extraordinary variety of family structures, patrilineal tribes, marriage systems, matrilineal organizations, polygyny, polyandry and similar matters – which have been successfully investigated by social anthropologists. This was the structured world of a Japanese audience which Kurosawa was addressing, which he thought he knew.

Such considerations led Lévi-Strauss and those who have followed him to explore the possibility of investigating the structure of human consciousness. This meant that different cultures have organized their cultural worlds into completely different patterns. So quite apart from language, the entire cosmos of other people, their worldviews, the categories of land, of animals, of plants, of their utensils, their catamarans, their forms of counting, etc. can be very different. In other words, starting from early on in life our cognition, our mental processes, are culturally patterned. This is the existential world that anthropologists have been writing about, showing us that such different ways of imagining the world around us have been part of the creative activity of peoples in very diverse geographical areas of our world. So the Inuit have created a particular way of life suitable for their surroundings, and the peoples of Australia created a totally different universe appropriate for them to survive in their particular surroundings. This much can be taken for granted.

But the observation that cognition patterns are culturally structured does not negate individual or collective creativity. On the contrary, just as the orderly grammatical and phonemic structures of language permit infinite permutations and combinations of newly formed phrases, similarly both individuals and collectively different cultures can and do change their outlook on their lives. The Iron Curtain and its physical presence in the form of the Berlin Wall may have appeared solid for many decades, but the dramatic events of its collapse in 1989 showed how such collective representations would become ephemeral if and when the mentality that supported them underwent significant changes. So collective mentalities, however structured, are always at the mercy of history.

Lévi-Strauss took these considerations concerning imagined realities to the next level: What is the relationship between their myths and ours? He writes of his astonishment at what our scientists have been telling us; that there are many senses in which reality is not what appears on the surface, just as in *Rashomon*. Just like the aboriginal peoples, our imagination also has the capacity to create myths which attempt to provide a sense of order to matters of grand mystery around us.

Lévi-Strauss wrote of his skeptics as follows:

> What is the use ... of analyzing ... a strategy that myths have repeated without renewal for dozens or perhaps even of hundreds of millennia at a time when rational thought, when scientific method and techniques, have definitely supplanted them in explaining the world? Did myths not already lose the game a long time ago?

That position may not be so 'certain any more', said Lévi-Strauss:

> In societies without writing, positive knowledge fell well short of the power of imagination, and it was the task of myths to fill this gap ... With us, positive knowledge so greatly overflows our imaginative powers that our imagination, unable to apprehend the world that is revealed to it, has no alternative than to turn to myth again. In other words, between the scientist who through calculations gains access to a reality that is unimaginable and the public eager to know something of this reality ... mythical thought ... becomes ... the only means for physicists to communicate with non physicists.
>
> (1995a: xii)

So, for Lévi-Strauss human imagination makes sense of the world by creating meaningful, orderly, often symmetrical structures which may or may not relate directly to what may exist out there. It is this deep imaginative impulse which renders the cultural worlds of different peoples so alien to one another, so difficult to penetrate. We are fortunate when a creative artist such as Kurosawa can find the common expressive language to be able to tap human emotions that lie beyond such cultural boundaries. Lévi-Strauss expressed even more profound skepticism about what most people take as self-evident: his own personal identity. In a challenging passage he says that he has always felt that his personality was as if he was living at a crossroads:

> I never had, and still do not have, the perception of feeling my personal identity. I appear to myself as the place where something is going on, but there is no 'I', no 'me'. Each of us is a kind of crossroads where things happen. The crossroads is purely passive, something happens there. A different thing, equally valid, happens elsewhere.
>
> (1995b: 3–4)

Those with familiarity with the speculations of the early Buddhist philosophers will recognize the disputes concerning the nature of the self (known as the *anatta* doctrine) had a very long trajectory in Indian philosophy: consciously or not, Kurosawa's work harks back to these traditions in Eastern thought which have not lost their speculative appeal.

Despite Lévi-Strauss' protestations in the concluding chapters of *The Savage Mind*, these ideas about the malleability of subjectivity, and the ambiguities involved in conceptualizing the sense of self and identity, brought him very close to Sartre's views about individual selves. Sartre was adamant about the fact that, despite the constraints of social norms, the future was always open to individual decisions, and that individual consciousness mattered. Indeed, individuals gained agency by becoming conscious of their circumstances: Then they could, and did, define their life trajectories for themselves. They would stand out from their background (just as the word *existens* means); this is why social structures and norms that appeared so solid in fact always depended upon the constant support of individuals involved.

These ideas concerning subjectivity and consciousness of individuals gained wide currency through the writings of two very different individuals who both followed Sartre's ideas: Both Fanon and Shariati were concerned to show how individuals could overcome their given historical circumstances. Frantz Fanon, a psychiatrist himself, wrote about his experiences in the devastating context of the colonial violence in Algeria. His remarkable work on psychiatry and revolution during the Algerian uprising, the *Wretched of the Earth*, became a handbook for young people who were in revolt against established authority everywhere. Sartre had written a highly controversial foreword to that volume approving of what Fanon was advocating. Similarly, Ali Shariati, who had also studied with Sartre in Paris, took these ideas of consciousness and agency in the direction of a revolutionary interpretation of Islam against the authoritarian regime of the Shah of Iran. Shariati can be said to have prepared the ground for the downfall of the regime, and although he died in 1977, that effort may have (partly) facilitated the return of Ayatullah Khomeini during those dramatic times in 1980.

Even though Sartre, Fanon and Shariati are not often mentioned among social scientists, our difficulties in dealing with individual subjectivity in troubled regions have returned to haunt anthropologists. In a recent lecture, speaking of Java and Sumatra, Byron Good returned to these very issues of psychiatry and violence in post-colonial circumstances. How should we understand the question of subjectivity? He spoke about subjectivity in the context of dangerous landscapes of explosions, noise, alienating silences, dissociation, fears and terror. This is the new place where we have arrived in writing about subjectivity in anthropology – a space and time quite different from those associated with earlier debates over the rationality of witchcraft, narratives of illness, and the lived experience of human suffering. Many anthropologists are working in settings of violence or post-conflict, and Good says they have to face enormous challenges for ethnographic research and writing, concluding,

> I no longer aspire to a single, unified theory of the subject or subjectivity, which was suggested by *Medicine, Rationality and Experience*. And I do not believe there is a single mode of inquiry that is adequate to the task at hand. The kinds of settings in which many of us, old and young, work these days, and the world in which we live, provoke a fundamental challenge to understanding. In a world of murderous rage and apparent death instincts, what Freud called *thanatos*, rationality seems an almost ludicrous presumption, an escape from the Ordinary.

(2010: n.p.)

I recall referring to these works of Lévi-Strauss, Sartre, Fanon and Shariati in my lectures on social theory at the University of Chicago in the 1960s. That experience is anticipated in the preceding chapter by Robert Anderson; it seemed to me at the time that anthropology would sooner or later have to come to terms with the Rashomon effect. The complexities of subjectivity on the part of both the people we were studying as well as the observers involved would, I thought, turn out to be a great challenge for the discipline. I realized at the time that we would be confronted with anthropological accounts of the same place and same setting, but reported by different experts with very different perspectives.

I was well aware of these kinds of differences between my reports about rural Sri Lanka (beginning in the late 1950s) and Edmund Leach's findings there at the same time. We were both studying the culture and social organiza-tion of Sinhalese villagers. Leach was working in the Anuradhapura district in the northern jungles, and I was quite far away in the Walapane area, later in Bintenne and the east, in larger villages which had been very isolated at the time. I visited Leach in his village and was very impressed by his simple accommodations in a little mud hut in close touch with the villagers. Leach later courteously returned the visit by coming to see me in the village where I had settled, walking to me over the mountains for two hours, far away from the nearest vehicle road. We had a very exciting discussion on all the new materials we were finding. We later continued the discussions in an elaborate correspondence when Leach returned to Cambridge. We seemed so much in agreement at the time. In our published work, however, the emphasis on land ownership on his part and on kinship traditions as systems of structured ideas on my part turned out to be strikingly different (Yalman 1967; Leach 1961).

These differences were soon echoed and amplified in the Cambridge Department of Social Anthropology. Leach found an ally in the late Stanley Tambiah to argue that kinship was really about land ownership, as Leach had reported in his 1961 book *Pul Eliya*. Leach and Tambiah were soon confronted by Meyer Fortes and Jack Goody. Following their own extensive works on West Africa, they argued for the moral, ethical and ideological basis of kinship systems (and not for land as tenure alone). In a similar vein the French anthropologists Lévi-Strauss and Louis Dumont had already drawn attention to the subtleties between thinking in terms of the primacy of infrastructures (i.e. land tenure and the hard practical matters of the econ-omy) as opposed to superstructures (i.e. the moral and ideological aspects of social life).

Could these theoretical differences be reconciled? Can *Rashomon* help us understand this? If understanding human motivations posed such conun-drums in the rarefied atmosphere of Cambridge University, what were the chances of agreement regarding the motives of ordinary people? Also, if even a subject as apparently technical as kinship systems was cap-able of generating such discord, one could imagine what difficulties a study of other political and economic formations would present to social scientists.

Given the ambiguities regarding how we understand other people, and how they understand each other, given the dynamics of subjectivity, and the role of myth in our lives and in history, I think we can indeed develop an existential anthropology in the way Sartre and Lévi-Strauss might have conceived it. This means being particularly attentive to the inner lives of individuals, all those who find themselves having to make difficult decisions in the matrix of history, those who are trying to change their lives and change and improve their surroundings. In fact, millions now find themselves in such circumstances: migration and the extraordinary cultural complexities it creates have become a major feature of social life. Social and political distinctions and structures of the past – nationalism, ethnicity, identity, class, power, etc. – cannot be disregarded because they are still confining our agency. But the future is obviously pregnant with unexpected new possibilities. An existential anthropology will have to include both agency and structure into its scope.

Kurosawa was well grounded in Japanese culture and history, adept with its nuances, but able to transcend its limits and speak to others in other parts of the world who do not know Japan at all (and certainly not its twelfth century). He understood the matter of different realities and different perspectives, anticipating an existential anthropology that is attentive to agency in history. These questions apply to other disciplines intent on understanding (*verstehen*) other people, no matter how far away the other is or was in space or in time. Being a keen student of the feature film industry, Kurosawa was influenced by ripples originating outside the circle called Japan.

This is how Kurosawa startled us with his brilliant work over sixty years ago, leading us back to these matters of empathy for the other today. *Rashomon* has now become an enduring metaphor for the human condition. With all our scientific rationality, there are still further mysteries which elude us. There is always much that we do not know. As the Russians say, the soul of another person is an unknown continent. Kurosawa knew that this was true even during that fateful incident in a forest grove in the mountains in medieval Japan. The filmmaker is gone, but his deeply moving images, and his exuberant imagination, continue to inspire our speculations about the ways of life and thought of other people.

---

Akira Kurosawa describing his inspiration for the film's musical score:
As I was writing the script, I heard the rhythms of a bolero in my head over the episode of the woman's side of the story.

(Kurosawa 1983: 138)

Publicity still featuring Toshiro Mifune as the bandit and Masayuki Mori as the samurai. The bandit's lie (promising to sell the samurai antique swords that do not exist as a ruse by which an attack may occur) is the first deception of many to occur in the film's chronological narrative. The film's exploration of the complex subjectivity inherent in how concepts like truth are understood is central to the Rashomon effect. (Courtesy of Kadokawa Corporation)

# 9  Screening truths

*Rashomon* and cinematic negotiation

*Blair Davis and Jef Burnham*

In Japanese narrative tradition, there is a long-standing murder mystery convention of providing the audience with the identity of the killer at the beginning of the tale rather than saving this revelation for the end, thus testing the ability of the detective-prosecutor, not the audience, to discover this identity. Akira Kurosawa subverts this process in *Rashomon* (1950) by constructing the viewer as a negotiator who must try to unravel the murderer's identity from among multiple suspects. The notion that there will in fact be conflicting versions, however, is withheld from the viewer until well into the story's progression. In establishing the audience's burden of negotiation in *Rashomon*, Kurosawa constructs the viewer as an external party whose knowledge is not as extensive as those involved in the conflict. It is not until later in the film when the narrative truths start to conflict, with the second account of the events (recounted by Machiko Kyo as the wife), that the audience will even begin to realize their role as negotiators. This adds the further handicap of not having been able to study the events in the first account with this newfound role in mind, and having to re-examine those events while at the same time being presented with new and conflicting information in the second account.

Kurosawa therefore took a significant risk with his predicted audience in Japan, standing their expectation about mystery narratives on its head. As such, viewers of *Rashomon* are placed in a particular role: the viewer-as-negotiator. It is a role that has increasingly been demanded of film audiences since *Rashomon*'s debut. The era of unflinchingly linear storytelling has now long passed. This can be seen as a classic example of a ripple flowing beyond the circle in which it originates.

Film scholar David Bordwell notes that *Memento* (2001) – a narrative told in reverse order from ending to beginning – 'is often considered a "puzzle film", and the emergence of this category in recent years testifies further to Hollywood's new pride in intricate narrative maneuvers' (2006: 80). Modern audiences are often required to solve puzzles or to negotiate one truth from the many presented to them during the course of a film. In addition to Bordwell, scholars such as Allan Cameron, Elliot Panek, Janet Staiger, George Wilson and Jan Simons have attempted to contextualize and codify this tendency in Hollywood toward films involving such intricate narrative maneuvers as *Memento*. When Thomas Elsaesser approached what he refers to as the phenomenon of the mind-game film that has persisted since the early 1990s, he traced the genealogy of this phenomenon back to the '1950s/1960s "art cinema" films by Akira Kurosawa' among others (2009: 16). He asserts that mind-game films point to 'a "crisis" in the spectator–film relation, in the sense that the traditional' spectator role of voyeur or witness is 'no longer deemed appropriate, compelling, or challenging enough' for viewers (2009: 16). One narrative device commonly employed in the mind-game film to challenge viewers, Elsaesser notes, finds the protagonist participating in or witnessing 'events whose meaning or consequences escape him: along with him, the film asks: what exactly has happened? There is a suspension of cause and effect, if not an outright reversal of linear progression' (2009: 17–18).

In precisely this way, Kurosawa challenges viewers of *Rashomon* through the suspension of conventional notions of narrative linearity and, by proxy, cause and effect. During the course of the film, the viewer is presented with four different versions of the same event and, lacking a resolution, is forced to come to their own conclusions as to which, if any, to believe. And if none is to be believed, what conclusions can the viewer draw from that? In spite of its complexity and adherence to the aforementioned mind-game film motif, however, Elsaesser points to *Rashomon* as an example of a film that fails to qualify as a mind-game film. According to the author, mind-game films employ narrative complexity in a way that specifically suspends 'the common contract between the film and its viewers, which is that films do not "lie" to the spectator, but are truthful and self-consistent within the premises of their diegetic worlds' (2009: 19–20).[1] Indeed, Kurosawa does not lie to viewers of *Rashomon*; any untruths therein originate with his characters. Kurosawa only obscures the truth from viewers insofar as he avoids an objective presentation of the events at the center of *Rashomon*'s narrative in favor of various characters' subjective interpretations of those events, but he does not lie to his audience.

The distinctions between *Rashomon* and the mind-game film are more numerous and complex than this, however. Mind-game films are distinguished from *Rashomon*, their genealogical predecessor, by the extent to which audiences retain agency in deciphering the complex narratives of such films. By exploring the relationship between Kurosawa and his audience as it relates to principles and strategies of the negotiating process, this chapter will attempt to demonstrate how both directors and audiences engage with nonlinear approaches to storytelling in cinema, and how the relative roles of directors and audiences in this process as applied to *Rashomon* and the mind-game film illuminate the distinctions between the two. Furthermore, this chapter will establish the process of cinematic negotiation between director and audience as one that can be directly compared to those forms of negotiation that are generally considered to be more traditional, such as that between labor and management.

In that regard, if it can be determined what the audience's needs are in viewing films, and what strategies might be employed in trying to determine narrative truth in *Rashomon*, then it must be in terms of what the audience might bring to the film, and what they will choose to take away with them. Of equal importance are what the director's needs, intent and risks therein may be in employing such unconventional storytelling methods, and how the construction of such negotiating strategies as (a) the tactical use of passion and (b) a sophisticated code can be deployed within these methods to better ensure their success. Finally, in dissecting the negotiation process at work in the making and viewing of a film, particularly one as structurally complex as *Rashomon*, it is possible to understand just how related and dependent upon one another the director and audience truly are in this process.

The idea of cinematic negotiation is not an established one, but clearly a constructed model from which an analysis of *Rashomon* may then proceed.[2] Cinematic negotiation can be seen on a surface level as being simply a metaphor for the act of a director's creation of a film and the audience's engagement with it. Yet when the theories and practices of traditional negotiation are applied to this metaphor, they reveal that there is in fact a relevant connection. What's more, the applicability of negotiation theory to cinema is even anticipated by negotiation theorists' 'universality principle', which asserts that 'many situations that are not considered to involve negotiation in the sense of formal, structured dialogue can be viewed as negotiation because they do, in fact, involve consensus development through interest-competitive dialogues' (Ramundo 1992: 129). To that end, when scrutinized according to negotiation theory, *Rashomon* reveals that Kurosawa left the powers of negotiation in the hands of his audience, while directors of mind-game films, which spring from Kurosawa's earlier narrative experimentation, restrict viewers' roles in the process of cinematic negotiation by stressing basic narrative comprehension over interpretation.

## Lights, camera, job action: the labor/management model

To begin, it is necessary to establish an ongoing comparison between our constructed model of cinematic negotiation and a more traditional model considered to have formal and structured qualities, namely that of labor versus management. In each of these models, it is a given that a long-standing history usually exists between both parties when they come to the bargaining table, and it is rare that they will not continue to be associated with each other long after a resolution has been negotiated. In the cinematic model, this can be seen in the fact that the director and audience have usually met each other before, if only in abstract terms. Whether or not a filmgoer is familiar with the works of Akira Kurosawa when approaching a work that requires negotiation as *Rashomon* does, he or she will likely have seen many films before and will also likely continue to see many more afterwards.

Similarly, most directors who make films tend to be experienced filmmakers and have made several others already. Even first-time directors of recent years are increasingly being recruited because of their experience with audiences in other formats, such as short films, television commercials and music videos. Kurosawa himself had made several films before *Rashomon*, and so was quite familiar with his audiences' preferences.

It follows then that 'when two individual actors negotiate repeatedly over time', as directors and audiences do, a 'social relationship is likely to develop', which 'is likely to be contingent on the social context giving rise to negotiations' (the movie theater), 'the strategic action people adopt in response to that context' (filmgoers' viewing habits) and 'the results they produce jointly' (either a successful or unsuccessful negotiating/viewing experience) (Lawler and Yoon 1995: 143). In this comparison between the cinematic and labor management models we are less interested in how either the director or the audience is able to control and obtain short-term victory over the other party than we are in how the process of negotiation between the two sides is a necessary and ultimately beneficial procedure.

If labor and management – or audience and director – are in harmony with one another, then there is of course no need for negotiation because there is no conflict to negotiate. However, in cinematic terms, a lack of conflict between audience and director may also refer to the effects of works reliant entirely on cinematic convention (i.e. straightforward linear storytelling). And as related above, the popularity of the mind-game films arose out of a ' "crisis" in the spectator-film relation', as the conventional roles filmmakers assigned to audiences were 'no longer deemed appropriate, compelling, or challenging enough' (Elsaesser 2009: 16). In cinematic terms, then, negotiation becomes necessary for some viewers to find reward in the form. In this model, then, harmony may only be achieved between director and audience insofar as directors adequately challenge audience expectations.

## Please take your seats: enter the audience

However, negotiation to the extent that mind-game films require is not always desired by viewers, as evidenced by mind-game films' typically minority audiences or cult followings (2009: 13). Therefore, such films may be met with either an adversarial or cooperative disposition depending on whether or not there are elements within it that indeed need to be negotiated, such as nonlinear devices. Far from attempting to alienate viewers, though, modern mind-game film directors rely on such devices to provide viewers with films that ideally 'are brain-teasers as well as fun to watch' (2009: 13), wherein identifying the 'rules of the game' they have created and solving their narrative puzzle are rewards unto themselves (2009: 34).

But in *Rashomon*, Kurosawa denies viewers such simple pleasures by incorporating a nonlinear narrative structure characterized by a refusal to provide an objective account of the events at the center of the film. In short, the solution to *Rashomon* does not lie in narrative coherence and therefore has the potential to frustrate viewers who are unwilling to engage with it to the extent that Kurosawa demands of them. Upon *Rashomon*'s release, 'several critics could make nothing of it' (Richie 1972: 5), while one American reviewer found that the film's 'repetition ... tends to become monotonous' (Beaufort 1952: 39). Donald Richie notes that even *Rashomon*'s Japanese audiences were 'quite ready to accept the story and its implications, but ... [often] could not understand the way the story was told' (1972: 6).

In presenting four different versions of a single event as he does in *Rashomon*, Kurosawa directly challenges the audience to take an active role in drawing their own conclusions, rather than waiting passively for one to be presented to them as it would be in a more conventional narrative. Each of the four main characters in *Rashomon* describes the murder in the film according to his/her personal interests in the event, and it falls upon the viewer to take these interests into account when analyzing and comparing the four versions. Dolores Martinez notes in *Remaking Kurosawa: Translations and Permutations in Global Cinema*: 'By making us watch this last set of events four different times, Kurosawa makes us, the audience, complicit through our silent viewing – like the woodcutter we are reduced to voyeurs and liars' (2009: 39). In this, Kurosawa ultimately places the burden of interpretation on the viewer.

The viewer is apt to take the first account of the murder (Tajomaru, the bandit's) at face value, being unaware of the unconventional narrative approach that is soon to follow. By the second account (Masago, the wife's), the viewer will probably start to question the seeming truth presented to them in the first account, and by the third (the dead husband Takehiro's, as told through a medium) and fourth (the woodcutter's) accounts will likely be unsure as to which version, if any, is entirely truthful. The film's lack of ultimate resolution, denying viewers an objective account of events, challenges the viewer to make sense of the four truths they have just seen, and to either consider the philosophical ramifications of this lack of resolution or to mediate the varying accounts into their own fifth version.

Kurosawa facilitates these four conflicting versions through the elaborate flashback structure presented in the film. In *Rashomon*, the film's narrative begins at the end, at the aftermath of the events that will eventually be depicted through various flashbacks. The first words spoken are those of the woodcutter: 'I can't understand it. I just can't understand it all.' This foreshadows the possible confusion to come on the audience's part. The scene soon transitions via flashback to the woodcutter's discovery of the body, and then to the sentencing of the bandit, who proceeds to give his account of the crime. It is only then, via an additional flashback, that the actual events in question are presented, allowing the viewer to understand what has happened leading up to the woodcutter's discovery. These varying structural layers by themselves are not particularly complicated for the audience to follow, as the first flashback of the woodcutter is fairly routine.

Maureen Turim, author of *Flashbacks in Film: Memory and History*, notes how 'Flashbacks typically hide their formal function ... by being presented as memories, dreams, or confessions' (1989: 6), and the woodcutter's flashback is indeed set up as a memory. The second flashback at the prison courtyard – constructed as a confession, given its testimonial context – is also relatively unproblematic in that it is a natural progression forward in time from the events of the first flashback. Yet when Kurosawa then moves on to the bandit's account, the viewer is led back in time to the actual events in question, which chronologically precede the first two flashbacks and become the first account of these events that needs to be negotiated by the viewer.

The fact that these opening structural layers must first be peeled away for the audience thus serves as a framing device for Kurosawa, who places the forthcoming events in a predetermined context before the viewer is exposed to them. Before the audience is even shown the events in question, they are treated to two different aspects of its aftermath – at the temple gate and the prison courtyard. The situation in which the film places the viewer is similar to that in labor/management negotiations, whereby one side has strategically held back information with the intention of later revealing it in order to disarm the other side and force them to re-examine events in light of this new information.

In employing such a strategy, one negotiator (Kurosawa) is using the leverage that it potentially creates in an attempt to shift the burden of negotiation to the other side (the audience). As Bernard A. Ramundo states in *Effective Negotiation*,

> the side made to feel that it has the burden of negotiation (i.e., that it needs the negotiated result more) will tend to be inhibited from taking substantive or procedural chances (e.g., making a very high demand or suspending the dialogue).
>
> (1992: 5)

The audience is thus more willing to accept or consider his demands of them, as Kurosawa places the burden of negotiation on his audience in *Rashomon* through use of this complex flashback structure. He forces viewers to take action: devise their own subjective, fifth account of events, reject the process of negotiation outright, or find thematic closure where the film offers no narrative resolution. In this, Kurosawa challenges viewers to consider the philosophical ramifications of the film's lack of an objective account of the murder as a commentary on truth and memory, reinforced by the very nature of flashbacks, which according to Turim represent the juncture of history and a character's subjective memory/interpretations of that history.

## Cut! – The risks of creativity

*Rashomon*'s complex narrative qualities can be seen as a direct challenge to the audience, demanding a level of involvement and engagement that some viewers may be unaccustomed to. With such a challenge comes a certain amount of risk, however, regarding how the film will be received and whether it can even be made in the first place. Indeed, it is not surprising that Kurosawa had difficulty securing funding for *Rashomon*. The film was viewed as a large financial risk to many companies, who feared major losses if they were to finance the project. The producer who eventually did finance *Rashomon* has admitted that 'he had no idea what it was about' when he agreed to produce the film (Richie 1972: 5). Instead, he put his faith in Kurosawa's artistic reputation.

This shows us that, as a negotiator, the director 'cannot avoid being influenced by his career stake in the outcome of negotiation' (Ramundo 1992: 4). Accordingly, before a film is made, a director, often feeling pressure from the producer, must develop a sense of whom their audience is. It is ultimately the concerns for this audience that 'are reflected in the judgements brought to bear in deciding whether to adopt a particular course of action' (1992: 33) in the making of the film, or whether the film gets made at all.

In 1950, film audiences had rarely seen a film with the unconventionally nonlinear approaches to storytelling that Kurosawa employed in *Rashomon*. Granted, Kurosawa was not the first to make use of these techniques. Film noir regularly utilized flashback structures in the 1940s, for example, in such films as *Stranger on the Third Floor* (1940), *I Wake Up Screaming* (1941), *Laura* (1944), *Mildred Pierce* (1945), *The Killers* (1946), *Out of the Past* (1947) and *The Lady from Shanghai* (1948). In Japanese filmmaking, the use of flashbacks can be traced back to 1909, just one year after pioneer American director D.W. Griffith began his experiments with the form (Richie 1987: 7). Griffith's epic spectacle *Intolerance* (1916) would require audiences to negotiate between four separate, interwoven storylines, ranging in period from ancient Babylon and Judea all the way up to modern-day America. A few years later, silent comedian Buster Keaton parodied *Intolerance* in his feature directorial debut, *Three Ages* (1923), which saw Keaton move between prehistoric days, ancient Rome and modern times. While these films were made in the silent era and would likely not have been seen by an entire generation when *Rashomon* debuted, Orson Welles made use of a flashback structure in the much admired *Citizen Kane* (1941), a structure that is arguably more elaborate than even that of *Rashomon*. However, *Citizen Kane* was not seen in Japan until several years after *Rashomon*'s premiere, and even in America it went largely unrecognized by the public for many years.

By 1950 nonlinear filmmaking was still a rarely practiced and little recognized cinematic form in Japan. The creative risks that Kurosawa took in *Rashomon* are therefore relatively large, hence the project's rejection by many producers, who, in Kurosawa's words, feel pressured to 'turn out films simply to feed the cinema chains' (Gadi 1972: 18) rather than produce cinematic works of art. One can certainly see from these financial concerns how a director 'will tend to be influenced by his [or her] career self-interest to push for a softer position' (namely less challenging and hence less controversial narrative or structural elements) which promotes 'quick consensus rather than one which risks dialogue breakdown in the effort to achieve a more favorable result' (Ramundo 1992: 20–1). Of course, modern directors need not worry as much about risking this dialogue breakdown when they adopt nonlinear structural elements, thanks to Kurosawa's pioneering effort. Twenty-first century audiences are by now usually well accustomed to the nonlinear devices used in film. Bordwell states that modern directors and screenwriters are rewarded 'for taking a chance in storytelling' (2006: 75). Films that challenge traditional narrative techniques such as *Reservoir Dogs* (1992) and *The Usual Suspects* (1995) 'have become classics dissected in film schools', and Bordwell describes how film students 'often hit on eccentric formal schemes before they have worked out the story action. (I want to begin and end my film with exactly the same scene, only it'll mean something different the second time.)' (2006: 75).

Compared to Kurosawa's work in *Rashomon*, however, modern directors crafting mind-game films such as *The Usual Suspects* play relatively safe games with their audiences at the negotiating table, asking only that audiences trust that all things will be answered in time. At their most structurally daring, mind-game filmmakers 'teach their audiences the new rules of the game, at the same time as they are yet learning them themselves' (Elsaesser 2009: 39). The chances these filmmakers take are indeed largely structural, but attentive viewers can nonetheless solve the films' narrative riddles. In this, mind-game films offer narrative closure, albeit closure requiring an elevated effort on the viewer's part, where *Rashomon* does not.

This owes to the 'concerns for the reputation of the negotiator' (Ramundo 1992: 33), which are always a factor for a director in trying to anticipate an audience's interests. The 'concern for the continuing relationship' between the two (meaning the director's potential for future work and the ability to draw future filmgoers) 'influences negotiating objectives, strategy, and tactics' (1992: 40). To resist providing viewers with narrative closure is to risk alienating audiences.

Yet 'subjective perceptions about the negotiating situations are just as important as its objective reality' (1992: 10). Ultimately, the viewer's interpretive approach to a film is more important than the director's true intentions, because audiences are rarely given explicit insight into the director's motivations behind a film in the work itself. This is certainly the case in *Rashomon*, for we are never made aware of Kurosawa's position on the four variations of the truth in the film, as evidenced by the film's ultimate lack of resolution. Nor does Kurosawa indicate whether or not there is in fact a solution to this narrative puzzle. In this, Kurosawa places greater value on the audience's subjective perceptions of the piece than he does his own, limiting his influence over viewers' interpretations of the narrative by denying them an objective account of the murder. The audience is challenged by Kurosawa to accept a role in the negotiating process wherein the burden of interpretation lies solely with them. Resolution for the audience then comes not with determining the director's notion of truth, but in understanding why this is not given to us by the director.

Kurosawa is concerned more with the process of negotiation here than he is with teaching viewers the narrative rules of the game necessary to uncover the truth of this central murder. It is hoped that the audience's commitment to *Rashomon* takes the shape of a negotiation process that will continue for the viewer long after the film is over (as they try to make sense of the four versions Kurosawa provides them with and to understand why closure was denied to them), and that by engaging with the process, a level of respect for it will develop. Kurosawa's goal in this negotiation, it would seem, is to persuade audiences that, though their interests may initially lie in achieving narrative closure, film can offer more rewarding experiences than that if they will only put forth the effort.

However, it is no easy task to bring an audience to this point. Filmgoers have usually seen enough films to have developed a 'shared mental model' about what a film should and should not be, an understanding of 'system purpose and form' (Thompson et al. 1995: 20) with regards to the standard conventions of filmmaking to which they have grown accustomed – what is known in the labor/management model as a collective agreement. 'We understand movies fairly easily because in many respects their conventions are easy to learn: they are simplifications of things we already know', says Bordwell (2005: x). Deviations from the abstract mental model that filmgoers share may be treated with skepticism or resistance unless the director is able to actively negotiate the changes to this model proposed within the film in question, as mind-game film directors do in providing viewers with the rules of the game. David Fincher's *Fight Club* (1999) contains a plot twist two-thirds of the way into the film that asks the audience to reinterpret all that has come before it in order to find narrative closure. Unlike Kurosawa in *Rashomon*, Fincher indeed openly provides viewers with the clues necessary to arrive at the singular narrative solution to *Fight Club*, for he cautions that 'if you trick people, it's an affront, and you really better be careful about what you're doing' (Smith 1999: 62). 'The need for conclusion' is one that is highly ingrained in the filmgoer's model of what a film should be; the viewer has 'a need for cognitive structure, which stems from an intolerance for ambiguity' (Thompson et al. 1995: 19). While it is true that 'mental models are dynamic' (1995: 20), and can therefore incorporate change, when that model is seen as being tampered with, the director must be highly persuasive in attempting to negotiate the change with the audience.

This persuasion often takes the form of 'creative advocacy', in which 'the use of positive perceptions concerning interest [are used] to sell consensus' (Ramundo 1992: 11). The amount of risk and effort inherent in the negotiation process must be met with equivalent rewards. If the audience is made to actively want to engage with the nonlinear storytelling devices in a film, the director will find it easier to sell audience's on that which he/she is artistically trying to achieve through the use of those devices, as in *Rashomon* where the nonlinear depiction of conflicting truths can serve as a statement about the juncture of history and memory. Likewise, in the labor/management model of negotiation, if an employee feels that a manager has their best interests at heart, or has at least demonstrated an understanding or allowance for those interests, the employee may be more willing to accept the manager's actions or decisions. Accordingly, if the audience can be made to feel that they have some control over the nonlinear organizational techniques, they will in turn be less likely to resist those techniques or their implications for the film's ultimate lack of narrative resolution.

## I want my audience to feel what the characters feel: reason vs. emotion

In persuading audiences to open themselves up to the negotiation process, a director can appeal to either the viewer's sense of reason or emotion. In using reason, a director,

> can find some value that the [audience] accepts, and that can serve as the premise from which to lead an argument. [The director] then works from the accepted value, showing logically that other values can be derived from it and coming eventually to a definition of the situation which ... will lead to the appropriate action.
>
> (Bailey 1983: 22)

In the case of *Rashomon*, this leads first to an understanding, or at the very least an acceptance, of the conflicting truths presented in *Rashomon*. This approach can be problematic, however, if the value from which a director seeks to progress goes against what the audience has come to understand based on their shared mental model of what the cinematic norms should be. Hence, viewers who take offence to Kurosawa showing the same event told four different ways, or to the director of *Fight Club* asking that the first two-thirds of the film be reinterpreted, will likely be unwilling to try to understand the director's creative motivations in these variations from convention. In this case, the negotiations will likely stall or fail, with neither party benefiting from the result, as the director's film fails to be understood and the audience leaves the negotiation unsatisfied.

To avoid such a failed negotiation a director can appeal to the viewer's emotions rather than to their sense of reason. This approach:

> seeks to eliminate the mind and the critical faculties. It provokes feeling rather than thought, [and can be used when the director], suspects that the logical steps in the argument will not survive critical examination, or when he [or she] can find no shared value that will serve as the premise for an argument by reason. The appeal to emotion may be designated either to create such a shared value or to provoke a direct connection between

feeling and action without the intervention of mind and its capacities for criticism.

(Bailey 1983: 23)

As a result, if viewers become involved in or captivated by the emotional content of a film, they may be less inclined to critique its unconventional formal aspects (thus accepting the film), just as the employee who is influenced by the manager's empowerment strategy will likely be less critical of that manager.

Kurosawa establishes this approach early in *Rashomon*, with the introduction of the commoner in the first scene. This character is the only one in the film whom Kurosawa has himself created, as the commoner is not found in either *Rashomon* or *In a Grove*, the stories by Ryunosuke Akutagawa upon which the film was based.[3] The commoner can therefore be seen as a construct through which the audience may make this leap from reason to emotion, because he is seemingly aware of the distinction between the two. He tells the priest in the first scene: 'I only wanted to know about this strange story of yours because it might amuse me while I wait out the rain. But I'd just as soon sit quietly and listen to the rain than hear any sermons from you' (Richie 1987: shot #20). Here, the need for amusement is paralleled with resistance toward any discourse promoting change (the sermon that the commoner seeks to avoid). Hence, Kurosawa recognizes the conflict that may lie ahead as the viewer's need for entertainment potentially clashes with Kurosawa's intention to place the burden of interpreting the film's nonlinear elements on that viewer, thereby requiring the viewer to put more effort into the film than they are willing to.

The commoner plays a vicarious role for the audience throughout the film, mediating between Kurosawa and the audience. He too is asked to negotiate the four versions presented, and so shares the same needs and concerns as the audience. After hearing the second version of the events, he states: 'But the more I listen, the more mixed up I get ... Now if I believed what she said, I'd be really mixed up' (1987: shot #256). The commoner expresses sentiments that the audience will likely also share, hence we can see how Kurosawa anticipates and acknowledges the audience's needs in this cinematic negotiation. Yet despite his confusion, the commoner also tells us, 'I don't mind a lie. Not if it's interesting', which draws attention to the audience's need for entertainment and intrigue. So, if the audience is confused by the conflicting truths, as the commoner is, it is hoped that they will follow the lead of their spokesman in the film and accept the lies in the name of intrigue, because they are in fact so interesting.

Hence the commoner embraces this approach of favoring emotion over reason, telling the audience that they should not worry about the logic of the conflicting tales Kurosawa presents them, but rather should derive what pleasure they can from the fact that each version is so interesting. The fact that the same event is being reinterpreted so many times in the film will therefore become frustrating for the viewer only in so far as it makes problematic their feelings or expectations for the characters in the film (a natural occurrence, for without conflict there is no story), rather than the actual viewing experience of the film itself.

This is not to say, however, that one must take only an either-or approach to reason and emotion. Negotiation theorists Edward J. Lawler and Jeongkoo Yoon reject a sharp distinction in favor of the notion that 'the two are intertwined', largely in the idea that 'positive emotion leads to more heuristic information processing' (improved performance through more practical means) (Lawler and Yoon 1995: 146). They describe how 'mild positive emotion leads people to view a situation more broadly and attempt to pull it together or interrelate more elements of it' (1995: 147). Therefore, if the audience is pleased with the content of the film, or at the very least finds it as interesting as the commoner does, they will likely be more accepting of the unconventional creative approaches that the director takes in presenting that content to them. Not unlike mind-game films that provide the viewer with fun in the form of a brain-teasing puzzle, Kurosawa then invites his audience to embrace the emotions that *Rashomon* stirs in them even as they struggle to reconcile the characters' conflicting testimonies.

This technique is employed early in the film, during the first flashback in which the woodcutter discovers the body. As the woodcutter makes his way through the woods, he eventually discovers a woman's hat dangling on a branch. This is the first of four items strewn about that the woodcutter discovers, followed by a man's hat, a piece of rope and an amulet case. As he goes to pick up the amulet case, he stumbles, and then jumps back with a look of shock on his face. Kurosawa cuts to a medium-shot of the horrified woodcutter, with the stiffly raised hands of the corpse that he has just discovered extended in the foreground up from the bottom of the screen. This is followed by an edit to a close-up of the woodcutter's face, as he screams, leaps back and turns to run.

The appeal to the viewer's sense of emotion comes in the level of curiosity that this scene continuously builds from beginning to end. The audience is shown the woodcutter's reaction to his horrifying discovery before actually seeing what he has found. Kurosawa sets the audience up from the beginning of the scene to expect something terrible, as per the discussion at the temple gate, but links that suspense to the audience's basic desire for more information to invest them in the events unfolding before them. The sequence begins with a suspenseful build-up of sixteen shots in which the woodcutter moves through the woods before he finds the first strewn object. This serves to create an ever-increasing anxiety or curiosity in the viewers' mind, as they are not rewarded immediately with the information they seek, but rather must engage with the process of the journey in order to arrive at that information (a metaphor for the negotiating process itself).

This curiosity is again maintained by the four strewn objects that the woodcutter finds. These serve as four clues for analysis, just as the viewer has four possible versions of the truth to choose from in the film. Yet when Kurosawa finally reveals what the woodcutter has discovered, our curiosity is still not fully satisfied, as we are only shown the victim's cold, stiff hands outstretched before us. We are not provided with the victim's identity, only with the knowledge that someone has died and that four clues were found that may direct us at length to more answers.

It is hoped that if the audience's emotions and curiosity are aroused by this sequence, and – if they want to know who has been murdered and why – that they will then be less critical of the nonlinear structural elements that they are asked to engage with in order for their questions to be answered (or not answered as the case may be). After the discovery of the body the scene shifts to the prison courtyard, where the woodcutter and the priest each gives his testimony. The priest testifies how he had seen the murdered man while still alive, and describes the road where the two had passed by one another. The scene then flashes back to this incident, with the man leading a horse upon which rides his wife, as they pass the priest on the road. Here, the audience is shown the murdered man in full for the first time, and is told that he had a sword, bow and arrows – more clues to his identity. It can be deduced at this point that he must be a samurai to be carrying such an arsenal.

As more and more information is slowly released, the viewer is taken deeper and deeper into the film's elaborate structure. By now the viewer is several layers removed in time from the original temple gate setting where the first flashback had originated, to which the film has not yet returned. The conventional approach to flashbacks in the decades prior to *Rashomon* dictates that you must soon return the viewer to their source so as to reorient him/her, and remind the audience as to the need of the flashback in the first place (often offering a summative form of punctuation to the flashback, ensuring that the viewer won't get lost in the plot). In the case of *Rashomon*, however, the story does not return to the temple gate until much later in the film.

After the priest's testimony, the police agent and Tajomaru, the bandit, are introduced. By this point, after having learned of the murdered man's identity, the audience will likely be curious as to who has murdered the man we have just met. Therefore, once the film starts to involve an even more elaborate flashback structure with the bandit's tale, it is hoped that the audience will be too caught up in the murder mystery to be concerned about the nonlinear structure that becomes more and more elaborate as the mystery unfolds. Thus, reason can be overcome by emotion. As a result, the viewer does not demand the logical return to the temple gate for the perceived clarity that this will seemingly provide, per the audience's shared mental model of how a flashback traditionally operates. Should Kurosawa succeed in thus appealing to emotion over reason, his audience may walk away from the experience satisfied to the benefit of both parties, as 'people experiencing positive emotion are more optimistic about future negotiations' (1995: 147). With this in mind, a director concerned about his or her continuing relationship with the audience will then likely try and stimulate these positive emotions in the viewer wherever possible.

## What's my line? – The sophisticated code

This concern for the continuing relationship between director and audience has often led to the lowest common denominator approach of crafting feel-good films with happy endings in Hollywood. This was obviously not the case for Kurosawa in *Rashomon*. The film is not necessarily a pleasant one to watch in that it deals with unpleasant situations, characters and emotions. Yet the director may please audiences in spite of unpleasant content if a sophisticated code rooted in an engaging nonlinear structure can be embraced by viewers.

Anthropologist F.G. Bailey describes the sophisticated code as containing 'rules for making discriminations' (1983: 110). In representing the same event from four different perspectives, Kurosawa openly encourages this discrimination from his audience, and establishes it as a necessary concept for fully engaging with the film's content. Bailey further states that the sophisticated code 'is suitable for debate and discussion, for thought and argument' (1983: 110), something that Kurosawa certainly seems to be encouraging of his audience. Kurosawa is not only promoting discrimination through his use of nonlinear filmmaking techniques, he also establishes discrimination as a basic requirement for engaging with the film; one cannot engage with the sophisticated code without meeting its fundamental requirement of discrimination.

The sophisticated code therefore rewards those who understand it, true of both directors and viewers alike. In a mind-game film, the sophisticated code might refer to those rules of the game that these films impart to their viewers as the narratives progress. The reward for understanding the sophisticated code of a mind-game film largely centers on basic narrative comprehension, as the viewer has been ostensibly trained by the filmmaker for the sole purpose of effectively and productively organizing the information presented throughout. The rewards offered to those who understand *Rashomon*'s sophisticated code, however, are more philosophical than they are useful in the practical organization of narrative events, given the lack of closure.

Indeed, the greatest fans of *Rashomon* seem to be those who can deconstruct the techniques that went into the making of the code, and who can appreciate these philosophical rewards. At the end of the bandit's version of the murder, we return to the temple gate setting from the beginning of the film. By this point, it must be remembered, the audience has been structurally removed several stages from this original foundational layer. When we return to the temple gate, it is not necessarily for clarifying purposes, but rather to set the stage for the negotiation still to come, when the wife's version soon begins to contradict that which the audience has come to accept as the truth up until this point.

This conflict is pointed out to the audience even before it occurs, as in between the bandit's and the woman's versions the woodcutter tells the audience: 'It's a lie! They're all lies! Tajomaru's confession, the woman's story – they're lies!' This is arguably the first time that the viewer will begin to understand the nature and very existence of this sophisticated code, for it is the first major seed of doubt planted in the viewer's mind that we may not be getting the truth from these characters. The previous account by the bandit has now been discounted, or at least thrown into question, as has the upcoming account by the wife.

However, not all viewers will pick up on these lines by the woodcutter, or grasp their full implication, and so they will not be able to anticipate the conflict that lies just ahead. Those that do are accepting and engaging with the sophisticated code that Kurosawa has constructed in the film and are being primed to accept the ultimate lack of narrative resolution, to question the significance of the lack of objective truth. Those who do not recognize and engage with the sophisticated code may be apt to become confused by the conflicting versions, and will resent not being warned in advance that they will be required to re-examine the events in the first account as the film progresses. Hence, those who are less enthusiastic about the film tend to have a poorer understanding or appreciation of the unconventional cinematic elements that went into the code's construction. Bailey points out that this is an inherent aspect of the sophisticated code, showing how the code 'is likely to become a private language restricted to the chosen', becoming 'a source of aesthetic pleasure to those who can handle it' (1983: 114). Hence the cult classification of the audiences drawn to mind-game films.

With specific regard to *Rashomon*, though, those in tune with this private language will be privileged in the film's final scene with something that rewards their continual attention to detail throughout. At the temple gate, when the three men discover the abandoned baby, there is a familiar item that has been left along with it. The woodcutter discovers the item: 'Look! Look here at the amulet case it has on. It's something the parents left to guard over it.' Discerning viewers will remember from the beginning of the film that the woodcutter discovered another amulet case, right before he discovered the dead body. The baby is acknowledged as a symbol of hope and rebirth in *Rashomon*, but sophisticated viewers will realize that the amulet case is as equally important a symbol in the film, serving as a framing device for nothing less than the dichotomy Kurosawa constructs between life and death. The amulet case found strewn by the dead man had failed to protect the husband and wife, while an amulet case now serves to protect the baby who has just been abandoned.

In an ironic twist of fate, responsibility for the baby's care falls on the woodcutter, whose decision to adopt the child is perhaps an attempt to make up for his passivity in the film's fourth version of events. The woodcutter had failed to intervene while watching the husband meet his demise, asserting that he ought to be ashamed for his part in these recent events. His role in the baby's survival parallels his undetermined role in the husband's death, and as such creates a bookending technique for the film's start and finish, involving the woodcutter, an amulet case and a helpless body (one at the end of its life, the other at its beginning).

Hence, in order to engage with the sophisticated code to the extent that such symbolism may be apparent to the viewer, it must be remembered that it is the little details that can be the most important in the negotiating process. That which is overlooked, or perhaps considered inconsequential because of its seemingly diminutive qualities, can often have crucial repercussions later on. As seen with the amulet case, one must never take any little detail for granted when negotiating, because it may well become important as the negotiations continue. Those who fail to do this will likely be unable to engage with the sophisticated code, which Bailey also reminds us is largely 'inaccessible' to those who cannot understand it, 'by reason of its complexity', and it therefore serves as 'a device for ensuring that the many – the irresponsible, the inexperienced, and the unwashed – are kept on the outside' (1983: 114).

This brings us back once more to the director's need for a continuing relationship with the audience. For if viewers fail to understand the film's sophisticated code, it is less likely that they will continue their relationship with the director in the future. This echoes Lavinia Hall's claim that the interests of the other negotiating party must be taken into account, even in the very construction of this sophisticated code, if there is to be hope for a future negotiating relationship with the audience (1993).

## Roll credits: the negotiated self

But what is the balance of power that defines these continuing relationships in this process of cinematic negotiation? Both parties are indeed dependent upon the other for the cinematic negotiation to be a success. If the director does not satisfy the audience's needs, or if the audience does not embrace the demands that the director places upon them, a successful film is unlikely. However, Lawler and Yoon describe how 'in repeated negotiations, the objective power dependence context that brings actors together to negotiate in the first place will bring them together time and time again to resolve problems through negotiation' (1995: 149). Each side has willingly come to the table, because each side enjoys the process of this cinematic negotiation enough to repeatedly return to it, even if it is not always a success. 'Stable structural-power conditions produce commitment in ongoing, repeated encounters' (1995: 149), which is why each side is usually willing to approach the negotiation with the interests of the other party in mind as well as their own.

It is this transcendence of selfish interests as an ideal quality that is of the most concern to the major tenet of this study of cinematic negotiation, that it is the engagement with the process of negotiation itself that is ultimately beneficial to both parties, not the outcome of individual loss or victory. Kurosawa reveals his stance in the final moments of *Rashomon* when the woodcutter criticizes the commoner (who, it must be remembered, is a construct by Kurosawa to represent the audience) as being selfish, and therefore evil, for stealing the baby's clothes. The commoner's response, which we may then transpose to the audience, asks: 'And what's wrong with that? That's the way we are, the way we live. Look, half of us envy the lives that dogs lead. You just can't live unless you're what you call "selfish"' (Richie 1987: shot #385). It is hoped that the commoner's attempt to defend his questionable actions will force the audience to examine and critique his moral position. Once doubt has been cast upon their spokesman, the audience must then also naturally question themselves, and their own role in this negotiating process that they have hitherto (perhaps unknowingly) been involved in.

It is hoped that through the process of negotiation, and the recognition by the audience of such a process, that one will be able to balance the needs of self with the needs of others. By becoming aware of the process, one may start to take action through it. In moving away from the selfishness that the commoner embodies, toward the spirit of selflessness that the woodcutter eventually embraces by the end of the film, the beneficial aspects of the negotiation process can then occur. The idea of the viewer-as-negotiator exemplifies how the Rashomon effect applies as a cognitive model to the act of film spectatorship. In *Transcultural Cinema*, David MacDougall describes 'an evolving relationship between the filmmaker, subject, and audience' in writing about the intersections of cinema and anthropology (1998: 76). Patricia Zimmerman further notes how MacDougall promotes the idea that 'the creative process of filmmaking is not about making a representation or an image but about two parties entering into a relationship that takes them into a liminal zone and, as a result, changes them' (2006: 120). It is this notion of the changing relationship between director and audience that is central to the idea of cinematic negotiation.

After all, as this exploration of cinematic negotiation in *Rashomon* shows, Kurosawa allows his audience more freedom in the process than do directors of the mind-game films, which evolved from the work of Kurosawa. His refusal to provide narrative closure places a heavy burden on audiences in the negotiation process, requiring more work from them than they may be willing to put forth to derive pleasure from or find reward in the experience. Rather than offering viewers the simple pleasure of finding narrative closure should they willingly engage with *Rashomon*'s sophisticated code, Kurosawa directs our attentions toward more philosophical puzzles regarding the nature of truth and subjective experience – determinations about which he leaves to the engaged audience.

By contrast, mind-game film directors, in educating viewers in the rules they establish in their films, maintain a greater level of control in the negotiation process than Kurosawa, and therefore over the messages their works impart to viewers. They allow viewers to engage with their sophisticated codes for the purpose of achieving satisfaction in narrative coherence, with this coherence serving as the audience's reward unto itself for time and effort invested in the negotiation process. While that may only specifically encourage viewers to engage with these films on superficial levels, this is not to say that these films do not serve a broader purpose. According to Elsaesser, mind-game films aid in 'reordering and realigning our somatic responses with the sensory overload of contemporary life' (2009: 32). On one hand, the complex organization of mind-game films can be seen as merely an accommodation of viewers who regularly engage with the complex organization of information in the networks, databases and archives that define modern information technologies. On the other hand, as Elsaesser asserts, such sophisticated codes embody Walter Benjamin's notion of cinema as 'training for the senses', 'reordering and realigning our somatic responses' to equip us with the skills necessary to properly engage with modern information technologies, or to refine our pre-existing skill sets in this regard (2009: 32).

As such, while those directors whose films have evolved from the work of Kurosawa retain greater control over their works' interpretation in the cinematic negotiation process than Kurosawa did in *Rashomon*, mind-game films capture the spirit of *Rashomon* insofar as they can be seen as providing modern viewers with valuable life lessons. In *Rashomon*, Kurosawa offered viewers a philosophical challenge by denying them narrative closure and challenged them to reconcile their understanding of history as objective truth with the subjectivity of memory through the use of flashbacks. Mind-game films, by contrast, offer more practical lessons in information organization which ease the strain of engaging with modern information technologies, thus serving as a sort of basic training in media literacy. As such, though *Rashomon* may not qualify for classification as a mind-game film, as Elsaesser suggests, the legacy of *Rashomon*, its creator, and the process of negotiation entailed by the film can still be felt by modern audiences in the mind-game film phenomenon, wherein filmmakers challenge us not only to remain flexible and to adapt to ever-changing rules, but also to actively search for truth.

## Notes

1 The notion of a diegetic world refers to the idea of the diegesis in film studies, which is

> the content of the narrative, the fictional world as described inside the story. In film, it refers to all that is really going on on-screen, that is, to fictional reality. Characters' words and gestures, all actions as enacted within the screen constitute the diegesis.

> (Hayward 2000: 84)

2 Much has been written about the use of Kurosawa's filmmaking techniques in *Rashomon*, in such authoritative works as Stephen Prince's *The Warrior's Camera: The Cinema of Akira Kurosawa* (1991) and Peter Cowie's *Akira Kurosawa: Master of Cinema* (2010). The model presented here focuses less on a detailed examination of the specific formal qualities enacted by Kurosawa in the film and more on using a non-cinematic field of study – negotiation theory – to

explore the ways in which directors and audiences conceive of and respond to one another.

3 The commoner can be compared to the wigmaker character in Akutagawa's '*Rashomon*' story, but Kurosawa and screenwriter Shinobu Hashimoto substantially revised the latter, in effect removing her from the screenplay (Richie 1972).

Akira Kurosawa reflecting on Fumio Hayasaka's score for *Rashomon*:
The mood created was positively eerie.

(Kurosawa 1983: 138)

# 10  Reflections on *Rashomon*, Kurosawa and the Japanese audience

*Donald Richie*

For Kurosawa, *Rashomon* was the first picture he had wanted to make since the beginning of his career that he was able to get the funds together to do – although he had to go to a different company to do it. Thus the whole thing was not done in the usual spirit of cozy cronyism that typically distinguishes the Japanese product. Instead, it was everyone going out there and trying to do extraordinary things. Daiei, the company that produced *Rashomon*, stated that they didn't make the film for foreigners, and questioned why it would be sent abroad (outside the circle of Japanese cinema). Giuliana Stramigioli insisted that it was a very good film and must be sent to Italy, and so against everybody's better judgment it was submitted to the Venice Film Festival.

The Golden Lion prize was treated like an Olympic victory, of sorts, in Japan. It was one up for our side. The producer, Mr. Nagata of Daiei, who sort of rubber-stamped everything his company did, had before this gone into print by saying in the Japanese press that he didn't understand what the film was about, and that he had no idea what on earth Kurosawa was trying to do. He then had to eat all of those words when it won the prize, and say things like, 'I'm so glad that I had the foresight to helm this marvelous masterpiece', and so forth (Kurosawa 1983: 140). Kurosawa, who was not asked whether he wanted the film sent to the festival, typically found something the matter with the prize. He indicated that he was happy to get it, but would have been much more pleased if he had won for a film that told something about contemporary Japan.

Yet Kurosawa himself also said at the time that he did not make historical pictures, no matter that *Rashomon* is set in the twelfth century. He has said that his pictures are entirely contemporary, and that he makes them entirely for a contemporary audience. Therefore he throws out the historical frame at once. In other words, his film *Rashomon* takes place in 1950. If you look at Kurosawa's own time frame, Japan was in shambles after the war. It had been absolutely destroyed, just as the Rashomon gate had been destroyed. There were no values that Kurosawa could see that he thought much of in 1950s society. He saw the carpet bagging, stealing babies' clothing and similar events. As such, this was a provocative statement about the present that he made in *Rashomon*.

This was a film to wake people up. It was a provocation to beware of what is occurring to you in this, your time. Whether this provocation actually worked or not, I don't know. The film was so engaging that people would often go to see it for its entertainment value alone, but as we have discovered, many decades later, it also has the ability to make us question ourselves. This kind of questioning of self is quite certainly what Kurosawa intended to achieve with this film. He intends it in all of his films, even those in which it is least apparent. The condition of making his films is that they ask a moral question, and that the film answers this. Stephen Prince notes that Kurosawa is not afraid to go into the darker realms, and to use negative exemplars, such as *Rashomon* and *Throne of Blood*, just to show you how bad things were. In putting all of this together, you can realize something about your contemporary state. I think that this was what Kurosawa thought the film was about. He had said that he was sorry that it wasn't about contemporary Japan. In that case, however, I think he meant to show something of how contemporary Japanese lived, because *Rashomon* is very much about the contemporary Japan of its time, and contemporary Japan now.

Actually, as we now know, *Rashomon* not only shows us typically Japan, it shows us typically ourselves. The film is one of those very rare things that encompass all races, all cultures and all inclinations. Everybody can hone in on *Rashomon* and get something out of it. It is the least parochial of films. One of the reasons for this is that the original author, Akutagawa, was the most cosmopolitan of authors. The other one is that the screenwriter, Hashimoto, was a man of great culture, a great liberal.

In something I once wrote, I decided that I could set out to solve 'The Great Rashomon Murder Mystery' and indeed, if you cheat a little bit, you can really reconcile these things – of course there are a few things left out of consideration, but you can do it. Yet solving the mystery of *Rashomon* is quite beside the point of *Rashomon*. The mystery doesn't make any difference. What the mystery – if you want to call it that – does demonstrate is that not only is truth relative, but reality is just as relative as truth is, since one is dependent upon the other. This is what I think is revolutionary about the picture. All of us have this sort of dumb idea about some kind of basic reality, which we have no proof for. But to question this in a popular entertainment is quite extraordinary. Nonetheless, this is done fairly regularly in Japanese art. Therefore when Kurosawa did this and then presented it in 1950, the audience quite accepted it, and I do not remember any critics complaining about this.

So all of *Rashomon*'s elements come together to make an extremely personal film that outdistanced its own Japaneseness. That is one Rashomon effect. It is very Japanese in its way, but the Japaneseness was left far behind. It is a film that speaks directly to all of us, and more amazingly, it speaks equally clearly after all these years, and gives pleasure. Most films get dated like everything else. I saw *Rashomon* quite recently, and it is as fresh as the day it was made. So it is an extraordinary thing, and it is even more extraordinary how a film that introduced an entire film culture to the world should become and remain a film that is eminently worth learning from.

While *Rashomon* speaks directly to all of us, many times when asked, Kurosawa said that he was making films for the only audience he cared about, the only audience he respected, and that was the young. He had the young Japanese in mind, and he wanted them to listen to him, to understand him, and he wanted to teach them – he taught morality. He spoke of this mostly when he was being accused of pandering to another audience, as he often was: accused, in fact, of pandering to the Western audience. This was the canard that Kurosawa's critics were especially fond of, and one which the director most resented. The press could always get a rise out of him by maintaining that he only made films for foreigners. The willingness of the press to repeat this over and over again became quite permanent.

True, Kurosawa's pictures are familiar in the West, and, to a certain segment of Japan, this is sufficient to create suspicion. Westerners are not supposed to be able to understand Japan – that is an underlying article of faith. Therefore, anything Japanese which they can understand cannot be very Japanese. Indeed, whatever the West understands must somehow or another have been made especially for it. Thus runs the canard.

There are many things the press has said about Kurosawa. These always drew from him gratifyingly angry statements; not only about who he was making his films for, but also the matter of his individualism. He was forthright, he was opinionated, he was notoriously unsuccessful at communal efforts, and he tended to be bossy. Furthermore, his pictures were all about individuals. From *Sanshiro Sugata* on, his protagonists always learned their lessons. They decided who they were, and – unless they were dead – ended up as better people.

The Kurosawa protagonist makes his or her own decisions, and does so very often in the face of public opinion. This is one of the underlying assumptions of the story. Even when the duty is communal, as in *Seven Samurai*, it is the individuality of each member that is stressed, and not the group effort. Indeed, in the Kurosawa films, group effort can even be viewed as immoral: the lengths to which the bureaucrats go to defend their traditional turf in *Ikiru*, or the greedy collusion between big business and the government in *The Bad Sleep Well*, or the awful groups of people in *Yojimbo*, and the even worse military aristocrats in *Sanjuro*.

To many Japanese, Kurosawa's message of individuality was and remains entirely grateful. He seemed to embody postwar democracy and the new freedoms which were promised after that disastrous group effort, the Pacific War. To a few, however, in the government, in the media, and among the many critics whose scribblings fill the popular press, the very idea of individuality and the very integrity that goes with individualism seem suspicious. One can understand this, after all, because individualism undermines worthwhile group effort. This being observed, even now there is the feeling that despite the popularity of the films, and despite the approval of the Japanese majority, the climate of opinion that formed and denied Kurosawa funding for his further films was not such a bad idea. It insured that Kurosawa would have to look to the West in order to find the money he needed, which was something that could then be used to prove that the director was only interested in his Western audience.

Given what Kurosawa had to go through, his hope for a legacy would ideally then return his films to those young Japanese whom he wanted to reach, to those who were in need of moral training, those to whom he could teach the true meaning of individuality, and of the humanism which animated everything that he did. These are the people who were like *Sugata Sanshiro* in Kurosawa's mind, or like the youngest samurai in *Seven Samurai*, or like the young intern in *Red Beard*, or the children in *Rhapsody in August*.

At the same time, one of the most commonly heard local complaints about *Rhapsody in August* was that the film was old fashioned and out of touch. That kids like those in the film – hardworking, sober, serious, studious – barely exist in modern Japan, and that's true. The children in this 1991 film behave as children used to behave in 1951. The changes in Japanese society over these forty years have been enormous, and its ambitions have changed.

Indeed, most young people nowadays are no longer interested in the moral and ethical concerns that Kurosawa had hoped to instill. The recipient of the director's preferred legacy is therefore no longer present, at least not in the numbers hoped for. His current reception in Japan is also reflected by the current status surrounding the rights to Kurosawa's films, which are highly problematic. On paper, the production company Toho owns the rights to whatever exists for those films that he had made for them, including *Ikiru* (1952), *Seven Samurai* (1954), *Throne of Blood* (1957), *The Hidden Fortress* (1958), *Yojimbo* (1961) and many other of Kurosawa's most popular films. Unfortunately Toho has taken an embattled position, and will not allow any Kurosawa material to be used unless you trade it for large amounts of money.

Martin Scorsese, for example, who is a great fan of Kurosawa, decided upon Kurosawa's death that something had to be done to save these films. He raised money to open a kind of archive, with the idea of striking copies of the original negatives to keep in California. The archive would then make those prints available for showings, for archival purposes rather than financial gain. Scorsese even traveled to Japan with his committee to meet with the Toho officials, and they got nowhere at all.

With that being the company's stance, Kurosawa's family has the rights to everything that was done after the original contract was satisfied. Everything after *Red Beard* – from *Dodeskaden* onwards – the family company Kurosawa Productions has the rights for. As is the case with other companies such as Shochiku for whom *The Idiot* (1951) was made, Kurosawa Productions doesn't charge nearly as much as Toho does, but on the other hand these films aren't nearly as popular. For the other films such as the big spectaculars, you still have to go to Twentieth Century Fox to get the rights for *Kagemusha*

(1980), and you still have to go to France to get the rights for *Ran* (1985). The family itself owns everything else, such as all of the scripts that weren't filmed and all of the archival papers, etc. As always, when a person dies, their remains are scattered. It is unfortunate from a film historian's point of view that so many of these remains are in the coffers of Toho. It is very hard to get still photos from them, just as it is extremely hard to get prints of Kurosawa's films because Toho insists on charging very large sums. I imagine that the prints that are often seen in the West are ones that happened to be in America. That is, someone in the early days when people could afford them had paid the necessary price that the company was asking. Right now everything at Toho is effectively frozen, however, and until some sort of breakthrough is made possible, nothing will change and access to Kurosawa's films will remain problematic at times.

Toward the end of his career, before he died, the director seemed to have lost all of his audiences, or vice versa. Almost everyone in Japan went to *The Hidden Fortress*, which was his greatest moneymaker. Almost no one went to see *Madadayo*, his final picture. One of the reasons was that the picture being painted by the media showed Kurosawa as a cantankerous old man who was out of touch with everything. Another was that these later films reflect few of the qualities that an audience expected from the director of *Yojimbo* and *Sanjuro*. Yet another was the way in which Kurosawa died. It was a long, drawn out, doubtless painful process, which lasted years. So the public tired of him before his death.

Once Kurosawa was safely dead, however, the apotheosis began. He was suddenly a national treasure, and the nation had experienced a crippling loss. All of the newspapers ran extras, all of the magazines released special issues, the television was filled with well-known media folk shaking their heads and reaching for their handkerchiefs. One remembers *Ikiru*: after the dead Watanabe has been vilified during the wake, then the detractors turn to praise, all of which was as empty as the condemnation which had preceded it. This scenario is paralleled by that inflicted on the dead Toshiro Mifune. Before he died, no insult was too vile. After his death, he suddenly became Japan's finest actor, the loss of whom was irreparable. This sort of thing happens everywhere, but in Japan it is accomplished with a definite certainty, and an almost breathtaking suddenness. The dead Mifune was, as a friend of mine said, turned overnight from ham to Hamlet.

So now, having been decided, the official legacy of Japan's finest film director continues. It has become accepted opinion, and certainly much of that previously mentioned popularity now rests here. When you watch *Seven Samurai*, you are watching Japanese culture, and this is deemed a good thing to do. At the same time, however, even such cursory attention does not preclude a natural appreciation. Those who use *Stray Dog* as a nostalgia trip, or those who use *The Bad Sleep Well* for a sitcom home drama, do just that – but they also, inadvertently as it were, learn something. It is here that, as far as the public is concerned, the lasting legacy of Kurosawa lies.

Moving from popular appreciation into the Japanese film world itself, Kurosawa is known as perhaps Japan's best director, but certainly the world's best editor. This emphasis upon the technique of the film indicates that the most visible of Kurosawa's legacies lies in his means and his methods, his style. For example, how his compositions reflect the situations of his characters, or how his camera moves to suggest their gaze, or how using more than one camera allows a spatial freedom, or how long focal lengths create visual atmosphere, or how images can be cut together to recreate actual motion. These are the things that young cineastes learn from Kurosawa, and now admire him for. Indeed, most of the young directors have learned from Kurosawa. Even Oshima, who originally mistook Kurosawa for the system, moved from criticism to open admiration.

Among the action-prone of the younger directors of course, his influence is enormous. Although the director is not that young, the films of Takeshi Kitano would be impossible without the influence of Kurosawa. Also, the new ultra violence created by a director such as Takashi Miike owes as much to the techniques of Kurosawa as it does to such directors as Quentin Tarantino. The fact that we can combine these names is indication enough that the moral fidelity for which Kurosawa stood and which he so fervently believed in is, in this legacy at least, no longer operative. We cannot compare a Kurosawa film to a Kitano film or a Miike film. You can only compare the means – how they use a lens, or how they edit. But influence is a strange thing. For all I know it was Kurosawa who inspired the style of a film-literate person such as Tarantino himself. However, the enormous foreign influence that Kurosawa has had outside Japan is for others to discuss, and I will restrict myself to the legacies of Kurosawa in Japan.

At present, Kurosawa runs the enormous risk in Japan of becoming a great classic. That means: omnipresent but dead. Already he has become something of an icon. Those whisky commercials that he did when he really needed the money have been revived for all of us to see again; his sipping Suntory and saying, 'Mmm … yup'. The scenarios have all been published, and there are a lot of new books coming out – 'Kurosawa: The Man', and the like. Posthumous orders have been given both by the government and by private institutions. A final script, called *After the Rain*, has been filmed by someone else. Other forms of resuscitation are afoot. A script that he only wrote part of, *Dora Heita*, has been filmed by Kon Ichikawa. This kind of notice continues.

When the dead become classics, they turn into monuments. They become whitened sepulchers, and what was most alive about them disappears. So the private is always defaced by the public, and to an extent this has happened to Kurosawa in Japan. But also to a certain extent, this has not occurred. Somewhere out there, some young Japanese is looking at Sugata Sanshiro up to his neck in the lotus pond, but still holding on. Or they are looking at Setsuko Hara deciding to go to live with her peasant parents, even though her husband is falsely accused of spying. Or they are looking at Yuzo Kayama, who is learning the hard way how to care for somebody else. The morality of the Kurosawa film is so strong, and so integral a part of the experience itself, that these seeds are bound to fall on open adolescent grounds, both inside and outside the circle of Japaneseness. Certainly not as many as the director had expected, and not as often as he had hoped for. But I do think, given the films themselves, that it might be possible for him, and for all of us as well, to continue to believe in this most personal of all of Kurosawa's legacies.

Akira Kurosawa describing the effect that *Rashomon*'s Grand Prix award at the Venice International Film Festival had on Japanese film production:

It was like pouring water into the sleeping ears of the Japanese film industry.

(Kurosawa 1983: 138–9)

# 11 Kurosawa's international legacy

*Stephen Prince*

Although the medium of cinema is more than a century old, and its history is full of outstanding and memorable artists, in this select company Kurosawa is a commanding figure and a relatively unique one. His work speaks eloquently to its postwar Japanese context – that daunting crucible of national collapse and social challenge – and it has transcended this context to move audiences and inspire filmmakers throughout the world. Before taking up the question of Kurosawa's international legacy, I want to emphasize a facet of his career that lends him a unique stature even among the giants of cinema. Kurosawa treated filmmaking as his life's work, and in doing so he managed to defy some of cinema's corrosive pressures that often defeat filmmakers who pass the peak of their careers. Cinema is a ferocious medium for those who work in it. It cannibalizes many of its artists. It is tremendously difficult to make films – it is hard, physical work accompanied by a lot of anxiety – and harder still to make good ones. When the painter faces an empty canvas or the writer faces a blank page, at the moment of creativity those artists are alone with their medium. Film directors, by contrast, never work alone. They depend on a host of collaborators and must accommodate their vision to the input of art directors and cinematographers, screenwriters, actors and sound designers, as well as producers and studio executives concerned about the money invested in a production. Kurosawa's battles with these latter are legendary. Directors face creative and financial pressures, which are an inescapable part of being a professional filmmaker, and they have to negotiate with an industry that survives by making profits, not art. It is no wonder that Kurosawa once compared the film director to a military officer. 'A movie director is like a front-line commanding officer', he wrote in his autobiography. 'If he doesn't command each division, he cannot command the whole' (1983: 95). The strain is tremendous, and as a result talent tends to burn out quickly. The strains that Kurosawa endured resulted in his bleakest period, following *Red Beard* (1965), when he could no longer secure funding in Japan. He found two filmmaking opportunities in the United States – *Runaway Train* for Embassy Pictures and *Tora! Tora! Tora!* for Twentieth Century-Fox – but both ventures were canceled when Kurosawa's behavior became erratic and he grew exhausted and overwhelmed with anxiety. He seemed to doubt his own abilities to work. Kurosawa abandoned *Runaway Train* at the last moment, one month before shooting was scheduled to begin. On the other project, Fox fired him when his conduct became bizarre and unprofessional and he failed to keep the production on schedule.[1]

Kurosawa returned home, directed a small film that failed at the box office and, convinced his career was over, attempted suicide. But he managed to climb out of this bleak professional and personal trough and to resuscitate his career. He continued working for two more decades and his output included two more great films, *Dersu Uzala* (1975) and *Ran* (1985). Most directors experience periods of peak artistry that are relatively brief, and cinema has few filmmakers who sustain their work across a lifetime – half a century of filmmaking – as Kurosawa did. Moreover, he remained open to the wellsprings of his creativity, to the interplay between life and film. He continuously reinvented his work, defining new aesthetic and philosophical periods that renew and refresh the work.

Beginning with *Sanshiro Sugata* (1943), the prewar films show Kurosawa's extraordinary command of the medium at the inception of his directing career, an impressive mastery of the tools of cinema that one rarely sees at this juncture in a filmmaker's career. The end of the war launched Kurosawa on the second and most significant phase of his career, from *Drunken Angel* (1948) to *Red Beard* (1965), when his powerful heroes undertake the challenges of postwar reconstruction. The pessimistic and tragic tonality that had long been an undercurrent in his work came to dominate Kurosawa's third period, from *Dodeskaden* to *Ran*, when he became enmeshed in personal and creative crises. Then, in his eighties – defying the short-term lease that cinema tends to give its artists – Kurosawa reinvented his work by taking it in three films – *Dreams, Rhapsody in August* and *Madadayo* – into a psychobiographical region where the stories and characters become relatively direct transcriptions of Kurosawa's attitudes toward the world and of his personal situation in the twilight of a life nearing its end. These last films perplexed critics. These pictures are unconventional, quiet, inward and so personal in their design, and so eccentric in their approach to narrative as to fall outside many of the traditional conventions of narrative cinema. In the last phase of his career, Kurosawa was creating a new kind of cinema, situated midway between narrative and essay and deeply informed by the psychological filter of the director.

To speak of Kurosawa's legacy for world cinema, we must ask, Why have other filmmakers found his work so impressive? Why has it been such an inspiration and influence outside the circle of Japanese cinema? Like the popular audience, filmmakers respond to Kurosawa's extraordinary stories and characters but they also see and respond to the cinematic design of his work. That is to say, they see things – Kurosawa's film technique – that the popular audience may not recognize so overtly. Kurosawa's films have a singular visual signature, derived from the way that Kurosawa uses his cameras, where he puts them, how he moves them, and the way that he edits his footage.

I would like to spend some time discussing this because these attributes of style are at the heart of his influence and legacy. Kurosawa always said he preferred not to talk about the meaning of his films because the meanings were in the films, that is, in the way he organized picture and sound to tell his stories.

Many directors rely on their cinematographer in defining the parameters of a shot and may acquiesce to his or her judgment about how to light a shot, what lens to use, and where to place the camera. The visual style of a director's films may shift as that director works with different cinematographers.

Kurosawa, by contrast, had such a sharply defined visual sensibility that his films retain their key signature elements of design no matter who he worked with – including such terrific cinematographers as Asakazu Nakai, Kazuo Miyagawa and Takao Saito. They found themselves adapting to Kurosawa, to his visual tastes, and to his preferences about how and where to place the camera. Teruyo Nogami served as the script and production supervisor on most of Kurosawa's movies, and in her memoir she wrote about Kurosawa's knowledge of cameras and his intimate involvement with cinematography:

> He would consult with his cameraman and decide the structure of every shot himself, peering through the viewfinder and even selecting the proper lens. As a result, he always knew the precise limits of the frame ... it was no easy matter to develop an eye as unerring as Kurosawa's.
>
> (2006: 77–8)

## Kurosawa and technique

How, then, do we as viewers know that we are in a Kurosawa film? Obviously, performers such as Takashi Shimura or Toshiro Mifune, or the remarkable stories about rebellious heroes, announce that we are in Kurosawa's universe. But, too, it is the cinematic language of the films that speaks unmistakably of Kurosawa. His formal designs help to define that universe, and while the casual viewer may not consciously see these techniques, they help constitute the language a filmmaker speaks and are among the things that other filmmakers notice and respond to.

Many elements of Kurosawa's cinema technique help to make his films so recognizable and unique. Particular emphasis should be placed on Kurosawa's use of sound and his reliance on telephoto lens, axial cuts, reverse field editing, the moving camera, ninety-degree multi-camera setups, and his emphasis on long takes as well as montage. His conjunction of the last two elements is somewhat unusual because many directors will favor one or the other but seldom both.

Among filmmakers of his generation, Kurosawa is unusual for the amount of attention that he gave to his sound tracks. He used sound aggressively and as an essential component of cinema. He believed that cinema resulted from the combination of picture with sound and that the effects of this combination were not merely additive – sound plus picture – but multiplicative.

'My pet theory,' he wrote, is that 'cinematic strength derives from the multiplier effect of sound and visual image being brought together' (1983: 107). Combined, sound and picture multiplied the meanings and effects that came from them.

Kurosawa was unusual in this regard because many filmmakers of his generation used sound simply to convey dialogue and basic effects, such as gunshots or doors closing. Today, with multi-channel digital sound, moviegoers are accustomed to an enveloping, three-dimensional sound experience in cinema and to an aggressive use of all channels. By contrast, the limitations of the optical track on film – the means by which sound was encoded in Kurosawa's day – greatly restricted what filmmakers could accomplish with it. So most used it for dialogue and basic environmental sounds.

Not Kurosawa. He was very adept at isolating key sounds and amplifying them in ways that create a striking combination with picture, as in *Throne of Blood* when a medium long shot of a castle gate swinging open is accompanied by a close-up audio perspective of creaking hinges. Sound also gave him a means for exploring the emotional and psychological perspective of characters, as in *Ikiru* (1952) when Kurosawa presents a busy street scene with no ambient sound effects in order to convey the inner distress of a character focused on a cancer diagnosis that he's just received. Working in a predigital era and at a time when sound was monaural and greatly restricted in its dynamic range, Kurosawa anticipated the active and expressive use to which filmmakers put sound today. Viewing his work, they find that it prefigures their own.

In the early stages of his career, Kurosawa seemed to favor wide-angle perspective, but with *Ikiru* onward, his choice of optics changed, with long-focus lenses used to flatten space and foreshorten perspective. This compression of depth, this foreshortening is one of the most recognizable attributes of his screen work. His optics is based on long-focus perspective so he doesn't create depth of field like most other filmmakers. He doesn't put objects into the face of the camera; instead, he puts his cameras well back from the scene and lets the optics of his long lenses transform reality. This transformation produces an emphasis on artifice and style, and if one responds to telephoto aesthetics, it can furnish a great source of pleasure.

The axial cuts – edits that move the camera nearer to or further from its subject with each camera position replicating the line of sight established at the onset of the axial sequence – are a unique, eccentric and striking feature of the films. Often at moments of climax, or at some other critical place in the story, Kurosawa will give us an axial series with each composition framed along the camera's line of sight as established in the first shot. When the shots are edited together, they drive a viewer percussively, explosively into a scene, as they do when he shows the mill's wheel in *Seven Samurai* or the cliff in the last shot of *Ran*. Usually, the axial shots occur in threes, but sometimes they do so in twos – as when Sanjuro spies the broken lock on the box in which he can hide in *Yojimbo* – and they usually move toward closer views of an object or character, but sometimes Kurosawa will use them to back out and away from a scene, as he does at the end of *Ran*.

Another favored editing pattern is reverse field cutting, where the field of view of two adjacent shots changes by precisely 180 degrees, which occurs throughout *Sanshiro Sugata* and *Seven Samurai*.

Kurosawa is one of cinema's great masters of the moving camera, used to electrify scenes with the dynamic excitement of motion perspective. In *Rashomon* and *Throne of Blood*, he gave us complex yet fluid tracking shots through dense forest. The last of his rapid camera moves occurs in *Red Beard* in 1965. Thereafter, he moved toward long takes and static, nonmoving compositions.

Kurosawa's preference for camera placement was always a highly angular one. He often favored camera set-ups at ninety-degree angles and especially so once he moved toward filming with multiple cameras running simultaneously. From *Stray Dog* to *Madadayo*, Kurosawa's ninety-degree set-ups remain a consistent and singular feature of his style. He also often conjoined these set-ups with a preference for long takes, shots of long duration that favor the performer and which, in his later work, are used to emphasize stillness and quietude.

Many directors, of course, use long takes in this manner, but what distinguishes Kurosawa is that he blends two cinema styles that ordinarily are not found within the same filmmaker. As he emphasized the long take and the quiet frame, Kurosawa also embraced a style featuring montage as a principal tool of scene construction. *Stray Dog* takes these antithetical stylistic templates to an extreme point, featuring an interrogation scene done largely in a single shot and a sequence showing the film's hero, Murakami (Toshiro Mifune), searching a black market district in a montage lasting over eight minutes. He is best known internationally for this latter style, for his choreography of action in thrilling montages such as those in *Seven Samurai*, *The Hidden Fortress* and the train sequence from *High and Low*. But it is the presence of both styles – the long take and montage, quietude and action – that makes Kurosawa such a striking filmmaker.

## International influence

Thus, to speak of Kurosawa's international influence is to describe the impact of a filmmaker who organized style in a uniquely compelling way. He defied the medium, and he defined it, by establishing a singular stylistic profile and by continuing to explore its secrets long past the point at which other filmmakers give up or are defeated and worn down by the sheer difficulty of making films. Conventional and clichéd wisdom holds that Kurosawa was strongly influenced by the American cinema, that his samurai films, for example, were inspired by Hollywood's Westerns. *Yojimbo* has the T-shaped street familiar from Hollywood Westerns and a showdown on this street that struck critics at the time as an apparently obvious transposition from the

Western – the samurai as gunfighter. To be sure, there is some borrowing by Kurosawa – the hammering of coffins may derive from *High Noon* and the scene where Toshiro Mifune is beaten up and escapes from his captors has its visual source in *The Glass Key*, a Paramount film noir of 1942. Critics have compared Kurosawa to Hollywood director John Ford, and, again, there is some truth here. Kurosawa admired Ford's work and was tremendously impressed when they met. However, in *Stagecoach*, Ford's Indians never shoot the horses pulling the stagecoach; in *Kagemusha*, depicting the Battle of Nagashino in 1575, during which samurai on horseback charged an enemy clan fortified with guns, Kurosawa made sure the horses were shot, overturning this Western cliché.

I want to suggest that this familiar critical paradigm – that has Kurosawa borrowing from Hollywood – drew the significant influences in the wrong direction. Kurosawa's borrowings from Hollywood are mostly trivial things and show the workings of a fertile, hybrid imagination. Kurosawa didn't make samurai films because Hollywood made Westerns; he would have made them anyway.

Furthermore, if we take the most obvious examples first, Kurosawa's films are a continuing inspiration for international filmmakers, who have remade his works, wholly or in part. *Rashomon*, *Yojimbo*, *The Hidden Fortress*, *Seven Samurai* and *High and Low* have spawned numerous English-language descendants, and this process continues. Director Martin Scorsese's production company, Cappa Productions, has been interested in doing English-language remakes of *Seven Samurai* and *High and Low*. Of all Kurosawa's films, *Seven Samurai* has inspired the greatest number of remakes across a wide variety of genres, including science fiction (*Battle Beyond the Stars*), children's animation (*A Bug's Life*), and, of course, the Western (*The Magnificent Seven* and all of the professional Westerns that came of it and Kurosawa, Westerns about groups of men on a dangerous mission, including *The Professionals* and *The Wild Bunch*).

One of the most famous of these remakes, Sergio Leone's *A Fistful of Dollars* (1964), was lifted, not so subtly, from *Yojimbo*. This is one of Kurosawa's most entertaining pictures, with a masterful visual design and sharp, biting social satire and a performance of pure star charisma from Toshiro Mifune. At the time that he made *Fistful*, Leone was a fledgling Italian filmmaker who had been looking for a subject with which to make his debut as a feature director. He had just seen *Yojimbo* in an Italian movie theater and was struck by the possibilities he felt it offered as a Western. Indeed, *Fistful* is virtually a scene-by-scene remake of *Yojimbo*, very closely patterned on Kurosawa's picture, the result of Leone spending many hours at a Movieola studying the scenes and details of Kurosawa's work. He didn't copy Kurosawa's camera style – Leone's camera style would be quite different – but he did transpose closely the content of Kurosawa's shots and scenes.

Leone defended himself against the suggestions of colleagues that he was plagiarizing Kurosawa's film by claiming that he was merely returning it to its point of origin in the Hollywood Western. This is an interesting claim because Leone did more than almost anyone to change the kind of Westerns that Hollywood made. Leone's Dollars trilogy – *Fistful, For a Few Dollars More, The Good, the Bad and the Ugly* – was released by United Artists in the United States in 1967, after which Westerns were never the same again. Moreover, though *Yojimbo* doesn't really have its origin in the Hollywood Western, Leone doesn't really take it back there anyway. He triangulates the Western with Kurosawa's samurai film and with an Italian cultural context to create a hybrid, an amalgamation of three quite different cinema and cultural traditions. *A Fistful of Dollars* is a true mongrel.

Whether it was due to the enthusiasm with which he worked or to willful neglect, Leone's production company failed to secure the rights to remake Kurosawa's film. Kurosawa threatened a lawsuit – Leone apparently oblivious to this threat because of his thrill that the great director had taken the time to write to him![2] – which was settled when Leone ceded to him distribution rights in Japan and a portion of worldwide box office. Years later, in 1990 when Clint Eastwood, the star of Leone's Dollars trilogy, met Kurosawa at the Cannes Film Festival, they are reported to have shared a laugh about Eastwood's career being launched with this piece of plagiarism.

Leone would go on to transcend the Kurosawa influence and to develop a very different and quite unique visual style of his own. Where Kurosawa favors the telephoto lens, Leone loved the wide-angle lens, with the result that each filmmaker's shot style looks quite different from the other. Kurosawa shot with multiple cameras; Leone did not. Moreover, whereas Kurosawa was a masterful storyteller, as Leone's style matured, he grew less interested in story and more interested in elaborating the rhetoric of the Western – the grizzled faces, the glaring eyes of antagonists, the archaic weaponry, and above all the ritualized behavior, such as that which composes the prelude to a gunfight. These would come to occupy more and more screen time as story came to occupy less in Leone's work, and the elaboration that he gives to this visual rhetoric reaches epic and astonishing proportions in *The Good, the Bad and the Ugly* and *Once Upon a Time in the West*. *A Fistful of Dollars* is interesting because it shows this style in embryonic form and for the startling maturity of Clint Eastwood's performance, his first as a lead in a feature film. These three filmic traditions – Japan, Italy and Hollywood –would never be quite the same again when Kurosawa and Leone had finished with them.

The remakes are, of course, obvious examples of Kurosawa's influence on filmmaking outside Japan. More significant influences, though, also go in the other direction, from Kurosawa to the West, and these are not small and isolated stylistic elements – such as the T-shaped street in *Yojimbo* – but are truly powerful designs that have helped to change the face of modern cinema. Of these, I would like to concentrate on two influences that seem to me of decisive importance. The first is Kurosawa's invention of what became for several decades the essential stylistic template for presenting scenes of physical violence. The second is Kurosawa's popularization of a visceral, kinetic approach to storytelling, which, beginning in the 1970s, became the predominant model of Hollywood blockbuster filmmaking and that has subsequently been exported throughout the world.

## Stylizing violence

Kurosawa's ability to stylize scenes of physical violence in memorable ways is an enduring feature of his work – one thinks of the slow motion and jump cuts in *Sanshiro Sugata*, the paint-splattered antagonists in *Drunken Angel*, the human porcupine riddled with scores of arrows in *Throne of Blood*, the severed hand and arm in *Yojimbo*, the geyser of blood in *Sanjuro*, the audible shattering of bones in *Red Beard*. These images (and sounds) linger because of their surprising, unexpected flamboyance – Kurosawa has consistently found new ways of presenting screen violence and of making it vividly cinematic.

In *Seven Samurai*, however, he did more than this. He found a device and its stylistic application and, in so doing, he helped to change the face of modern cinema. In the scene where the hero, Kambei (Takashi Shimura), kills a thief who has kidnapped a child, Kurosawa shot the scene with multiple cameras running at different speeds. He then intercut the footage – slow motion shots of the dying thief crashing through a door, rising up on tiptoes, and falling to the ground – with normal speed shots of fascinated onlookers. He made the essential discoveries here about how to use slow motion to accentuate moments of violence. The slow motion inserts have to be brief, otherwise they will be a drag on the energy of the sequence. By keeping the slow motion shots brief, Kurosawa can easily negotiate the changes of speed and time in the sequence, and he can give the slow motion a charge of energy that it would not possess by itself. In this regard, the editing of slow motion in *Seven Samurai* is leagues beyond what he accomplished with slow motion in his first film, *Sanshiro Sugata*. In that film, Kurosawa simply inserted a slow motion shot into the body of a normal speed scene. The insert is interesting and surprising and vivid, but, because it's only one shot, Kurosawa cannot create a dynamic contrast of different frames of time and space by extending them across the length of an edited sequence, as he does in *Seven Samurai*. Nor did he seem to be thinking of doing that in *Sugata*. He seemed curious about the juxtaposition of different camera speeds but not interested enough to examine the technique and extend it across several shots. As a result, in *Sugata* the technique has a minimal relationship to the surrounding material. In *Seven Samurai* it's an integral part of the structure. Watching the two scenes, you feel the difference. In *Sanshiro Sugata*, the effect is surprising and interesting. In *Seven Samurai*, it is exciting and dynamic.

The consequences of this for world cinema have been enormous. Although Kurosawa would show only an occasional interest in this kind of editing, subsequent filmmakers found here, in this brief scene, the modern textbook on movie violence. They have been remaking this scene ever since and in ever-grander terms.

Kurosawa's demonstration deeply influenced the two films and filmmakers whose work served to popularize and disseminate his approach. The first of these was Arthur Penn and his presentation of the slaughter scene that climaxes *Bonnie and Clyde*, as automatic weapons cut down the gangsters in a multi-camera montage juxtaposing different camera speeds as Kurosawa had done. Penn said that he knew how to do it because he had seen Kurosawa (Crowdus and Porton 1993).

*Bonnie and Clyde* offered the most elaborately stylized cinema violence yet seen, and it brought Kurosawa's technique into the mainstream, setting off a race among subsequent filmmakers to outdo each other in elaborating and exaggerating this technique. The following year, in *The Wild Bunch*, Sam Peckinpah determined to surpass Penn. To make sure he would go beyond what Penn had shown, he had a print of *Bonnie and Clyde* shipped to his Mexican location for screening a few days prior to the start of principal cinematography on *The Wild Bunch*, and, indeed, he filmed two slaughter scenes opening and closing the film that used slow motion in a multi-camera montage to extend the ferocity of the action to a then-unprecedented degree.[3] Like Penn, Peckinpah was a keen student of Kurosawa, and Peckinpah's production crew regularly spoke of his editing as a Kurosawa effect. Peckinpah's elaboration of Kurosawa's design was to amplify its scale, taking Kurosawa's brief shot series and Penn's brief montage and extending these into an edited sequence of much greater duration.

From the elaboration given to it by Penn and Peckinpah and because of the visibility and popularity of their work, Kurosawa's technique – of multi-camera montage incorporating slow motion – passed to virtually every modern filmmaker seeking to make screen violence vivid and poetic. It is not an exaggeration to say that the device became a canonical structure of contemporary cinema, widely dispersed across a range of films and filmmakers on an international scale. Like all formal conventions, however, this one eventually faded from continuous usage, and today is not so prevalent as in decades past.

Moreover, the convention trapped many filmmakers drawn to it for whom the device became its own end, a fetish of technique, as did the fascination with doing violence for the camera. Kurosawa, by contrast, maintained only an occasional interest in slow motion, and while he continued to study the phenomenon of human violence, in films such as *Ran*, he refused to present it so as to glorify it, to pump it up with a false grandiloquence. Instead, he saw where violence has taken humanity and where graphic violence would take cinema and its filmmakers. He refused to go there, and so his work transcends its own flamboyant violence because Kurosawa retained a moral control and perspective over his material and style. But, despite this difference, and if we construe one measure of artistic legacy as that which falls at the level of style itself, of formal structure, we can see that Kurosawa bequeathed to modern cinema an essential stylistic design for movie violence. In this regard, he altered the face of contemporary film.

## Kinesthetic filmmaking

Kurosawa also influenced contemporary cinema in a second profound way. Since the 1970s, Hollywood has been heavily invested in a model of popular film that is fast-paced, sensual and sense assaulting, and it has exported this model across the globe. This style of film was tied to the emergence of a new generation of filmmakers in 1970s Hollywood, including directors Steven Spielberg, George Lucas, Martin Scorsese and Brian De Palma. Collectively, they practiced a visceral and kinetic brand of moviemaking that was more insistent and aggressive in its visual design than previous generations of American film had been and that used these aggressive designs to deliver stories in the most adrenaline-enhancing manner possible.

I am calling this style of filmmaking kinesthetic because of its dynamic properties, its use of film style to convey sensations of motion and tension and the elicitation of excitement at a nearly physical level, in the nerves and muscles and joints of its viewers. These directors broke with existing traditions of narrative filmmaking, which were less aggressive and were pitched at a less emphatic level of style. They used elaborate camera moves, montage editing and swift transitions between unique and non-repeating camera set-ups to maintain continuous visual stimulation for the viewer, an ongoing audiovisual excitement.

Taking cinema in this direction, in Kurosawa they found a filmmaker who was a master of sensual camera movements, of montage, of non-repeating camera set-ups, and of arresting sound-image juxtapositions and who used these techniques to tell remarkable stories with crispness, momentum and grace. In this regard, it is instructive to recall that the tremendous impression that *Rashomon* made on international critical opinion was due to Kurosawa's filmmaking style as much as to the remarkable theme of the film. In review after review of *Rashomon*, critics remarked upon the film's strikingly pictorial qualities. Not since the silent cinema had critics encountered such an aggressively designed visual experience, where the story had been conceived in terms of the pure flow of imagery and where Kurosawa's camera movement, editing, lighting and sound fully exploited the properties these tools can contribute to the experience of cinema. Nobody shot forests the way Kurosawa did, and the woodcutter's walk through the forest, followed by a gliding, serpentine camera, is one of the high accomplishments in modern cinema.

To return to the main line of our discussion, the sensuality of Kurosawa's style, and the elegance of his storytelling and its profoundly popular appeal, deeply impressed this emerging cohort of American filmmakers, each of whom remembered his first encounter with a Kurosawa film as being one of the most cherished cinematic memories of youth. These filmmakers openly acknowledged the importance and the appeal of Kurosawa's work for their own films.

The historical irony here is impressive. At that point in his career, after *Red Beard*, when Kurosawa's ability to secure funding for Japanese productions had faltered and stalled, threatening his very ability to continue as a film-maker, he was adopted as a mentor figure by this emerging generation of American directors, most of whom would go on to secure considerable power within their industry. Doing so, they paid their debt – George Lucas and Francis Coppola helped Kurosawa make *Kagemusha*, Steven Spielberg and Lucas' effects house, Industrial Light and Magic, assisted with *Dreams*, and Lucas and Spielberg ushered Kurosawa onstage at the 1990 Academy Awards where he received a special Oscar.

Kurosawa thus stands – stylistically – behind the turn toward movie blockbusters that Hollywood commenced in the 1970s, and it was *Seven Samurai* – with its racing, powerful narrative engine, breathtaking pacing, and sense-assaulting visual style – that was the clearest precursor of this new, visceral brand of moviemaking. Spielberg, Lucas, Scorsese and De Palma aimed to create a more kinesthetic cinema, rooted in physical action and the use of camerawork and editing to take the audience inside that action, to evoke it at as close to a physical level for viewers as film can, and to give it a relentless pace. The box office results that followed from this approach to cinema were extraordinary. *Jaws* (1975) and *Star Wars* (1977) inaugurated the new blockbuster phase of Hollywood moviemaking and made more money than anyone thought it was possible to make from movies. As examples of action filmmaking and exciting visual design – as examples of kinesthetic cinema – the distance from *Seven Samurai* to *Jaws* is not so far, though we all know that *Seven Samurai* is much more than a thrill machine. As for *Star Wars*, the debt to Kurosawa was more explicit, as will be demonstrated anon.

Having identified Kurosawa as the father figure for the 1970s generation of new American directors, I must add two qualifications. First, although Kurosawa aimed for a popular audience, it was not for the same reason as the Hollywood directors did, namely to make a lot of money. Kurosawa wanted to use film to transform the imaginative and cultural horizons of his audience, to reach his viewers socially and morally by offering visions of lives well lived, and he wanted to accomplish this in the broadest possible frame by reaching as many viewers as he could. Popular storytelling was a means to this end, and Kurosawa felt only disdain for the marketing side of film.

Second, in important respects, *Seven Samurai* is quite an atypical Kurosawa film. He was not a director of fast-paced movies. Like nearly all of cinema's great filmmakers, he favored a measured pace and at times a slow one. As we have seen, he was a master of long takes. He never again made a film like *Seven Samurai*, where the narrative engine is so driven and so powerful and where the entire audiovisual design is calculated for the greatest possible narrative momentum. That film hurtles along, and the viewer can but hang on with astonishment and joy at so masterful a display of action-based storytelling.

But, as with Kurosawa's intercutting of multi-camera slow motion into the texture of a normal tempo sequence, he needed only to demonstrate once, in especially pure form, the model for a cinema of visceral, sensual, rapid-fire storytelling. Having done it, Kurosawa then left it as a legacy for other filmmakers to take up, and in the 1970s his American admirers did so, even as Kurosawa's own work was then shifting to a greater emphasis on stillness and quietude. The most famous of these in terms of the Kurosawa influence, of course, is George Lucas in his *Star Wars* films. It has been widely acknowledged that he lifted some characters and the general story situation from *The Hidden Fortress* and used these in *Star Wars*. In both films, a resolute princess and her band of loyal retainers are in flight across enemy territory, and Lucas transposes Kurosawa's feuding peasants, Tahei and Matakishi, into the bickering R2-D2 and C-3PO.

What is not as generally known, however, is that Lucas found Kurosawa's narrative methods to be a great inspiration. In *Seven Samurai*, *The Hidden Fortress*, *Yojimbo* and his other period films, Kurosawa visualizes in rich, dramatic and vivid terms the historical setting of the tales – often it is sixteenth-century Japan and the social upheavals wrought by prolonged civil wars – but he never explains much to the audience about this context. Instead, he begins his stories in the midst of things – Tahei and Matakishi on a desolate plain surrounded by bloody fighting; the bandit horde galloping toward the village of farmers in *Seven Samurai*; Sanjuro striding into a town already piled high with corpses in *Yojimbo*. Kurosawa plunges his viewers into rapidly unfolding action and a gallery of larger-than-life characters. Sanjuro, the hero of *Yojimbo*, is specific to the time frame of the tale – he is a ronin or unemployed samurai who feels disdain for the merchant class. Yet he is so stripped of a personal biography – he has no name, no past, not even a reliable age – as to become mysterious and abstract. This is to say that Kurosawa reaches deeply into the historical to find myth, and it was this narrative stratagem – the evocation of myth – that tremendously impressed Lucas. He emulated this approach in his films, envisioning a huge and hugely detailed universe of characters and places that is already fully animated when the film series begins and that aims these details to evoke the powerful generalities of myth. Kurosawa and his period films, then, stand as a key inspiration for the mythic substrata and narrative richness of the *Star Wars* series, and this is a more significant and pervasive influence than is implied by the obvious overlaps of character and story between *Star Wars* and *The Hidden Fortress*.

In these two ways – by demonstrating a sensual and kinesthetic approach to popular storytelling and by showing what multi-camera filming methods could accomplish in montages of physical action – Kurosawa provided contemporary cinema with two of its most enduring templates. These have been used by directors throughout the world but most especially and vividly by Hollywood filmmakers, whose products dominate world markets. It is not an exaggeration, then, to suggest that, in these ways, Kurosawa redefined the language of modern cinema, and this legacy transcends its incarnation in any single film or filmmaker. Thus, though his extraordinary films have been, and will continue to be, remade, Kurosawa's deepest influence and most enduring legacy is here, in having changed the language of cinema and having done so in a body of work that stretched, with distinction, across a lifetime. In this way, his work becomes a part of the heart of the medium and his career an essential moment in its history.

## Markets, mass audiences and the mechanics of global cinema

Kurosawa's place in film history is no small accomplishment, and required that he overcome the medium of cinema and its laws about the duration of career and creativity. Having done so, his example and his work reaffirm the artistic potential of cinema and do so at a time when, sadly, the cinema is disappearing on a landscape of digital media and interactive entertainment and a fragmenting audience. In Kurosawa's day, cinema was a medium housed in large theater auditoriums. He made movies for the big screen, not television. From 1958–75, for example, he worked almost exclusively in anamorphic widescreen. Seven of the eight pictures he made during that period he shot in a Tohoscope 2.35:1 aspect ratio, which is not a picture ratio that can be accommodated by the television screen. This preference of his indicates how important the big screen – the movie theater – was for the design of his work.

Today, the cinema theater exists mainly as a way to service the ancillary markets. The ancillary markets are all the nontheatrical contexts in which people watch movies – video sales and rental, cable television, web-based streaming video – and they are more important to the film studios, and the big communications corporations that own them, than theatrical film. Movies today are only released to theaters because that kick-starts performance in the ancillary markets.

Furthermore, as film production has been gobbled up by global media companies, the distinguishing characteristics of national cinemas have eroded. Kurosawa made his great films by responding to Japan's postwar context, and the Japanese cinema supported not only his work but also that of many fine directors. Today, by contrast, just as the McDonalds' hamburger I might eat in Tokyo would be like the one I could eat in New York, many of the most popular films in Japan are the same commercial Hollywood pictures that dominate other national cinemas. Hollywood blockbusters typically earn more revenue in overseas markets than in the United States and Canada. Marvel's *The Avengers*, for example, the top-grossing film of 2012, earned nearly $900 million in overseas markets compared with $623 million domestically. (In Japan the film grossed $45 million.) At this level of financing and distribution, cinema is less about artistic expression than the servicing of global entertainment markets. These markets, serviced by American media companies, are no longer film specific because film, as Kurosawa understood it – a sprocketed celluloid strip run through a projector – no longer exists during production or distribution. Cinema today is a set of electronic video formats. Moreover, as the retail tie-ins to the *Harry Potter* movies demonstrate, movies are an engine that drives an enormous amount of related product merchandising.

How would Kurosawa have regarded these changes? Almost certainly with hostility. He would have been distressed and disillusioned. We know that he felt mostly disdain for the marketing side of cinema. Kurosawa once said that his goal as a filmmaker was to make movies for the people, for all the people. This goal was tied to a particular historical moment in the life of cinema, one that is now gone. That moment was the period when cinema was the predominant medium of popular visual culture, when rivals such as television had not yet eroded its base of appeal and new forces such as the Internet had not yet appeared to claim the audience, and when filmmakers could make movies for a mass audience that included adults as well as children and teenagers, the latter being today the most desirable and coveted audience segment for big budget moviemakers.

These components of an earlier period helped to make cinema a medium that embraced diverse audiences. The existence of that mass audience, hungry for films and reachable by talented and ambitious filmmakers, was the essential precondition of Kurosawa's work. The universalizing aspects of cinema – its status as the most popular medium of mass visual culture and as a global medium of influence – were essential to his work, to his desire that his characters be role models for audiences both inside and outside the circle of Japanese cinema. The entire ethical project of his filmmaking – the desire to reach a popular audience with visions of how life could be lived to its fullest human potential – presupposed the existence of a mass medium that embraced everyone.

Cinema no longer does so. The mass audience is gone, having been replaced by a fragmented audience, by niche groups targeted by specialized movies, many of which are aimed at teenagers. Furthermore, these niche audiences are now dispersed among many different media experienced by viewers using web-linked and often mobile devices. These media are engines of the consumer economy, proffering virtual worlds that hold out an ideal of fulfillment through consumption that Kurosawa had always been so critical of in his films.

How does a filmmaker today aim for the universal audience that Kurosawa went after? A filmmaker can only do it today by manufacturing a commercial blockbuster, a *Harry Potter*, a *Lord of the Rings*, an *Avengers*, and doing that requires cooperating with the multinational communications corporations that command the machinery for global film distribution. Typically, such a film will be heavy on visual effects and will contain characters that can be franchised across many different media categories and product lines – home video, cable television, recorded music, fast-food hamburgers, T-shirts. The most successful such characters are those who are, like the Hobbits, fantastical or are, like the Avengers, essentially toys. It is difficult to imagine Kanji Watanabe, the hero of *Ikiru*, replicated on T-shirts or fast-food wrappers. Even to try imagining this is nonsense and shows the great distance between Kurosawa's cinema and the mechanics of global movie merchandising in our own age.

Kurosawa could work as he did, and make the kind of films that he did, because of the peculiarities of cinema in his time. It was the medium of an epic embrace – movies for everyone but not for a global market of franchised products. That time, though, is over, and it may be that no one is again going to use cinema in Kurosawa's grandly ambitious way. Kurosawa's legacy endures, then, at the very moment when the medium in which it flourished is vanishing and its great auteurs have been eclipsed in time and swept away, like the *Seven Samurai*, by the winds of time and history. Standing below the graves on that hill, we can feel the weight and density of their accomplishments, even as we see that golden period of great deeds receding farther into the past.

## Notes

1 Hiroshi Tasogawa provides a detailed history of these episodes in *All the Emperor's Men: Kurosawa's Pearl Harbor* (2012).
2 Christopher Frayling recounts this episode in his biography (2000: 148).
3 I discuss this in more detail in *Savage Cinema: Sam Peckinpah and the Rise of Ultraviolent Movies* (Prince 1998).

---

Akira Kurosawa reflecting on the implications of *Rashomon* winning the Academy Award for Best Foreign Film in addition to the Venice Grand Prix:

Japanese critics insisted that these two prizes were simply reflections of Westerners' curiosity and taste for Oriental exoticism, which struck me then, and now, as terrible. Why is it that Japanese people have no confidence in the worth of Japan? Why do they elevate everything foreign and denigrate everything Japanese? Even the woodblock prints of Utamaro, Hokusai and Sharaku were not appreciated by Japanese until they were first discovered by the West. I don't know how to explain this lack of discernment. I can only despair of the character of my own people.

(Kurosawa 1983: 139)

---

# 12 Dialogue on Kurosawa

## Nationality, technique, lifework

*Donald Richie and Stephen Prince*

### Remembering Donald Richie

I met Donald Richie briefly in 1997 and more substantially in 2000 at the Simon Fraser University conference during which this conversation about *Rashomon* took place. Of course, I knew Donald's work long before this conference. I owned a copy of his book on Kurosawa and had read it thoroughly, along with his other books on film. When my own book on Kurosawa was published in its first edition in 1991, I received a big package in the mail one afternoon. I opened it to find a large, orange sweatshirt emblazoned with the artwork for Kurosawa's *Dreams* which was just then in release to theaters. There was a note from Donald. It offered congratulations on the Kurosawa book. He added, 'I was very glad to see it appear.'

This sentiment says so much about Donald, especially his generosity. He was a remarkably big-spirited man. After his own book appeared, nobody had published in English another substantive book on Kurosawa. When mine came out, rather than feeling a need to protect intellectual territory that many had come to associate with him, Donald welcomed this new publication. I was touched by his gesture and impressed.

Two years later I was in Japan speaking on Kurosawa at the Tokyo American Club, and Donald, too, was on the program. That's where we bonded and then shared a close friendship that over the next decade went well beyond our mutual interest in Kurosawa. I visited Donald numerous times in Japan. He took me to his favorite haunts, some of which were very personal indeed, and he was very candid about his reasons for preferring Japan to the United States. We journeyed throughout Tokyo and beyond. One of my favorite trips was a visit to Kurosawa's grave, accompanied by Teruyo Nogami, Kurosawa's long-time production supervisor. I acquired one of Donald's paintings. He took my hand, and we walked to the gallery where they were on display and asked me which I liked. He was pleased by my choice, and it hangs today, as it has for years, over my breakfast table. He was an unfailingly warm and welcoming host who lived in a tiny apartment overlooking a giant lotus pond. I once asked him how he managed to write so many books, and he replied, simply, 'I get up early.'

In all of these ways – his generosity, his depth of emotion, his intellect, his sense of poetry and aesthetics, his embrace of life in all its forms, and the enormous outpouring of writings, films, photographs and paintings that he authored – Donald Richie was a truly remarkable man. I was so fortunate to have known him and to have shared the time with him that we had. I miss him all the time.

– Stephen Prince

## Nationality

*Stephen Prince:*

Donald, you've written about how Kurosawa's films have been felt by many to be un-Japanese. One of the key frameworks to studying Kurosawa is through the context of national identity. For many Westerners, it can be somewhat difficult to understand how Kurosawa could have been considered un-Japanese within his own nation. Some Westerners will even say that their very perceptions of Japan and the Japanese people were founded through Kurosawa's films as they were growing up.

*Donald Richie:*

The trappings of the films, of course, are all Japanese, such as when you have samurai wearing their traditional samurai costuming. So for Western audiences the films look very Japanese, yet the construction methods are not Japanese. Kurosawa also ignores many of the things that pass for local narrative. For example, in Japan a cliché is not considered a bad thing but rather a good thing, because it is reassuring. It reassures the majority of the people to have somebody acting the same way all the time. This of course spills over into all popular entertainments. Japanese television, for instance, is nothing but stereotypes from morning to night. This is found very reassuring in Japan; however, in the same way, things that we wouldn't say in the West without a layer of irony are said innocently there.

Can anybody really say 'have a nice day', for instance, with any feeling of integrity any longer? All you can do is camp it up and smirk when you say it, or else say it mechanically as though it has no meaning, which indeed it does not. But 'have a nice day', or the equivalent Japanese expression, has been alive and well for the last thousand years in Japan. There is no sense of the fact that a cliché exists, or that something has become a cliché. A cliché to us means that something is overdone. Yet as long as it carries its social weight, it is used in Japan.

Therefore when you put such seemingly clichéd ideas together to construct a narrative, then you have a whole way of reading reality that, from the individualistic Western view, is not worth doing. But from an Asian point of view, it is quite different. You might go to an ordinary period film and see the lovers walking around as the cherry blossoms are falling. This of course means true love, but it won't last for long. You see the lovers crossing a brook, which means they will soon be divided. You hear a crow calling during a sword fight scene and you think: Ah, he's going to die. These are all clichés, yet Kurosawa has fun with this a lot of the time.

If you remember the scene in *The Lower Depths* where just before an angry Mifune kills the landlord, there is a crow cawing. Someone in fact mentions the crow cawing in the film. Kurosawa is playing with the cliché because the landlord really does not deserve to live. Another famous example is in *Yojimbo*, where the convention in samurai films is that the man having been slashed from stem to stern calls for his mother as he falls: *o-kaa*! In *Yojimbo* this is done in three ways. First a little boy is imitating sword fighting, and he cries *o-kaa*! The second time, a young man says *o-kaa*, only to be viciously slapped in his face by his mother, played for its humor. But the third time occurs when there is a big fight. The samurai dies, and cries *o-kaa*! with horrific intensity. Suddenly, Kurosawa returns to this completely overused cliché some of the pathos that it must originally have had.

Kurosawa loves to play with these kinds of conventions. Clichés are always used with a kind of irony in his films, which is something that people who are more conservative don't often like. Japanese narrative can therefore be, in the wrong hands, a tissue of this sort of stereotyped characters, stereotyped dialogue, and the things that continually reassure. One of the reasons for the lowered state of Japanese film abroad is that we in the West have reached the point of only liking novelty. If we've seen it before, we don't like it anymore; that's a problem. Now imagine a civilization where if something is a novelty, they don't like it. They only like what they've seen before, which is also a problem.

**Stephen Prince:**

You have also referred to a canard that critics put about concerning who exactly should be able to understand Japanese films. At some point in recent history it was said that people who weren't Japanese couldn't understand Japanese culture, and therefore if Kurosawa's films were understandable he must have made them with an eye on these other audiences outside the thick boundary that is the circle of Japaneseness. At what point did that argument fade from sight, if ever, and how did the director himself deal with it? How did Kurosawa engage with that question of what it might mean to understand Japan?

**Donald Richie:**

If you have been to Japan, or if you live in Japan, you will realize that the Japanese are, like most people, of several minds about their own culture.

These are island people who, as it was said, only opened up to the West over one hundred and fifty years ago. Therefore, as in the case of Great Britain or other islands, the national hold on who they are, on their idea of identity, remains strong and exclusive. We all have this in times of moral struggle, such as in America when they are trying to decide who is going to run the country, and there is talk about We Americans, speaking in a very exclusive way about one's own country. Japan is just like that, in that they have We Japanese as an expression that is built into the language. On television you hear *ware-ware no kuni* instead of Japan – our country – and it is said very seriously. It is quite possible to say this is in a camp humorous manner, but that is not intended.

Everyone is of two minds about whether they are international, or really their own people. As in most countries, one group decides that they are a unit and that they are exclusive, and must keep people out without caring whether or not they are being xenophobic. The other group is more encouraging toward other people. In Japan we notice the former: because Japan is simply more open, it sweeps less under the carpet. Other countries have been hiding this sort of thing, but Japan sees nothing to be ashamed of in being xenophobic. So consequently, what we do have in Japan is xenophobia, as people who do not like that outlook will call it. This xenophobic impulse is, of course, one of the things which prompts criticism, such as the criticism of Kurosawa, that he has gone over to the enemy, to the other side, has neglected his own people.

This is built into the language, and until a lot of things change this will undoubtedly maintain. We have in Japan the concept that certain kinds of words are purely Japanese, called *Yamato kotoba*. Such words are not tainted, as it were, by Western associations. This idea of what is polluted and what is not polluted may have been lost in England, where they do not care which words are French and which are not anymore after the Norman conquest. That was a long time ago, however, and the opening of Japan through the invasion of Commodore Perry is a fairly recent thing as history goes, and naturally people are still very touchy about this.

Hence there is a continual war of opinion going on in Japan. Obviously Kurosawa himself wanted a strong moral character, but he did not want it at the cost of xenophobia. On the other hand, a lot of politicians, particularly people who have agendas of their own, are very happy to use this. So we have this push and pull, which you can see even from here in North America. You can see this pattern of opinion going back and forth in Japan. It is a very real issue, particularly in the twenty-first century with the country's economy being such that there is drastic restructuring, and whole ways of thinking are simply going to have to change for that most imperative of all reasons – money.

I mention this only in regard to how the public in general is swayed by these conflicting arguments in its assessment of Kurosawa. As to how he managed to cope with this canard, he did not cope with it. He paid no attention to it, saying that it was *bakabakashii*, which means foolishness. He would say: It's not true that I did this for the foreigners. I don't care any less for the Japanese because I also care for foreigners. It's nothing like that. It is just nonsense. He saw through the intent and saw through the agenda at once. But of course, when an agenda is this popular, with our side versus their side, that is very difficult to do.

## Is there a rape scene in *Rashomon*?

### Stephen Prince:

One particular cultural concern that bears further scrutiny has to do with the subject of rape in *Rashomon*, which Janice Matsumura raises in an earlier chapter. Some viewers respond very strongly to the subject of rape, thinking that is what is portrayed in the film. Discussions often arise about the woman's tactical use of seduction versus the bandit's aggression. The larger question concerns what would constitute rape in the film and for a 1950 audience in Japan. Some viewers are convinced that there is no question that rape occurs in the film, while others are doubtful. Do we know anything about Kurosawa's intent, and how might this idea of rape have been understood socially in 1950?

### Donald Richie:

There is both a geographical frame as well as a time frame at work here concerning the subject of rape in *Rashomon*. Things haven't changed in Japan, being a country where rape is still permissible on the screen, if not in life. It is said to be too bad, but it has always been too bad. It's not questioned with the same kind of moral concern as it is now, certainly in North America, and increasingly in Europe. The powers that have managed to change the male mind in these particular countries simply did not exist yet in Japan, and so we still have the usual suspects committing the usual kind of rapes in entertainment films. We don't have a lobby, if that is the word for it, to examine this violation. Women who are concerned with being empowered are not choosing rape as a theme or as a challenge to take action against.

If you look at the recent Japanese films that are coming that are aimed at male audiences, frequently they are extremely violent. This is particularly true of the films of Takeshi Kitano or Takashi Miike, which are misogynist to a degree that would be impermissible in the West today. Machismo was riding strong in Japanese films, so much so that in *Rashomon* it is still routine among Japanese to see the woman as a troublemaker, to see her actions as machinations. She is seen as trying to get the bandit to murder her husband, which means that she's an evil woman, ergo all women are evil. If she hadn't shown her face to the bandit none of this would have happened, or so on and on goes this reductive pattern of thought.

This is rather typical of the male construction of this picture, and one that females are unfortunately too busy doing other things to really contradict. As such, political correctness did not factor into Japanese culture when *Rashomon* was first released and in much of its subsequent circulation. Political correctness in the movies was certainly not discussed, certainly not in the manner that it occurs in Europe, America or Canada. Consequently, when speaking of frameworks, we should consider geographical frames as well as temporal ones, as to how they affect current readings of the possibility of rape even in an old classic such as *Rashomon*.

### Stephen Prince:

Such questions obviously come from a more contemporary perspective. Certainly in cinema, actions such as rape have undergone tremendous reevaluation in the way that they are presented, especially in how actions such as rape are presented by male filmmakers. We can see an evolution in the world of cinema in this regard, in that a male filmmaker in the 1950s would have felt a certain prerogative to portray incidents in a storyline, such as rape, without the kind of consciousness or awareness that a director would inevitably have today or be subjected to today. Consequently there is a sort of disjunction in terms of historical frames of reference, so that when contemporary viewers debate the question of rape in *Rashomon*, they're asking a question that has resonance today, and that a filmmaker today cannot escape. When looking at older films, however, the somewhat paradoxical challenge becomes the need to think oneself back into the circumstances of the period. To do so involves a moment when you suspend your contemporary frame of reference, in an attempt to meet the work on its terms, and then assimilate it and create access to it within the contemporary frame, but also respecting the conditions of the time.

As a male filmmaker, Kurosawa has therefore been quite indifferent to most of his female characters. His world is a very male-centered world. There is a spectacular exception to this, however, in *No Regrets for Our Youth*. Here his protagonist is a young bourgeois woman who overthrows her class heritage and social standing to live and work as a peasant, getting her hands rough and coarsened. Yet for the most part, Kurosawa as a filmmaker doesn't manifest something that has become a contemporary standard for evaluating films: namely a sort of gender inclusiveness in the way the characters are presented. His was a world of adventure, a world of men, and Kurosawa himself has acknowledged this. He has said that he finds his female characters to be relatively peculiar, as indeed they sometimes are.

## Cinematic technique

### Donald Richie:

Stephen, you have made reference elsewhere to Kurosawa's sensual and kinesthetic techniques that gave us a kind of template for modern cinema. In regard to Kurosawa's final three films, you mention that his film style changes in that he developed something that you called a psychobiographical approach, which relied more on techniques of narrative and the personal essay. This would almost seem to be a literary approach to filmmaking.

### Stephen Prince:

Kurosawa's film style does change quite bit in his later films, in that it slows down considerably. There is less that happens in these later movies, whereby there is less going on, less physical activity. The characters in his last films are sitting around and talking about things that are happening off screen, and referring to things in the past that have already happened. On the dramatic level, there is less of the energy and the tensions that we find in the earlier films. At the same time some of his techniques do carry over, and again it is very clear who directed these pictures.

In his later career, Kurosawa loved to shoot with two cameras set at right angles to one another, and then to just let those shots go on for a very long time, so the intervals between the edit points become very lengthy. Yet when these edits do occur, you get a shift in the composition and a shift in the camera's line of slight by ninety degrees. You can see that kind of relation in camera set-ups throughout his career, but it becomes much more pronounced in the later films. The axial cuts, where he will set up a composition and then cut in two closer or two farther away shots along the line of sight established in the initial setup, is there in his first film, *Sanshiro Sugata*, and he is still doing it in his last film, *Madadayo*.

To see someone maintaining this sort of visual identity in his or her work across so many years is tremendously exciting. Kurosawa may have changed cinematographers, but the essentials of how he is filming don't change. Kurosawa doesn't strike me as a director who had to ask his cinematographer where he should put the camera. In terms of the reflective qualities in the late films, I think that there are certainly many filmmakers throughout the world whose movies go in that direction. What I find very striking about Kurosawa is the degree to which it is a stylistic change. This is a different tone that correlates with a different period in life. The reason why this is so striking is that we so rarely see it in cinema, due to the relative brevity of a typical director's career. To be making films across half a century as Kurosawa does is relatively rare, and to have made so many films, so we are able to see that rhythm of the filmmaking change. The rhythms of the shooting and the editing begin to slow down, and I would correlate that with the rhythm of Kurosawa's life.

In his later films he's reflecting upon issues of mortality that are much more personal. He previously made *Ikiru* because he was thinking about death, but it still did not have an existential closeness. In the later films there is a mellowness that takes place, correlated with the artist's aging. With it being unusual in cinema to see that, I think critics were unprepared for it. Yet even at the end of his life, where he was not the filmmaker that he used to be, and where he could not command the medium in the total fashion that he once did, he could still create extraordinary sequences and passages of beauty, and showed us that cinema can be a very personal medium.

### Donald Richie:

We are also provided with a template for modern cinema through Kurosawa's use of sound in his films. His films regularly display a kind of transcendence of reality, particularly through this use of sound. *Throne of Blood*, for example, feels quite dream-like at times, as if everything has slowed down, with the use of both sound effects and silence in the film helping to create this.

### Stephen Prince:

Of all the elements of cinema in the last fifty years, sound has been the one that has undergone the most transformation. Filmmakers today can work with multi-channels – six or seven channels in the final mix. It's routine for modern filmmakers to think in terms of aggressive sound, as a part of the experience. In Kurosawa's day, of course, they worked with one channel of sound, which was of relatively poor quality. The optical track was on the print, and you couldn't have very low noises because they would vanish into the hiss of the film as it goes over the sound head. Really loud noises would exhaust that physical space on the film for the encoded information, and then turn into noise.

Consequently, for most of its history, sound has been a rather recessive element in the aesthetics of cinema. There are really only a handful of filmmakers who used sound in a fully elaborated and very conscious fashion, and Kurosawa was one of those. Kurosawa felt very strongly that sound and image didn't add to one another, but rather multiplied one another. So, as with all the elements in his repertoire of style, he used sound in a very aggressive fashion. It is relatively unusual to notice discrete sound effects on the track in a 1950s film. Typically, dialogue is what would be emphasized in the sound mix, along with the musical score. In Kurosawa's films, however, you remember sound effects. You remember the thudding of horses' hooves, which are unnaturally amplified in *Throne of Blood*, and you remember the whizzing of those arrows. Kurosawa attends to specific effects, and does so to create a very physical audio environment on the screen. Again, in historical terms, he's relatively unique in doing this, because filmmakers didn't have the technological capability for really elaborating the sound dimension of motion pictures. He was ahead of his time in this regard. Imagine what a Kurosawa film would be like today in digital multi-channel sound.

## Literary source material

### Donald Richie:

With regards to *Throne of Blood* and Kurosawa's other Shakespeare films, where the original story becomes transported to another place and time, how do you see Kurosawa's rendering of Shakespeare as compared to other directors, such as Orson Welles?

### Stephen Price:

Kurosawa completely transforms the source material in his Shakespearean adaptations, rendering it into thoroughly indigenous terms. In contrast, Welles feels the need to be faithful to the text. Kurosawa is freed from that, so he is able to think in terms of the cinematic equivalents of the imagery that Shakespeare offers in *Macbeth* and *King Lear*. Furthermore, Kurosawa intuits the historical parallels between his own time, the turmoil of the sixteenth century, and the kind of internecine ongoing patterns of bloodshed that you have in the historical tragedies. Most notable in both cases, Kurosawa darkens the Shakespearean material. In transposing it to a Japanese context, he changes the plays and makes the characters darker. He eliminates some of the moral uplift that is there in *King Lear* and *Macbeth* to create a more timeless view of human perdition and depravity.

These are significant alterations. In cinematic terms, I think one could clearly make the argument that Kurosawa's are the best versions of Shakespeare. It's ironic because you don't have the language, but on the other hand if cinema is a visual medium, and it's the image that counts, then that frees you up. It allows you to think in visual terms, and the visual metaphors that Kurosawa finds for the issues from *Macbeth* in *Throne of Blood* are just stunning – the forest, the patterns of circular movement, and the fog.

### Donald Richie:

Concerning this role of the visual in cinema, there is a distinct sense of realism in Kurosawa's films as compared to a lot of other work. This is created not only through the kinds of visual imagery that you mention, but also in the types of acting, and the content, or the stories. Kurosawa was a masterful storyteller, and the stories that he told always seemed to lose something in the translation when remade by foreign directors. At the end of *Seven Samurai*, for example, Toshiro Mifune makes a comment that the farmers aren't these little innocent bumbling people that he thought they were, but have probably got food stored away, as indeed they did. Yet in the American remake, *The Magnificent Seven*, they're just bumbling.

### Stephen Price:

Yes, because you don't have the historical parallel, and you can't transplant that. You can copy the physical action, and you can copy the set pieces, such as the wood-chopping scene. You can do that, but you can't copy the class structure, because there is no equivalent for that in the American West. The gunfighters were not a class, and it wasn't a hierarchical relationship that they had with farmers. Those things can't be transplanted, and as a result you lose the richness of the original film.

Interestingly, Kurosawa could be maudlin, and in some of his movies he does give vent to that. The end of *The Bad Sleep Well*, for example, becomes tremendously maudlin, and I think there is a little bit of that at the end of *Rashomon* when the woodcutter goes off with the baby. It's hard as a film-maker to strike the right kind of emotional balance. There is a narrative elegance with Kurosawa. He swiftly sets up the premise of his movies, and he often does so in very visual terms. Then the remainder of the film becomes the elaborate working out of that pattern which we intuit from the opening of the film.

It is a narrative grace that many filmmakers today do not have, and one could suggest that there has been a certain loss of narrative skill, a certain loss of the storytelling art in contemporary cinema. This is perhaps largely because you can use technology today to cover up the holes in your story, so to the extent that viewers come to look for effects, rather than characters or situations, there is a loss of that kind of filmmaking. Indeed, Kurosawa's tremendous skill as a storyteller is one of the things that impressed American directors. Certainly there are few things more important in the Hollywood tradition than story, than the narrative.

### Donald Richie:

I also wonder what you think about the idea of the adventure story, and how a lot of the time it would bury some of the trite things in the story in a literary sense, though of course not cinematically.

### Stephen Prince:

What attracted Kurosawa to the adventure story, and so many of his films are adventure stories, is the tremendously fluid set of situations that it gives you as a storyteller. It allows you to take a character who is unformed in some ways, and put them into a situation that is going to test them, and allow them to undergo changes – often radical changes. For Kurosawa, the adventure story becomes a kind of social laboratory, where he can portray his visions of a new, alternative kind of social world by dramatizing the growth of reformist values in characters working for the betterment of other people.

The adventure story offered him a structure in which he could do this. As compared to a director such as Steven Spielberg, who has a sort of adolescent's sense of adventure, for Kurosawa it was the fluidness of the situations and their unpredictability. He has always been attracted to chaos and upheaval, and he feels that from these things character develops, growth occurs, and that enlightenment can result. The adventure story therefore allows him to put his characters in these tremendously unsettled kinds of social worlds, and then show the audience what can come from that.

## Lifework

*Stephen Prince:*

Donald, you provide in Chapter 10 your assessment of what Kurosawa is likely to leave to viewers both in the East and in the West. I would like to hope, as you do, that those qualities in the films that have spoken to each of us so directly, and with such compassion, will continue to do so. What remains finally is the work. The individual, the artist, passes on, and after all it is the work that will last and will continue to speak to new generations. Art sometimes manifests a utopian impulse. The artist tries, in their art, to work through problems that are often very difficult to work through in life, and I think that Kurosawa's films show this.

You raise the question of Kurosawa's moral legacy, because for him cinema was a vehicle for instruction. It was also a vehicle for entertainment, as he used popular storytelling to reach his large audience. But it wasn't for the same reason that so many directors today want to reach a large audience, which is to make a lot of money. For Kurosawa, it was to reach out and to impart lessons. Lessons in the nature of responsible living, which so often come down to the scenario of an individual working for the benefit of others. The master/pupil, teacher/pupil relationship recurs in so many of the films, and became Kurosawa's vehicle for illustrating the transmission of utopian values, and also by implication for sharing them from film to viewer.

Therefore in *Drunken Angel*, we have the doctor and the gangster locked in a kind of struggle, where one is attempting to show the other that life can be different. In *Seven Samurai*, those are Kambei and Katsushiro, the leader of the samurai and the youngest of them. In *Red Beard*, Niide and Yasumoto, the doctor and the intern, give us this pattern of learning and change. In the pessimistic films such as *Throne of Blood*, we do not have a master/pupil relationship. In that kind of film, Kurosawa instructs by way of negative example, by showing a world that is given over entirely to the forces of destruction, the passion for ambition, power and violence.

I agree very much with your assessment that it is this moral legacy that is the important thing of Kurosawa's films. Many directors who were influenced by Kurosawa do not share that utopian impulse. We are left, in the end, with the films, and while audiences may have changed I am still hopeful that people will continue to see the worthy things that Kurosawa has shown us in his work.

I wonder if you could speak further about Kurosawa's legacy in light of how he was regarded by other directors. Nagisi Oshima's most recent film, *Gohatto*, was an homage to Kurosawa. How do you relate this to the notion those directors such as Oshima and Immimura were reacting in their films against the older directors such as Ozu and Kurosawa?

*Donald Richie:*

There was a strong feeling among many of the younger directors in Japan, particularly when Ozu died, that it was time to do something else. There was a definite reaction against Ozu, but this did not last all that long after his death. Now Ozu is the most appreciated of all the Japanese film directors, though sometimes for the wrong reasons. This has also occurred to Kurosawa. The reason for the initial turn against him was that the younger group of directors, or rather the Shochiku Motion Picture Company which was behind that group, decided that they needed a new slogan, or a new logo. The company called them *la nouvelle vague Japonaise*, although they were no such thing. They were billed as Young Turks who were out to make the world a better place by making better cinema.

Indeed, one such member from another company, Yasuzo Masamura, climbed on any number of soapboxes stating that Kurosawa was himself what's wrong with Japanese cinema, and that therefore they had to destroy the system. Certainly there was an establishment, but it was an establishment that you would never have heard of, full of second-rate directors doing the same things over and over again. This was the proper target of the newer generation, but they did not see that until much later. Oshima eventually felt quite badly about his treatment of Kurosawa. He never treated Kurosawa badly directly, but he treated him badly in the press. Hence when Kurosawa won the Kyoto Prize and a dinner was held for him, all of a sudden there was Oshima, practically in full formal obeisance on the *tatami*, saying, Sensei, Sensei, forgive me, forgive me!

Obviously the climate of opinions has changed, and Oshima changed even more. Oshima had been through a lot, suffering a disabling stroke that would have killed anyone else, and yet through sheer willpower and courage he managed to pull himself back from the brink. He got the use of his right hand and then his right leg, and then he stopped the sag on his face. He got it together somehow to make the film *Gohatto*. The film is filled, as you can imagine, with experience and with a kind of severity, but he's still up to his old tricks. It's an extremely subversive film, but very successfully so in the way that he does it. He has sword fights in it because it's a period film, and these duels owe a lot to Kurosawa. He even used the same sword master that Kurosawa used. Oshima aimed in *Gohatto* for that kind of authenticity for which he originally scolded Kurosawa. This, plus the fact that he worked extremely hard on the film's color schemes to give it a kind of autumnal beauty, plus the severity of the film's seriousness and the dedication with which it was made, indicates a rapprochement to the ideals of Kurosawa, which allows me to say that it is a kind of homage. I don't think he'd mind my saying that.

## Does Kurosawa reveal much about himself?

*Stephen Prince:*

As you know, Kurosawa's autobiography – *Something Like an Autobiography* – only goes up to 1950. It would be interesting to learn his version of his life after 1950. Were there ever any plans to work on a second part to his autobiography?

### Donald Richie:

I don't believe so. I know that he was very dissatisfied with that autobiography, hence that down-putting title, which is even worse in Japanese. He hated that kind of revelation. It was originally run as a series of newspaper installments. He did it because a newspaper offered him a lot of money at a time when he really needed it. It's extraordinarily well done, but his heart wasn't in it, and when he got to *Rashomon* he'd had enough. I don't believe he ever did write more, nor ever intended to, nor ever regretted that he hadn't done it.

### Stephen Prince:

It's a curious autobiography, and having what we do have gives us an instance of the artist narrating their life as if they were a character in the movie that they make. You read the book and you're struck again and again by scenes that have the kind of visual quality that you find in a Kurosawa film, and incidents that you could easily envision him dramatizing. It's the aestheticizing of the life that is the fascinating part of the autobiography. Not so much whether it is factually true or not, but the aesthetic filter through which his memories are passing is so strongly like the artistic profile that we know in the film that it's almost as if there is a fictionalized tendency that comes in to the autobiography. It becomes a story that he is telling as much as a life that he is remembering.

I was once asked what I thought Kurosawa considered to be his greatest screen achievement in his career. Kurosawa always said that he liked his last film best.

### Donald Richie:

That's right. Or better yet, he always liked the one he was going to make – the next one.

### Stephen Prince:

The nature of filmmaking is such that you watch the footage again and again and again, especially if you're an editor. You watch it again and again and again. This is perhaps why directors often say that they don't go back and look at their movies after they have finished with them. They have internalized it and they can see it in their minds, and also at some level they are tired of it. Hence they go on to make the next one.

***Donald Richie:***

In the case of Kurosawa, he didn't even want to talk about his old films. When I was writing a book, I would go talk to him and ask him, 'but didn't this really mean something?' He always got very impatient and said, 'look, if I have to tell you this, then I didn't do a very good job in doing the film, did I?' On the other hand, if you were willing to talk about the next film – that is, to listen while he told you about the next film – then he was available for hours on end.

Kurosawa gave almost no small talk at all when you spoke to him. He could only talk about his work. He didn't pass the time of day. He couldn't do it really, because he wasn't interested in anything except what he was involved in. He was truly, absolutely hands-on with the films, and he just didn't have any more hands left for small talk. I have never known anybody so absolutely what we could call a workaholic. He absolutely plunged into whatever it was that he was doing.

Publicity still featuring Machiko Kyo as the samurai's wife and Toshiro Mifune as the bandit. The bandit Tajomaru points deeper into the grove, deceiving the samurai's wife into believing that her husband is in trouble and needs her help. Finger-pointing in *Rashomon* may be seen as symbolic of deceit and self-exoneration through placing blame on others. When Rashomon was released in 1950, Japan had experienced a series of war crimes trials. Was Kurosawa using mythic history to remind his audience of the films' connection with the present? (Courtesy of Kadokawa Corporation)

# 13 Conclusion

## Ripples and effects

*Robert Anderson, Blair Davis and Jan Walls*

When Rashomon entered the arena of international cinema it made a splash which resulted in ripples, and its ripple effects are still expanding well into the twenty-first century. *Rashomon* has been rescreened, studied and discussed for over sixty years. The conversation about the film has co-evolved with the international understanding of Kurosawa himself. In addition to his other successes and his astonishing rise to prominence, the meanings of *Rashomon* have spread to cultural domains beyond film. Although this is concurrent with the appearance of a wider cinematic influence in modern culture itself and part of its globalizing tendencies, the spread of meaning cannot be explained by globalization alone, nor does globalization subtract from the extraordinary reach of Kurosawa's specific influence. Our conclusions focus first on the filmic influence, and then on the other wider dimensions touched by *Rashomon*, and finally on the transcending power of Kurosawa and his art.

To begin, a personal anecdote serves to allow us to explore several dynamics of Kurosawa's legacy. One of us, Robert Anderson, used stills from *Rashomon* in a university lecture in Tokyo in 2003; an image of the confrontation in the forest was used to remind the audience about negotiation, and an image of the men under the rainy gate was used to remind the audience about dialogue. After the lecture, a man came up to talk, accompanied by his twelve-year-old grandson. I have not seen it for years, he said, but your pictures brought it all back. He continued, prodding his grandson forward: He has not seen it, and he really should, said the man of his grandson. Oh, and why? asked Anderson. Because it has become part of our history, flashed the grandfather without hesitation. Grinning, he added, I will go to the video shop tomorrow and get it for him to see, I am sure we can find it.

This is an example of one way in which *Rashomon* can be passed down to new generations of viewers. Yet as Donald Richie tells us, Kurosawa's work has not had a lasting moral or ethical impact on contemporary Japanese youth, as the director had hoped. Andrew Horvat, a veteran journalist based in Japan, notes how at a branch of Japan's largest video rental chain (*Tsutaya*) the young staff do not know about *Rashomon*, and have to ask customers to spell the title so as to look it up on the computer. Horvat notes that while it would be an exaggeration to suggest that *Rashomon* has been forgotten in

Japan, it can be said that the film has not had the same lasting impact either intellectually or culturally in Japan that it has had abroad. He sees an enormous gap between Kurosawa's international reputation as one of the twentieth century's greatest film artists – with intellectuals and critics continuing to value the moral-ethical questions posed by his films – and his legacy at home in Japan as an eccentric cultural icon (Horvat 2006).

### *Rashomon*'s media legacies

In addition to its intellectual legacy the film has had an enormous impact on popular culture, inspiring a multitude of adaptations and remakes and becoming reimagined in a number of different film genres (see Appendix II *Rashomon*'s Media Legacies for an annotated list). In fact, *Rashomon* has become part of the lexicon or vocabulary of modern entertainment, serving as the inspiration for a multitude of creative projects in a variety of media. Within ten years of its initial release two adaptations of the film's story emerged, each in a different medium. One came from Broadway, the other from the confines of a television studio, yet each remains relatively obscure. As discussed in our Introduction, 1959 saw the debut of *Rashomon* on Broadway in a play adapted from the Akutagawa stories by Fay and Michael Kanin. The cast featured such renowned Hollywood actors as Rod Steiger, Claire Bloom, Akim Tamiroff and Oskar Homolka. The play is still performed by modern theater companies, having been adapted by several American theater companies, including the Interactive Asian Contemporary Theatre in 1997, the University of Pittsburgh Repertory Theatre in 2005, and the Mad Cow Theatre in 2011. Furthermore, British playwright Glyn Maxwell adapted *Rashomon* to a contemporary setting in his play *Broken Journey*, which was premiered in America in 2006 by the Phoenix Theatre Ensemble. American playwright Eric Mikes Glover also created a musical in 2006 entitled *See What I Wanna See*, drawing upon Akutagawa's *Rashomon* and *In a Grove* for much of its narrative.

The success of the Kanins' play in 1959 attracted the attention of producers in both film and television. *Rashomon* reached an even larger audience in 1960 when the play was adapted for television. Directed by Sidney Lumet, who had previously dealt with notions of crime, truth and memory just three years earlier in the 1957 film *Twelve Angry Men*, the TV *Rashomon* again starred Oskar Homolka, along with Ricardo Montalban of *Fantasy Island* fame. In 1961, the BBC offered its own television production of *Rashomon*, again based on the Kanins' play. Unfortunately, there is scant opportunity to study this notable broadcast; little has been written about it, and neither episode is available on video, although archival prints are available.

*Rashomon* has also been transported to several Hollywood genres. The Kanins' play was adapted into a Western for director Martin Ritt's *The Outrage* (1964), with Claire Bloom reprising her Broadway role – though now in a different cultural context – alongside stars Paul Newman, Edward G. Robinson and William Shatner. With other remakes of Kurosawa's films such as *The Magnificent Seven* (1960) and *A Fistful of Dollars* (1964), it has become impossible to speak of Hollywood remakes of foreign movies without mentioning Kurosawa. Articles about the remakes of Asian horror films such as *The Ring* (2002) and *The Grudge* (2004) commonly describe the phenomenon as part of a larger trend which began with the aforementioned remakes of Kurosawa's films.

Far less well known than these Western retellings is the low-budget biker film remake of *Rashomon* from 1971 entitled *Angels Hard as They Come*, which also has the distinction of being Jonathan Demme's first film. The future director of *Silence of the Lambs* (1989) wrote and produced this story of a Hells Angels motorcycle gang out to avenge a rape in a small town. While the film is only a very loose adaptation (and was not particularly well received nor well remembered), Demme insists that it was indeed inspired by the Kurosawa film.

In July 2001, *Variety* reported that *Rashomon* might be transported to yet another film genre, as Kurosawa's son Hisao sold the remake rights to his father's film to a Los Angeles production company for a sum in the high six figures. Initially budgeted at $40 million, the remake was proposed as a thriller set in the present day, with the tentative title *Rashomon: Where Truth Lies* (Dunkley 2001). The film did not reach the production stage, and while some might decry the idea of such a remake it is nevertheless emblematic of the continued interest in and relevance of Kurosawa's film in modern Hollywood. *Rashomon* became reimagined, for example, as a computer-animated cartoon-musical in the 2005 film *Hoodwinked*, adapting the story of Little Red Riding Hood into *Rashomon*'s flashback structure. The fairy tale is examined from four different perspectives via a police investigation, with flashback retellings told by Red, the wolf, granny and the woodsman. The film offers a whimsical approach to the relativism of truth and the unreliability of memory with such lines of dialogue as, Let's just say that if a tree falls in the forest you'll get three stories – yours, mine and the tree's.

A 2006 episode of *CSI: Crime Scene Investigation* entitled 'Rashomama' utilized on television a similar flashback structure as a mother's death is investigated. Replacing the gate setting with CSI headquarters, a dialogue occurs among the various investigators as they sit around an evidence table comparing witness interviews. The episode is therefore largely divided into two settings: the crime scene and the aftermath back at the lab, in keeping with *Rashomon*'s forest/gate dichotomy. In a larger sense, the episode's title and narrative structure serve as a sort of commentary on how CSI constantly utilizes speculative what-if flashbacks while they attempt to recreate how crimes could have occurred. That the show would title one of its episodes after *Rashomon* is seemingly an acknowledgment by the producers of just how much this central structural element of the show is indebted to the film.

## Rippling Rashomon effects

*Rashomon* has already been turned into a Broadway play, TV movie, a Western, a biker film and an animated musical, yet the original film still retains its enduring cultural and cinematic relevance. As the *CSI* television episode title indicates, *Rashomon* has become part of the common parlance of the entertainment industry. But the influence does not end there – there is reference to *Rashomon* in news, in courts, in universities and in the streets. And the idea of the Rashomon effect appears again and again in unusual places, such as in a well-informed observer's interpretation of the differences between the Israeli Cabinet and the Chiefs of Staff regarding Israel's military interventions in Lebanon in July–August 2006. The editor-in-chief of the Tel Aviv newspaper *Haaretz* said that listening to the two groups explaining their reasoning and justification 'was like *Rashomon* – they [the Chiefs of Staff and the Cabinet] were talking about the same thing but had quite different versions' (Landau 2006: n.p.). Now you may conclude that this extension of the awareness of a Japanese film made in 1950 is simply a corollary of the profound interpenetration of modern cultures and international cinema, that they are co-evolving, and this is proof of it. But that would gloss over a world of detail in which this particular film has been screened and discussed, and rescreened and debated in countless specific circumstances, each contributing incrementally to *Rashomon*'s reputation. This energy generates what we are calling the ripple effect. When by the end of the twentieth century, producers, directors and screenwriters combined to tilt films (or parts of them) toward the sensibilities of different audiences in various countries, we must remember that there was no such tilting in *Rashomon*, and no intention to transcend the specific audience before which it was set in 1950. So in that sense its influence was unintentional.

But even as a modern silver screen film, it might have had a standard, predictable exposure lasting a short period, in which it just earned for its producers twice as much money as it cost them to make the film. After a standard release for Japanese audiences it was put on the shelf until the Italiafilm representative, Giuliana Stramigioli, who had no great personal interest in it, happened to view it, liked it, and urged that it be nominated to one of the most prestigious film festivals in Europe. Ms. Stramigioli's effort succeeded, and so it was subtitled and then screened in Italy before it was appraised at Venice. So an Italian initiative succeeded in spite of indifference and doubt in Japan's official and industrial circles concerning the film's merits. This very bounded creation was suddenly unbound. The filmmakers had both steeped themselves in the literary and artistic traditions around them, and mastered the cinematic techniques and conventions available across the world. They were in a position to innovate, but had no intention to do so beyond the film industry in Japan.

It was precisely the intersection of domestic innovation (Kurosawa's new techniques and conventions for conveying Japanese contents) and international communication (selection and screening in Italy and Venice, and then the huge US market) that brought an ancient Konjaku tale, Akutagawa, Kurosawa and Mifune into world cinematic history. This process of amplification continues, and includes the way in which the film has been transported to a variety of different media (including stage and television within ten years) and genres (Western, biker film, detective film), and has become a subtext in the lexicon of popular culture (*CSI*, *Hoodwinked*, *Simpsons*, etc.). Here we see again how the ripples that *Rashomon* created have extended outward ever since its debut.

Two fields of endeavor, translation and international circulation, have dramatically enhanced interlingual, intercultural and intermedia fertilization and cross-cultural inspiration such as we have examined with regard to the evolution of *Rashomon* and the Rashomon effect. We may cite just one other example: Kurosawa himself has stated that a major source for the plot of *Yojimbo* (1961) was *The Glass Key* (1942), a film adaptation of Dashiell Hammett's 1931 novel, and other scholars have suggested that the plot of *Yojimbo* is actually much closer to another Dashiell Hammett novel, *Red Harvest* (1929) (Desser 1983: 33). Three years after the release of *Yojimbo*, Sergio Leone directed its remake as a spaghetti Western starring Clint Eastwood in his first appearance as the Man with No Name. Dashiell Hammett's seminal influence has continued with *Last Man Standing* (1996), an authorized remake of *Yojimbo* as a prohibition era gangster film directed by Walter Hill and starring Bruce Willis. Interestingly enough, Bruce Willis is featured in the 2006 film *Lucky Number Slevin*, which has been described by many as a contemporary updating of *Yojimbo* (Total Film 2006). But that study would be the stuff of another book. Martinez calls these interlingual and intercultural effects 'permutations' of *Rashomon* (Martinez, 2009: 65).

## Concluding remarks

When a stone is cast into a pond, the water is inevitably affected. If cast with great force, the ripples created by the stone will be substantial and so reverberate through the pond with visible results. But if cast with only minimal force, the stone will have a relatively minor effect in the pond and may not produce an observable impact. In spite of the varying amount of force used in each case, the stone has undoubtedly altered the water: so too has cinema been forever altered by the appearance of *Rashomon* in 1950. Its initial impact on Japanese filmmaking was relatively minor because its ripples had not yet reached foreign shores. But when cast into the waters of international film festivals, audiences and awards, the film's impact on world cinema and Japan soon began to be felt. This impact initially took the form of the numerous awards that *Rashomon* received, and soon led to the film being adapted into new media and genres. Eventually, *Rashomon*'s distinctive formal elements and narrative strategies came to be utilized not only by countless filmmakers, but also by artists working in a wide variety of media and art forms around the world.

*Rashomon*'s impact was not just in the creative processes of others, however. Its ripples extended beyond the realm of the arts into such academic disciplines as philosophy, sociology, anthropology and literary studies, among others. Few films have been so regularly drawn upon by as wide an array of scholars as *Rashomon* has. Yet the film has had an effect not only on how academics think, but also on intellectuals and professionals in an ever-growing number of social contexts. As shown throughout this book, the Rashomon effect has been used by those in the fields of law, journalism, the military and a host of others as a way of describing a universal human phenomenon.

We have shown how *Rashomon* has had multiple effects on its audience, changing not only how we think about cinema, and how we think about the human condition, but also how we have come to see it through a cinematic lens. *Rashomon*'s impact rippled outward after its debut over sixty years ago and will undoubtedly continue to extend even further outward for generations to come.

# Appendix I: The Rashomon effect in the social sciences

The movement of the core ideas in *Rashomon* into the social sciences was gradual but eventually profound. Anthropologists, among others, encountered, spoke and wrote about the Rashomon effect since the 1960s, having received quite divergent accounts of the same communities and cultures from two (or more) different individuals. Sociology, psychology, law, history, philosophy slowly followed this pattern; some references to *Rashomon* were slight, others more carefully studied.

Irving Louis Horowitz tried to use the Rashomon effect in his 1987 sociological study of the IMF, but lacked a detailed grasp of how the effect actually works. Other social sciences gradually adopted this metaphor from a literary source: an early use of the Rashomon effect was Sarah Halperin's 1991 book in Hebrew on *Rashomon*'s influence in Israeli fiction writing. Allan Mazur's book about the Rashomon effect at Love Canal in New York appeared in 1998. I have already referred to the work of legal academic Orit Kamir who provided a feminist viewing of *Rashomon*, on a scene-by-scene basis.[1] About the same time Ann Althouse, senior law professor, assembled in 2000 evidence of the recent uses of *Rashomon* in the political culture of the United States; she tried to rescue her more nuanced viewing of the film from popular simplifications.[2] See also psychoanalyst Herbert Stein's 2001 analogy for *Rashomon* as a therapeutic séance. Another important conversation, this time between philosophers including Ludwig Wittgenstein, Karl Popper, Bertrand Russell (among others), suggested a Rashomon effect treatment to authors David Edmonds and John Eidinow. In October 1946, Popper came to Kings College at Cambridge University to give a talk to a group dominated by Wittgenstein. Russell attended out of curiosity along with other distinguished philosophers. In the middle of Popper's short presentation Wittgenstein picked up a poker, handled it (and either brandished it, fondled it, made a point with it, gestured with it, etc.), and then suddenly left the room. This short incident, understood from different points of view, is richly captured in thick description by *Wittgenstein's Poker: The Story of a Ten-Minute Argument between Two Great Philosophers* (Edmonds and Eidinow 2001).

A field study in 2001 of two high school shootings in Kentucky and Arkansas relied on the interpretive quality of the Rashomon effect (the authors called it interpretivism) and was published in 2002, though its treatment of *Rashomon* is rather slight (Roth and Metha 2002). There is a 2003 study about the relation of *Rashomon* to the interpretation of press treatments of repression of the Black Panther party in 1967–73 called 'A Multi-Source Analysis of Contentious Events Based on Five Newspapers' (Davenport and Litras 2003: n.p.). Continuing the theme of using film as the material for thinking about philosophical concepts, Burton Porter's work in 2004 focused on understanding epistemology by thinking about *Rashomon*. The list grows and grows, and can best be seen on various sites on the Internet.

## Notes

1  Kamir 2000; 2005: 269; 2006.
2  See also Brion 2006.

# Appendix II: *Rashomon*'s media legacies

*Rashomon* has been transported to numerous different media, genres and cultural forms, having been adapted by (or serving as the inspiration for) screenwriters, playwrights, musicians, novelists and many other such creators. The film's influence is thus truly global, with artists from around the world presenting the narrative logic and/or themes of *Rashomon* to local, national and international audiences in new ways, often using new forms that Kurosawa could not have anticipated. In this way we see the second Rashomon effect at work, as the film begins to reach wider audiences by way of these new interpretations: the power of the film begins to transcend its source material as new artists discover new aesthetic strategies through which they can relate *Rashomon*'s meanings to new audiences.

What follows is a selected compendium of the many ways in which *Rashomon* has been brought to different media.

## Films

In the decades following *Rashomon*'s release, the film was adapted into a variety of genres, including the Western, biker film and animated musical. In doing so, *Rashomon*'s themes have been introduced to a wide variety of audiences in new countries, using different cultural traditions of storytelling and filmmaking. In so doing, *Rashomon* proves not only its malleability as a narrative, but also the universality of its content.

*Rashomon* (1950) 88 minutes, Japan, alternate title *Rasho-Mon* (USA); Akira Kurosawa, director; Akira Kurosawa and Shinobu Hashimoto, screenplay; adapted from Ryunosuke Akutagawa's *Rashomon* and *In a Grove*; Minoru Jingo, producer; Masaichi Nagata, executive producer; Fumio Hayasaka, music; Kazuo Miyagawa, cinematographer; Akira Kurosawa, editor; George W. Davis and Tambi Larsen, art directors.

Cast: Toshiro Mifune, Tajomaru; Machiko Kyo, Masago; Masayuki Mori, Takehiro; Takashi Shimura, woodcutter; Minoru Chiaki, priest; Kichijiro Ueda, commoner; Fumiko Honma, medium; Daisuke Kato, policeman.

*The Outrage* (1964) 97 minutes, USA; Martin Ritt, director; Michael Kanin, screenplay; adapted from Fay and Michael Kanin's play *Rashomon*, Akira Kurosawa and Shinobu Hashimoto's screenplay *Rashomon*, and Ryunosuke Akutagawa's stories *In a Grove* and *Rashomon*; A. Ronald Lubin, producer; Michael Kanin, associate producer; Alex North, music; James Wong Howe, cinematographer; Frank Santillo, editor; Daniel McCauley, assistant director; Don Feld, costume design.

Cast: Paul Newman, Juan Carrasco; Claire Bloom, Nina Wakefield; Laurence Harvey, Colonel Wakefeld; Edward G. Robinson, con man; William Shatner, preacher; Howard Da Silva, prospector; Albert Salmi, sheriff; Thomas Chalmers, judge; Paul Fix, Indian.

While it has been overshadowed by other films such as *The Magnificent Seven* and *A Fistful of Dollars*, Martin Ritt's *The Outrage* also adapts a Kurosawa film to the Western genre. Here the Rashomon gate becomes an old train station, with the forest setting replaced by the desert. Paul Newman plays a Mexican bandit, introducing issues of race as well as class into the murder of the Caucasian military officer Wakefield. Claire Bloom once again plays the character of the wife, after starring in the 1959 Broadway production.

*Angels Hard as They Come* (1971) 85 minutes, USA, alternate titles *Angel Warriors* (Europe: English title); *Angels*; *Angels, Hell on Harleys*; Joe Viola, director; Jonathan Demme and Joe Viola, screenplay; Jonathan Demme, producer; Roger Corman, executive producer; Stephen Katz, cinematographer; Jack Fisk, art director; Richard Hieronymous, music.

Cast: Scott Glen, Long John; Charles Dierkop, General; James Inglehart, Monk; Gilda Texter, Astrid; Gary Littlejohn, Axe; Gary Busey, Henry; Don Carerra, Jucier; Brendan Kelly, Brain; Janet Wood, Vicki.

While appearing to be a lurid biker B-movie on the surface, producer/writer Jonathan Demme declares that this film was directly inspired by *Rashomon*, depicting the consequences of a murder that occurs in a hippie commune. The film is very loose in its adaptive strategies, at times bearing only a very casual connection to the original film, yet Demme has been adamant about his passion for *Rashomon* and his desire to embed as many of its themes as possible into this low-budget production.

*Iron Maze* (1992) 104 minutes, Hiroaki Yoshida, director; Tim Metcalfe, screenwriter; adapted from Ryunosuke Akutagawa's story *In a Grove*; Ilona Herzberg and Hidenori Ueki, producers; Taiichi Inoue and Janet Yang, associate producers; Edward R. Pressman, Oliver Stone, Katsumi Kimura and Hidenori Taga, executive producers; Morio Saegusa, cinematographer; Gary Kosko, art director; Stanley Myers, music; Bonnie Koehler, editor.

Cast: Jeff Fahey, Barry Mikowski; Bridget Fonda, Chris Sugata; Hiroaki Murakami, Sugito; J.T. Walsh, Jack Ruhle; John Randolph, Mayor Peluso; Peter Allas, Eddie; Gabriel Damon, Mikey.

A suspense thriller loosely adapted from Akutagawa's *In a Grove* about the attempted murder of a Japanese businessman in a small American town. The investigation turns up conflicting accounts of the crime that are explored through various flashbacks. The film's advertising features the obviously *Rashomon*-inspired tagline: Passion. Betrayal. Murder. Three different stories. Three different lies.

*Rashomon: Where Truth Lies* (2001) Kurosawa Productions, Harbour Light Entertainment.

This film project was announced in 2001, although it stalled early in development and there are currently no plans for its continuation. Production was expected to begin in 2002 with a budget of $40 million, for a planned 2003 release. Promoted as a crime thriller, the project was imagined as an English-language remake of *Rashomon* set in the contemporary period. No cast, director or screenwriter was ever announced.

*Hoodwinked* (2005) 80 minutes, USA, alternate title *Hoodwinked! The True Story of Red Riding Hood*; Cory Edwards, Todd Edwards and Tony Leech, directors; Cory Edwards, Todd Edwards and Tony Leech, screenplay; Maurice Kanbat, David Lovegren, Sue Bea Montgomery and Preston Stutzman, producers; Katie Hooten, associate producer; John Mark, painter; Kristin Wilkinson, music; Tony Leech, editor; Dan Malvin, production supervisor.

Cast: Anne Hathaway, Red (voice); Glenn Close, Granny (voice); James Belushi, woodsman (voice); Patrick Warburton, wolf (voice); Anthony Anderson, detective Bill Stork (voice); David Ogden Stiers, Nicky Flippers (voice); Xzibit, Chief Grizzly (voice); Chazz Palminteri, Woolworth (voice); Andy Dick, Boingo (voice).

This computer-animated film plays like a cartoon-musical version of *Rashomon* using the children's story of *Little Red Riding Hood*. Like *Rashomon*, the criminal events of the story are examined via a police investigation, with each of the four participants telling a different version of the proceedings.

## Plays

Theater was in fact the first medium that saw *Rashomon* adapted to it, and it has proven to be a dynamic form through which artists have reinterpreted the film in numerous ways. While Fay and Michael Kanin's 1959 adaptation of *Rashomon* for the stage has remained the most popular version, many other playwrights have created new stage adaptations of the film and Akutagawa's stories, utilizing bold formal strategies in their presentation of the Rashomon effect.

*Rashomon* (1959) Fay and Michael Kanin, authors; adapted from Ryunosuke Akutagawa's *Rashomon* and *In a Grove*; published in 1959,

New York: Random House; opened 27 January 1959, closed 13 June 1959, Music Box Theatre, New York; Peter Glenville, director, David Susskind and Hardy Smith, producers; Michael Abbott, associate producer; Laurence Rosenthal, music; Peter Glenville, staging; Oliver Messel, scenic and costume design; Jo Mielziner, lighting design.

Cast: Rod Steiger, bandit; Claire Bloom, wife; Noel Willman, husband; Akim Tamiroff, woodcutter; Oskar Homolka, wigmaker; Michael Shillo, priest; Elsa Freed, medium; Ruth White, mother.

The Kanins' 1959 adaptation of the Akutagawa stories proved to be extremely popular, serving as the basis of two 1960s television productions and the 1964 film *The Outrage*. The 1959 Broadway run starred several Hollywood actors: Rod Steiger (*On the Waterfront, Doctor Zhivago, In the Heat of the Night*), Claire Bloom (*Richard III, The Haunting, The Spy Who Came in from the Cold*), Akim Tamiroff (*For Whom the Bell Tolls, Touch of Evil, Ocean's 11*), and Oskar Homolka (*Sabotage, Ball of Fire, The Seven Year Itch*). It was nominated for three Tony awards: Peter Glenville for direction, and Oliver Messel for both scenic design and costume design. The play is still regularly performed by modern theater companies.

*Rashomon* (2000) Pangea World Theatre (Minneapolis, Minnesota), Meena Natarajan and Luu Pham, authors; Dipankar Mukherji, director; adapted from Ryunosuke Akutagawa's *Rashomon* and *In a Grove*.

This adaptation of Akutagawa's stories is set ten years after the disputed crime from *In a Grove*, using a judge as the central character who must navigate the case's conflicting testimonies. His doubts about the case reemerge after a chance encounter with a woman who is passing through Kyoto. The play features only three actors in its examination of the Rashomon effect.

*Broken Journey* (2005) Phoenix Theatre Ensemble (New York City), Glyn Maxwell, author; adapted from Ryunosuke Akutagawa's *In a Grove* and Akira Kurosawa's film *Rashomon*; Ted Altschuler, director.

A contemporary reimagining of *Rashomon*, British playwright and poet Glyn Maxwell's *Broken Journey* presents a police investigation into the death of wealthy playboy Andre and the possible rape of his girlfriend Chloe on a deserted highway the previous night. A biker named Troy is the primary suspect, and a psychic is brought in to channel the departed Andre. Maxwell uses iambic pentameter for the characters' dialogue as they explore the multiple versions of the event that are recounted.

*See What I Wanna See* (2006) The Public Theatre (New York City), Michael John LaChiusa, author and music; Ted Sperling, director; adapted from Ryunosuke Akutagawa's *In a Grove* and *Rashomon*.

A musical based on Akutagawa's stories, LaChiusa's *See What I Wanna See* balances scenes in medieval Japan and 1950s New York, as well as in New York in 2005. Conflicting versions of events are recounted in these parallel stories of murder and deceit.

## Television productions

*Rashomon* first appeared on American television ten years after the film's debut in Japan, and was quickly transported to British television. In the decades that followed, television creators would pay tribute to the film by using the basic *Rashomon* structure of conflicting accounts of an event, often playing with the film's title in the episode names.

*Rashomon* (1960) USA, 60 minutes, Series: Play of the Week, original airdate 12 December 1960, Season Two, Episode 12; Sidney Lumet, director; based on Fay and Michael Kanin's play *Rashomon* and Ryunosuke Akutagawa's stories *In a Grove* and *Rashomon*.

Cast: Ricardo Montalban, bandit; Carol Lawrence, wife; James Mitchell, husband; Michael Higgins, woodcutter; Oskar Homolka, wigmaker; Michael Shillo, priest; Osceola Archer, medium.

The first production to adapt Fay and Michael Kanin's play to another medium, this television version of *Rashomon* was directed by Sidney Lumet who had previously explored notions of truth and legality in the film *Twelve Angry Men* (1957). Oskar Homolka and Michael Shillo reprised their respective roles as the wigmaker and the priest from the play's initial run on Broadway.

*Rashomon* (1961) Britain, 90 minutes, original airdate 3 March 1961; Rudolph Cartier, director; based on Fay and Michael Kanin's play *Rashomon* and Ryunosuke Akutagawa's stories *In a Grove* and *Rashomon*; Rudolph Cartier, producer; Laurence Rosenthal, music; Clifford Hatts, production designer.

Cast: Lee Montague, bandit; Yoko Tani, wife; Robert Hardy, husband; Richard Pearson, woodcutter; Cyril Shaps, wigmaker; Roy Patrick, bailiff; Hira Talfrey, mother; Eileen Way, medium.

Produced for the BBC, this was the second television production of the Kanins' play. It is available at the BBC Television archives.

*All in the Family* (1973) 'Everybody Tells the Truth', original airdate 3 March 1973, Season 3, Episode 58, Production no. 321.

Inspired by *Rashomon*, and with a title indicative of the Rashomon effect, this episode of the hit show starring Carroll O'Conner centers around a broken refrigerator, with each member of the Bunker family recounting very different versions of what happened that day.

*Diff'rent Strokes* (1983) 'Rashomon II', original airdate 22 October 1983, Season 6, Episode 3.

With its title imagining itself as a kind of sequel to *Rashomon*, this episode of the popular sitcom starring Gary Coleman features different accounts of a burglary.

*Mama's Family* (1983) 'Rashomama', original airdate 3 November 1983, Season 2, Episode 5.

A spin-off from *The Carol Burnett Show*, this sitcom portrays two spinster sisters who take in several family members to their home. This episode features the multiple accounts of various characters when Mama has an accident.

*Hooperman* (1987) 'Rashomanny', original airdate 1 February 1989, Season 2, Episode 8.

This comedy-drama starred John Ritter as a police officer who inherits an apartment building. This episode centers on a compromising incident with a female suspect whose version of the events differs from Hooperman's.

*Star Trek: The Next Generation* (1990) 'A Matter of Perspective', original airdate 10 February 1990, Season 3, Episode 14.

This episode of the popular science fiction program stemming from the original *Star Trek* series of the 1960s finds the characters recounting different perspectives about a murder and explosion. The testimony of each witness is displayed visually via the virtual reality capability of the holodeck room.

*Players* (1997) 'Rashocon', original airdate 5 December 1997, Season 1, Episode 7.

A drama about three con artists recruited by the FBI, this episode features an interrogation that results in multiple accounts of an armored truck robbery.

*The Simpsons* (1999) 'Thirty Minutes over Tokyo', original airdate 16 May 1999, Season 10, Episode 226.

In this episode of the popular animated sitcom, the Simpsons travel to Japan and compete on the game show *The Happy Smile Super Challenge Family Wish Show*. Along the way they encounter sumo wrestlers, work in a fish-gutting plant, and get attacked by the giant monsters Godzilla, Mothra and Rodan. When Marge tells Homer, "Japan will be fun! You liked *Rashomon*!" He replies, "that's not how I remember it!"

*Cover Me: Based on the True Life of an FBI Family* (2001) 'Rasho Mom', original airdate 4 March 2001, Season 1, Episode 23.

A drama about an undercover FBI agent, this episode depicts protagonist Danny Arno being wrongfully accused of shooting his wife.

*CSI: Crime Scene Investigation* (2006) 'Rashomama', original airdate 27 April 2006, Season 6, Episode 21.

Popular drama about a team of Las Vegas forensic investigators, this episode centers on the murder of a wealthy mother. *Rashomon's* gate/forest settings are here replaced with the laboratory and crime scene.

*Naturally Sadie* (2006) 'Rashomon', original airdate 10 September 2006, Season 2, Episode 13.

A children's comedy series about fourteen-year-old Sadie Hawthorne, this episode presents conflicting versions of what happened during a food fight.

*Leverage* (2010) 'The *Rashomon* Job', original airdate 22 August 2010, Season 3, Episode 11.

An action / crime drama series about a team of high-tech thieves who select corrupt targets. In this episode, each member differently recalls the details of a past heist of an antique dagger.


## Operas

In more recent decades, operatic adaptations of *Rashomon* have appeared in both Asia and Europe, often incorporating a given country's traditional cultural forms in their staging of the opera.

*Rashomon* (1987) National Fu Hsing Chinese Opera Troupe (Taiwan) based on Akira Kurosawa and Hashimoto Shinobu's screenplay *Rashomon*, and Ryunosuke Akutagawa's stories *In a Grove* and *Rashomon*.

*Rashomon* (1997) ZKM, Karlsruhe, Germany, premiere 31 October 1997, based on Ryunosuke Akutagawa's stories *In a Grove* and *Rashomon*; Alejandro Viñao, composer; Henry Akina, director.

An opera composed for five singers, mixed choir and computer, commissioned for ZKM (Centre for Art and Media Karlsruhe) for their grand opening in 1997.

*Rashomon* (2002) Northern Kunqu Opera Troupe (Beijing) based on Akira Kurosawa and Hashimoto Shinobu's screenplay *Rashomon*, and Ryunosuke Akutagawa's stories *In a Grove* and *Rashomon*.

Numerous operatic versions of *Rashomon* have been performed in China in recent decades, such as the 1987 staging. In 2002, the Northern Kunqu Opera Troupe staged a version of the opera blending Kunqu opera arias with kung fu and traditional Chinese kickboxing.


## Radio productions

While a traditional radio adaptation of *Rashomon* has proven elusive to the editors of this collection, some radio dramatists have used the film as the inspiration for their work, such as this 2001 broadcast.

*This American Life* (2001) 'Rashomon', Station WBEZ, Chicago, original airdate 5 October 2001, Episode 196, Ira Glass, Host.

A weekly series blending together journalism and drama, this episode recounts three different perspectives on 9/11, recounting the events in New York City on 11 September 2001 and their meaning in three acts. Act one, '1001 Arabian Newscast Nights', features a news report on a Palestinian teenager from Chicago; Act two, 'Bombs over Baghdad', centers around an Iraqi father unwillingly drafted into Saddam Hussein's army during the Persian Gulf War; Act three, 'Toto, I Don't Think We're in Vietnam Anymore', depicts the American military operation in Somalia in 1993.

## Fiction

*Rashomon* has served as a likely inspiration for the following book of detective fiction written by an American author:

*Rashomon Gate: A Mystery of Ancient Japan* (2002) Ingrid J. Parker, New York: St. Martin's Press.
Story of a Japanese government clerk (and amateur sleuth) Akitada Sugawara as he deals with a case of blackmail and multiple murders. The book is set in the eleventh century in the then-capital city of Heian Kyo.

*The Rashomon Principle* (2011) Alex Radcliffe, Provocative Publishing (e-book).
Story of a jury member named Chloe who participates in the trial of a rape and murder, with four conflicting witness accounts.

## Music

*Rashomon* has also served as the basis for numerous musical pieces, often in conjunction with dramatic adaptations. Occasionally, though, the film has inspired artists who seek to create new sounds untied to any other medium, such as the Leeds group who took the film's name as their own.

*The Rashomon Quartet* (1996) Christopher Donison, composer; four movements: I The bandit, II The woman, III The husband, IV The woodcutter.
Composed for string quartet, this piece was commissioned by the Shaw Festival in Niagara-on-the-Lake to accompany their 1996 production of Fay and Michael Kanin's play *Rashomon*. This piece was premiered at Brock University by the Tristan Quartet in the spring of 1996. The play's rehearsals were filmed by director Anthony Azzopardi for his documentary *Making Theatre*, with the quartet being used as the sound track for the film.

*Rashomon* (2006) Richard Ormrod, Chris Sharkey, Dave Kane, Matthew Bourne, Nick Mills and Sam Hobbs, Leeds, UK.

The group *Rashomon* is a sextet that specializes in eclectic music using a variety of instruments, including saxophone, clarinet, flute, accordion, trombone, guitar, keyboard, double bass and drums. The band states that their music is tangential and capricious; this bricolage approach might be said to symbolize a Rashomon effect approach to music, whereby variation and divergence become the basis of their compositions.

*Rashomon* (album) (2010) Show Luo.

Taiwan pop singer Show Luo titled his 2010 album *Rashomon* (aka *Lover's Puzzle*).

# Bibliography

Akira Kurosawa Dokyumento (Akira Kurosawa Documents) (1974) *Kinema Junpo Zokan*.

Akutagawa, R. (1952) *Rashomon and Other Stories*, Kojima, T. (trans.), New York: Liveright.

———(2006) 'Kirishitan stories by Akutagawa Ryūnosuke,' *Japanese Religions*, vol. 31, no. 1, p. 23.

Althouse, A. (2000) 'Invoking *Rashomon*', *Wisconsin Law Review*, pp. 503–18.

Ashizawa Gould, K. (2006) 'The evolving role of American foundations in Japan: An institutional perspective,' in Tadashi, Y. Akira, I, Makoto, I. (eds.) *Philanthropy and Reconciliation: Rebuilding Postwar U.S.–Japan Relations*, Tokyo: Japan Center for International Exchange, pp. 101–33.

Babarczy, E. (2002) 'The Nobel dilemma – now is the time to speak', Szeky, J. (trans.), viewed 4 March 2014, <www.transcript-review.org/en/issue/transcript-1-contemporary-historical-novels-part-1/imre-kertesz/-now-is-the-time-to-speak–says-eszter-babarczy-in-the-wake-of-imre-kertesz-s-nobel-prize>.

Bailey, F.G. (1983) *The Tactical Uses of Passion*, London: Cornell University Press.

Beaufort, J. (1952) 'Focus on *Rashomon*', *The Christian Science Monitor*, 2 January, p. 39.

Befu, H. (2001) 'Symbolic vacuum', *Hegemony of Homogeneity*, Melbourne: Trans Pacific Press, pp. 86–104.

Berlin, Isaiah (1998) *The Proper Study of Mankind: An Anthology of Essays*, New York: Farrar, Straus and Giroux.

Bethe, H., Gottfried, K. & Sagdeev, R.Z. (1995) 'Did Bohr share nuclear secrets?' *Scientific American*, May, pp. 85–90.

Bierce, A. (1918/2012) *Can Such Things Be?* Auckland, NZ: Ariel Books IOBA.

Bock, A. (trans.) (1983) *Something Like an Autobiography*, New York: Vintage.

Bordwell, D. (2005) 'Foreword', Anderson, J.D. and Anderson, B.F., *Moving Image Theory: Ecological Considerations*, Carbondale: Southern Illinois University Press, pp. ix–xxi.

———(2006) *The Way Hollywood Tells It: Story and Style in Modern Movies*, Berkeley, CA: University of California Press.

Braidwood Commission of Enquiry (2010) Government of British Columbia (hearings in February–March 2010, decision in June 2010).

Brion, B. (2006) 'Pluralism: *Rashomon* and contested conceptions of criminality', *Washington and Lee Legal Studies Research Paper*, September.

Browning, R. (2001) *The Ring and the Book*, Peterborough, ON: Broadview Press.

Cameron, A. (2006) 'Contingency, order, and the modular narrative: 21 grams and irreversible', *The Velvet Light Trap*, vol. 58, no. 1, pp. 65–78.

Commissioner for Public Complaints Against the RCMP (2011) Chair's Final Report [re: Dziekanski], 11 February.

Cowie, P. (2010) *Akira Kurosawa: Master of Cinema*, New York: Rizzoli Publications.

Crowdus, G. & Porton, R. (1993) 'The importance of a singular, guiding vision: An interview with Arthur Penn', *Cineaste*, vol. 20, no. 2, spring, pp. 4–13.

*Daiei Junenshi (A Ten-Year History of Daiei)* (1951) Tokyo: Daiei, Inc.

Davidson, J.F. (1954) 'Memory of defeat in Japan: A reappraisal of *Rashomon*', *Antioch Review*, December, pp. 492, 497–8 [reprinted (1969) *Rashomon: A Film by Akira Kurosawa*, New York: Grove Press].

Davenport, C. & Litras, M. (2003) '*Rashomon* and repression: A multi-source analysis of contentious events', viewed 28 March 2014, <www.pcr.uu.se/Rashomon_Repression>.

Desser, D. (1983) 'Toward a structural analysis of the postwar Samurai film', *Quarterly Review of Film Studies*, vol. 8, no. 1, pp. 25–41.

Dhillon, S. & Keller, J. (2015) 'Judge acquits RCMP officer in airport Taser case', *The Globe and Mail*, 1 May, n.p.

Dresner, M. (2006) 'How true to history is Tom Cruise's *The Last Samurai*?', viewed 1 May 2006, <www.willamette.edu/~rloftus/LastSamurai.htm>.

Dunkley, C. (2001) 'Rashomon in a New Light', *Variety*, 9 July, <http://variety.com/2001/film/news/rashomon-in-new-light-1117802485/>.

Edmonds, D. & Eidinow, J. (2001) *Wittgenstein's Poker: The Story of a Ten-Minute Argument between Two Great Philosophers*, London: Faber and Faber.

Elsaesser, T. (2009) 'The mind-game film,' Buckland, W. (ed.), *Puzzle Films: Complex Storytelling in Contemporary Cinema*, Malden: Wiley-Blackwell, pp. 13–41.

Fassbender, B. (2004) 'The better peoples of the United Nations? Europe's practice and the United Nations', *The European Journal of International Law*, vol. 15, no. 5, p. 860.

Frayling, C. (2000) *Sergio Leone: Something to Do with Death*, New York: Faber and Faber.

Frayn, M. (2002a) *Copenhagen: A Play in Two Acts*, London: Samuel French Company.

———(2002b) *Forum on Physics and Society*, October, pp. 36–42.

Fujiwara, C. (2009) *Jerry Lewis*, Urbana-Champaign: University of Illinois Press.

Futamura, M. (2011) 'Japanese societal attitudes towards the Tokyo Trial: A contemporary perspective', *The Asia-Pacific Journal*, vol. 9, issue 29, no. 5, July 18, viewed 30 March 2014, <www.japanfocus.org/-Madoka-Futamura/3569>.

Gadi, R.B. (1972) 'An afternoon with Kurosawa', Richie, D. (ed.) *Focus on Rashomon*, Englewood Cliffs, NJ: Prentice Hall, pp. 8–20.

Gammel, I, & Epperly, E. (eds.) (1999) *L.M. Montgomery and Canadian Culture*, Toronto: University of Toronto Press.

Good, B.J. (2010) Theorizing the 'subject' of medical and psychiatric anthropology, R. R. Marett Memorial Lecture, Exeter College, Oxford University, 30 April.

Government of British Columbia (2010) 'Braidwood Commission of Enquiry' for the hearings in February–March 2010, decision in June 2010.

Griffiths, O. (2002) 'Need, greed, and protest in Japan's black market, 1938–49', *Journal of Social History*, vol. 35, no. 4, p. 825.

Hall, L. (1993) *Negotiation: Strategies for Mutual Gain*, Thousand Oaks, CA: Sage.

Halperin, S. (1991) *Zaner ha Rashomon ba – siporet ha – Yisre-elit / The Influence of Rashomon in Israeli Fiction*, Yerushalim: R. Mas.

Hayward, S. (2000) *Cinema Studies: The Key Concepts*, 2nd edn, London: Routledge.

Heider, K.G. (1988) 'The Rashomon effect: When ethnographers disagree', *American Anthropologist*, vol. 90, no. 1, March, pp. 73–81.

Henderson, D.F. (1965) *Conciliation and Japanese Law: Tokugawa and Modern*, Vol. I & Vol. II, Seattle: University of Washington Press.

Hirano, K. (1992) *Mr. Smith Goes to Tokyo*, Washington: Smithsonian Institution.

Hodell, C.W. (1908) *The Old Yellow Book*, Washington: Carnegie Institution, viewed 22 March 2014, <https://archive.org/details/oldyellowbookso00hode>.

Hollywood Reporter, The (1959) Advertisement, 10 February, p. 18.

Horikawa, H. (2000) *Hyoden Kurosawa Akira / Kurosawa Akira – An Appraisal*, Tokyo: Mainichi Shimbun Sha.

Horowitz, I.L. (1987) 'The Rashomon effect: Ideological proclivities and political dilemmas of the IMF', Meyers, R. (ed.) *The Political Morality of the International Monetary Fund*, Piscataway, NJ: Transaction Publishers, pp. 93–110.

Horvat, A. (2006) Personal correspondence, 20 November.

James, W. (1907) *Pragmatism: A New Name for Some Old Ways of Thinking*, New York: Longmans, Green, and Co.

Kamir, O. (2000) 'Judgement by film: Socio-legal functions of *Rashomon*', *Yale Journal of Law and the Humanities*, vol. 12, no. 39, pp. 86–7.

———(2005) ' "Why law-and-film" and what does it actually mean? A perspective', *Continuum: Journal of Media and Cultural Studies*, vol. 19, no. 2, June, pp. 255–78.

———(2006) *Framed: Women in Law and Film*, Durham: Duke University Press.

Keller, J. (2015a) 'Mountie who fired Taser perjured himself, judge rules', *The Globe and Mail*, 21 February, n.p.

Kamir, O. (2015b) 'Mountie in Taser case guilty of perjury', *The Globe and Mail*, 21 March, n.p.

Kurosawa, A. (1983) *Something Like an Autobiography*, Bock, A. (trans.), New York: Vintage.

———(1984) *Gama no Abura-Jiden no Yo na Mono / Something Like an Autobiography*, Tokyo: Iwanami Shoten.

———(dir.) (1950) *Rashomon*, DVD, Tokyo: Daiei.

———& Cardullo, B. (2008) *Interviews*, Jackson, MS: University Press of Mississippi.

Landau, D. (editor-in-chief) (2006) *Haaretz*, CBC Radio, 15 August, n.p.

Lawler, E.J. & Yoon, J. (1995) 'Structural power and emotional processes in negotiation', Kramer, R.M. and Messick, D.M. (ed.) *Negotiation as a Social Process*, Thousand Oaks, CA: Sage, pp. 143–65.

Leach, E. (1961) *Pul Eliya: A Village in Ceylon*, New York: Cambridge University Press.

Lévi-Strauss, C. (1995a) *The Story of Lynx*, Tihanyi, C. (trans.), Chicago: University of Chicago Press.

———(1995b) *Myth and Meaning: Five Talks for Radio*, Toronto: University of Toronto Press, pp. 3–4.

MacDougall, D. (1998) *Transcultural Cinema*, Princeton, NJ: Princeton University Press.

Macfarlane, A. (2004) Personal communication, October.

Martinez, D.P. (2009) *Remaking Kurosawa: Translations and Permutations in Global Cinema*, London & New York: Palgrave Macmillan.

Maurizi, A. & Ciapparoni La Rocca, T. (2012) *La figlia occidentale di Edo – Scritti in memoria di Giuliana Stramigioli / The European Daughter of Edo – Papers in Honor of Giuliana Stramigioli*, Milano: FreancoAngeli.

Mazur, A. (1998) *A Hazardous Inquiry: The Rashomon Effect at Love Canal*, Harvard: Harvard University Press.

Mellen, J. (1975) *Voices from the Japanese Cinema*, New York: Liveright.

Molasky, M. (1999) *The American Occupation of Japan and Okinawa: Literature and Memory*, New York: Routledge.

Nishimura, Y. (2000) *Kurosawa Akira wo motomete / In search of Akira Kurosawa*, Tokyo: K.K. Kinema Junpo Sha.

Nogami, T. (2006) *Waiting on the Weather: Making Movies with Akira Kurosawa*, Carpenter, J.W. (trans.), Berkeley, CA: Stone Bridge Press.

———(n.d.) *Satsuei Oboegaki* (Miyagawa's 'Cinematography Notes').

Orr, J. (2001) *The Victim as Hero: Ideologies of Peace and National Identity in Postwar Japan*, Honolulu: University of Hawaii Press.

Oshima, N. (2013) 'Interview with Akira Kurosawa, *Waga eiga jinsei / My Life in Film*', viewed 3 March 2014, <www.youtube.com/watch?v=7igkjzR9q8I>.

Oxenboell, M. (2005) 'Images of "Akutō"', *Monumenta Nipponica*, vol. 60, no. 2, p. 259.

Panek, E. (2006) 'The poet and the detective: Defining the psychological puzzle film', *Film Criticism*, vol. 31, no. 1/2, pp. 62–88.

Petrovich, C. (2014) 'Justice William Ehrcke in the case of K. Millington', *CBC News*, 27 November, n.p.

Porter, B.F. (2004) *Philosophy Through Fiction and Film*, Upper Saddle River, NJ: Pearson Prentice Hall.

Prince, S. (1991) *The Warrior's Camera: The Cinema of Akira Kurosawa*, Princeton, NJ: Princeton University Press.

———(1998) *Savage Cinema: Sam Peckinpah and the Rise of Ultraviolent Movies*, Austin: University of Texas Press.

Ramundo, B.A. (1992) *Effective Negotiation: A Guide to Dialogue Management and Control*, Westport, CT: Quorum Books.

*Rashomon* (2002) Criterion Collection DVD.

*Rashomon* (2008) *The Journal of the Bar Association of Queensland*, <www.hearsay. org.au>.

Redfern, N. (n.d.) 'Film style and narration in *Rashomon*', Academia.edu, viewed 21 March 2013, <www.academia.edu/3241863/Film_style_and_narration_in_Rashomon>.

Richie, D. (ed.) (1972) *Focus on Rashomon*, Englewood Cliffs, NJ: Prentice Hall.

———(1987) 'The continuity script', *Rashomon*, London: Rutgers University Press, pp. 35–96.

———(1990) *Japanese Cinema: An Introduction*, Oxford: Oxford University Press.

———(1996) *The Films of Akira Kurosawa* (3rd edn), Berkley, CA: University of California Press.

Roth, W.D. & Metha, J.D. (2002) 'The Rashomon effect: Combining positivist and interpretivist approaches in the analysis of contested events', *Sociological Methods and Research*, November, pp. 131–71.

Ryuza, M. (1998) *Kurosawa Akira den – tenno to yobareta eiga kantoku / The Story of Akira Kurosawa – The 'Emperor' Film Director*, Tokyo: Tenbosha.

Salzberg, S. (2000) The Legacies of Kurosawa Conference, Vancouver, BC, Canada, 14 October.

Sartre, J.-P. (1963) *Search for a Method*, New York: Knopf.
Sato, T. (1969) *Kurosawa no sekai / The World of Kurosawa*, Tokyo: San-ichi Shobo.
———(2002) *Kurosawa Akira sakuhin kaidai / Annotated Reviews of the Works of Akira Kurosawa*, Tokyo: Iwanami.
Simons, J. (2008) 'Complex narratives', *New Review of Film and Television Studies*, vol. 6, no. 2, pp. 111–26.
Smith, G. (1999) 'Inside out', *Film Comment*, September/October, pp. 58–68.
Souryi, P.F. (2001) *The World Turned Upside Down: Medieval Japanese Society*, Roth, K. (trans.), New York: Columbia University Press.
Staiger, J. (2006) 'Complex narratives: An introduction', *Film Criticism*, vol. 31, no. 1/2, pp. 2–4.
Stein, H. (2001) '*Rashomon*: The analyst who came in from the rain', *Psychoanalytic Association of New York Bulletin*, vol. 39, no 2, summer, viewed 28 March 2014, <http://internationalpsychoanalysis.net/2011/08/16/rashomon-the-analyst-who-came-in-from-the-rain>.
Supreme Court of British Columbia (2013) R. v. Bill Bentley; McEwan, J., 29 July, p. 45.
Surak, K. (2013) *Making Tea, Making Japan: Cultural Nationalism in Practice*, Stanford: Stanford University Press.
Tanaka, T. (1996) *Eiga ga Kofuku Datta Koro / When Movies Were Happy*, Tokyo: Japan Design Creators Company.
———(2002) *Japan's Comfort Women: Sexual Slavery and Prostitution during World War II and the US Occupation*, New York: Routledge.
Tasogawa, H. (2012) *All the Emperor's Men: Kurosawa's Pearl Harbor*, Milwaukee, WI: Applause Books.
Thompson, L., Peterson, E. & Kray, L. (eds.) (1995) 'Social context in negotiation', *Negotiation as a Social Process*, Thousand Oaks, CA: Sage, pp. 5–36.
Tonomura, H. (1990) 'Women and inheritance in Japan's early warrior society', *Comparative Studies in Society and History*, vol. 32, pp. 592–623.
———(1999) 'Sexual violence against women: Legal and extralegal treatment in premodern warrior societies', in Walthall, A., Wakita, H. and Tonomura, H. (eds.), *Women and Class in Japanese History*, Ann Arbor, MI: Center for Japanese Studies, The University of Michigan, pp. 140–2.
Total Film (2006) '*Lucky Number Slevin*', The modern guide to movies, reviews, viewed 1 April 2014, <www.totalfilm.com/reviews/cinema/lucky-number-slevin>.
Tötösy de Zepetnek, S. (2005) 'Imre Kertész's Nobel prize, public discourse, and the media', CLCWeb: *Comparative Literature and Culture*, vol. 7, no. 4, viewed 4 March 2014, <http://docs.lib.purdue.edu/clcweb/vol7/iss4/9>.
Tsuruta, K. (1970) 'Akutagawa Ryūnosuke and the I-Novelists', *Monumenta Nipponica*, vol. 25, no. 1–2, p. 14.
Turim, M. (1989) *Flashbacks in Film: Memory and History*, New York: Routledge.
Tykwer, T. (1999) *Run Lola, Run*, viewed 28 March 2014, <www.sonypictures.com/movies/runlolarun/>.
UP Report from Venice (1951) *The Mainichi Shimbun Newspaper*, Evening Edition, 12 September, n.p.
Ury, M. (ed.) (1979) *Tales of Times Now Past: Sixty-Two Stories from a Medieval Japanese Collection*, Berkeley, CA: University of California Press.
Wikipedia (2014) Rashomon effect, viewed 1 March 2014, <http://en.wikipedia.org/wiki/Rashomon_effect>.

Wilson, G. (2006) 'Transparency and twist in narrative fiction film', *Journal of Aesthetics and Art Criticism*, vol. 61, no. 1, pp. 81–95.

Wilson, S. (2013) 'Film and soldier: Japanese war movies in the 1950s', *Journal of Contemporary History*, vol. 48, no. 3, pp. 548–9.

Yalman, N. (1967) *Under the Bo Tree: Studies of Caste, Kinship, and Marriage in Interior Ceylon*, Berkeley, CA: University of California Press.

Yamada, M. (2006) 'Adapting Akutagawa: Kurosawa's *Rashômon* and the problem of narration', *The Film Journal*, viewed 1 May 2006, <www.thefilmjournal.com/issue9/rashomon.html>.

Yodogawa, N. (2008) Filmed interview, viewed 3 March 2014, <www.youtube.com/watch?v=iyTJXDBVptY>.

Yoshimoto, M. (2000*)* *Kurosawa: Film Studies and Japanese Cinema*, Durham, NC: Duke University Press.

Zimmermann, Patricia (2006) 'Revisiting and remixing black cinema', *The Moving Image*, vol. 6, no. 2, fall, pp. 119–24.

# Index